מסורה

ArtScroll Series®

Rabbi Nosson Scherman / Rabbi Meir Zlotowitz

General Editors

MORE

EFFECT-

IVE

by
Miriam Levi

Published by

Mesorah Publications, ltd

JEWISH
PARENT-
ING

FIRST EDITION
First Impression . . . February 1998

Published and Distributed by
MESORAH PUBLICATIONS, Ltd.
4401 Second Avenue
Brooklyn, New York 11232

Distributed in Europe by
J. LEHMANN HEBREW BOOKSELLERS
20 Cambridge Terrace
Gateshead, Tyne and Wear
England NE8 1RP

Distributed in Israel by
SIFRIATI / A. GITLER — BOOKS
10 Hashomer Street
Bnei Brak 51361

Distributed in Australia & New Zealand by
GOLDS BOOK & GIFT CO.
36 William Street
Balaclava 3183, Vic., Australia

Distributed in South Africa by
KOLLEL BOOKSHOP
Shop 8A Norwood Hypermarket
Norwood 2196, Johannesburg, South Africa

THE ARTSCROLL SERIES®
MORE EFFECTIVE JEWISH PARENTING
© Copyright 1998, by MESORAH PUBLICATIONS, Ltd.
4401 Second Avenue / Brooklyn, N.Y. 11232 / (718) 921-9000

ISBN
1-57819-189-0 (hard cover)
1-57819-190-4 (paperback)

Typography by Compuscribe at ArtScroll Studios, Ltd.

Printed in the United States of America by Noble Book Press
Bound by Sefercraft, Quality Bookbinders, Ltd. Brooklyn, N.Y.

*In memory of
my dear parents*

Henry and Irma Wechsler ע״ה

*who by personal example
taught me the meaning of chesed*

APPRECIATION

By Rabbi Shimon Schwab

"She opens her mouth with wisdom and the law of lovingkindness is on her tongue."

This *pasuk* is an appropriate description of this beautiful book by Mrs. Miriam Levi. She has become a teacher of contemporary Jewish parents and all her lessons have one common denominator — namely, she draws from reliable Torah sources and her own pedagogical experience in how to cope with most of the common problems of childrearing. The secret is the re-education of parents by introspection into their own emotional life. The mitzvos of honor and respect for parents are clearly defined as well as the methods of teaching obedience to children.

This is a very fascinating and valuable book for which we have to be deeply grateful to the author.

בית המוסר

ע"ש ר' חיים מנחם להמן ע"ה
רח' הרב סורוצקין 39 ירושלים
מיסודו של תנועת שוחרי מוסר, ירושלים

Institute for Torah Ethics
IN MEMORY OF R'CHAIM MENACHEM LEHMANN
39 Harav Sorotzkin St., Jerusalem

בס"ד _____

וינקר אל זה אדם/וי' עד עינינק הוא אונגר המליאות (נעו
גתעונד באר! יאפל. המינק כית הוא צלן נא מין, ופל גהוינץ
הינרמית מאמנעינת מאפל (א נראמו, ואהגלונות הקצורת מאנק
הוא לאמור את השלמון שההגאעצה ההרס/ית ושאה תנמול, אן לעמוד
הרעונק המינק אל וין' בל נב מאף העוים יוצלים אהו "המינק"
ונגד למנק.

וינקר אל זה לוי אבריק את ההוים בזמוה (לאה בילנ (עת
המינק לבעוה, ואני גבאה הידאה של אילן לב הצעונת המינונות
העצונות להגמות. יש לקומה סטוק אג יצון ליבי על ההגורים, גהנולוים
שואן זלה לראות א נהוהגת שלא אג ילוהו לעל לבעה
שאג הן למן /וי' עיוי סעג אן!

שאגא עלם

APPROBATION

by Rabbi Shlomo Wolbe

*M*rs. Miriam Levi's book on education is a *must* ... Home education is a matter of vital importance, in this generation in particular, when permissiveness has penetrated all areas of life, and we face the holy and difficult task of guarding our children from outside destructive influences. Yet in confronting the need for proper and effective education, *so few* parents know *what* education is, and *how* to educate.

In her book, Mrs. Levi provides wonderful guidance to parents in the proper approach to bringing up their children, and effective methods for treating all educational problems they are likely to encouter. It is to be hoped that this book will be found in every home, and that parents will find, *be'ezras Hashem*, that through the guidance contained in it they will succeed to raise their children in a pleasant spirit and a warm atmosphere to have good character traits, filled with love of Torah.

FOREWORD

by Rabbi Nachman Bulman

generation ago, the challenge faced by parents and educators in the Torah community seemed centered on matters of faith and practice. The tide of that battle has turned spectacularly in our favor and not only within the observant community. Unknown thousands are today magnetically drawn to mitzvah-observance from utmost alienation.

In the sphere of character and values, today's challenge is all the more threatening, precisely because its roots are less easily perceived.

The thirteen principles of our faith are definable. The halachah indicates which deeds are commanded and which prohibited. Today's parents are not on equally safe ground when they encounter the will, emotion, and habit patterns of their children. They face obvious questions.

Are they models of Torah authority or bullying tyrants?

Is their child rearing a reflection of neurotic complexes, or of Torah insights?

Conversely, when they rely on exclusive voluntarism based on "explaining it to Moishele or Sarale," are they educating their children, or surrendering to the values of a secular society and its unbridled permissiveness? In which case, a new generation might grow to adulthood, whose mitzvah-behavior might seem exemplary, but whose ego, emotions, and habits (in the sphere of non-formal mitzvah-practice) might be wildly unresponsive to Torah judgment. Can we remain oblivious when much of the above is no longer mere apprehension, but painful reality?

To harmonize those extremes, a high order of parental self-knowledge is necessary, as well as the keenest of insight into the soul of the child and the dynamics of his growth.

Coupled with such understanding — in fact, preceding it — a systematic exposition is vitally needed of Torah perspectives on the function of emotion, instinct, and habit in child and adult, and especially on how those soul and body powers may be "educated" and refined.

There is a particular difficulty in the matter of bringing Torah wisdom to bear on the issues at hand.

Classical Torah sources reflect different principles of organization and exposition from those that are familiar to most Jews in the west. The idiom of those sources, for all their perfect applicability, makes Torah guidance not easily accessible to all but deeply initiated students of Torah. On the other hand, the pervasive message of secular educational theory all but floods our consciousness. For many, the temptation to distort Torah values, by "tailoring" seemingly "liberal" Torah sources, becomes the more difficult to resist. Nor does a protective authoritarianism insulate a minority of children against being deeply affected by the wild permissiveness of today's majority of children.

In either case the parent loses control, and the child may be deprived of the noblest aspects of his heritage.

What alternative remains for those who have total faith that a clear exposition of the teachings of Torah on the "inner" upbringing of our children would immeasurably enhance our function as parents; that such an exposition would verify beyond dispute that our "authoritarianism" is the means to our children's matchless liberty, while our "libertarianism" leads to the pitiful enslavement of our own offspring?

Miriam Levi has authored a major work on the subject for which many will be grateful.

The chapters of *More Effective Jewish Parenting* are a wide-ranging digest of Torah teaching on the challenge of contemporary upbringing of Jewish children. Mrs. Levi's sources are painstakingly researched and listed. Her seeming simplicity of style is rooted in elemental clarity, not mediocrity. She does not preach, but engages in a genuine teaching dialogue with her unseen readers. Her theory does not remain suspended in abstraction, but is always applied with a wealth of illustration. Not the least achievement of the authoress is her judicious use of the theory of cognitive psychology, to convey in contemporary idiom much that illustrates Torah thought on respective issues — all in total faithfulness to Torah, without apologetics.

The parent is initially moved to introspection into his own emotional life, prior to consideration of how to instill the mitzvah of honoring parents. He is then led to seek a balance between firmness of position and stimulating a child's self-motivation; between love, discipline, mutual understanding, and consideration.

Training for orderly home behavior is next considered, and is followed by problems of emotional expression (jealousy, fighting, crying).

The cultivation of a supportive attitude to the child's schooling is explored. The work includes suggestions on six widespread problems that parents face from time to time.

In this expanded edition, chapters have been added dealing with the issues of preparing children for a Torah life, parenting difficult children, and relating to teenagers.

It is the hope of the writer of these lines that *More Effective Jewish Parenting* will come to be recognized as a wonderful means for the most precious of goals: rearing the coming generation of the People of the Torah.

On the way to that noblest of achievements, not a few parents may discover that they are re-educating themselves as well; that the proverbial, elusive hope, "if we could only relive some of our childhood," need not be an epitaph of despair, but a prod to heroic striving. "And he shall restore the heart of the fathers *through* the children" (Rashi, *Malachi* 3:24).

If in the process of raising our children we feel impelled to *teshuvah* in deed, in character, and in soul, can there be a more striking indication that our final redemption is near?

ACKNOWLEDGMENTS

*W*ords cannot express my gratitude to my husband Yehudah, who established the Torah foundation of this book, provided unstinting encouragement, invaluable counseling and editing help, and composed the notes at the end of the volume. He has made a major contribution without which the book could not have been written.

Warm thanks are due to my sons Yoseph, Shlomoh, and Hillel for the patience they exhibited as young children while Mother was working on the first edition of this book. My special thanks to my beloved son Hillel, who managed our household during the writing of this new edition, freeing me from virtually all time-consuming tasks.

My heartfelt appreciation goes to David Hornik for his expert editing on the first edition.

I am deeply grateful and indebted to Sarah Rosenblat for her valuable editing and extensive feedback on the manuscript.

I want to thank Miriam Adahan for reviewing Chapter 1 and making many helpful suggestions.

I am grateful also to the mothers who read some of the material and offered their reactions.

I thank the parents who shared with me their experiences and contributed their stories, which have so enriched this book.

It has been a privilege and pleasure to work with the staff of ArtScroll. A special thank you to Shmuel Blitz, manager of the Jerusalem ArtScroll office, for his helpful advice, and to Devorah Rhein for her skillful editing of the final draft.

Above all, I am thankful for having been afforded the merit of helping parents in their vital and holy mission of bringing up the next generation of Torah Jews.

AUTHOR'S PREFACE TO THE REVISED EDITION

With gratitude to the Almighty, I present this new, revised and expanded edition of Effective Jewish Parenting. As in the original book, published over a decade ago, the parenting workshops I conducted have served as a catalyst for the ideas and concepts presented. In those workshops mothers come together and discuss parenting issues of concern to them. Some of the issues raised have become the nucleus for several new chapters.

Parents have requested more information about inculcating Torah values and training children in mitzvah observance. Chapter 7, Education for Torah Living, deals with this.

Parents have always been aware that some of their children were more difficult to raise than others. Yet they were often at a loss to understand why this was the case. Chapter 14, The Difficult Child, presents new research to help parents determine if their child is in this category, and offers helpful guidance and management methods.

So many people asked for more information on teenagers. There is now an entire chapter devoted to the subject. Chapter 15, The Teenage Years, discusses adolescence, what parents can expect, and what they can do to ease this transitional period.

One issue raised by several readers was that not enough material was included on the importance of love, and the need to liberally demonstrate it to our children. If no separate chapter was devoted to this subject alone, it's because love is an integral part of every aspect of child rearing, and must permeate the entire parent-child relationship.

It is my hope and prayer that the reader will find answers here to the many questions arising daily in child rearing, and the guidance in raising the children from whom they will have much *nachas* and joy.

TABLE OF CONTENTS

INTRODUCTION

*P*arents have been raising and educating children for thousands of years, but never has there been so much interest in this subject as in our time. Hundreds of authoritative books on child care have been written, yet parents seem to be having more difficulties with their children than ever before. Disciplinary problems in particular are on the rise, and many parents are at a loss as to what to do about this.

In previous generations, mothers and fathers largely followed the example of their parents. Traditional practices went unchallenged. Parents were clearly in a position of authority; children were aware of their duties. Our generation, however, has rejected many of the structures of the past, including most of the time-honored child rearing methods. New principles of child-rearing, based on the idea of complete equality between parents and children, have been formulated. There are experts who theorize that children can no longer be expected to obey their parents, but must be encouraged into voluntary cooperation. Moreover, psychologists have alarmed everyone about the dire effects of inept parenting on the vulnerable psyches of young children.

Thus stripped of their authority, parents have become increasingly uncertain and confused. Whereas parents once trusted their capacity to raise children, many now self-consciously re-examine their decisions, their actions, and their conversations for parental misdemeanors which could implant insecurities and neurotic complexes in their children. For these parents, child-rearing has become a tense, guilt-ridden ordeal rather than the satisfying and creative experience it was meant to be.

Fortunately, Jewish parents who have Torah as their guide still believe that parenthood is a position of authority and control. Judaism cannot accept any relinquishment of parental responsibility. Torah teaches parents to see their children as a Divine trust.[1] Their task, to educate their child to live a life of service to God, is a sacred one.[2] Primarily, it requires the parents to set for the child a lofty example of those character traits they wish to develop in him. But this alone is not enough. There will always be occasions when, in order to provide the necessary guidance, parents must assert their authority. Furthermore, the mitzvah of honoring and revering parents precludes any egalitarian relationship. While Torah does see parents and children as equal in value, it assigns them different roles and responsibilities.

Still, many Jewish parents have, to some extent, been influenced by our times, and are confused and uncertain about their role. Moreover, while it was never an easy task to raise children, today's affluence and moral decay have made the job more difficult than ever before. Thus, many Jewish parents need clear guidance on child-rearing problems, based on Torah teachings.

Modern guidance books for parents have criticized the "old" methods of child rearing as harsh, oppressive, and insensitive. Yet if we examine the Torah approach to child discipline, we will find, quite to the contrary, that it is warm and loving, and it grants the child great freedom within certain limits. The *Gaon* of Vilna, famed Torah Sage of the 18th century, wrote that children should be admonished with "soft words and reprimands which will be willingly accepted."[3] The noted educator, Rabbi Samson Raphael Hirsch writes, "Never give your child orders that are unnecessary or unimportant. Never forbid him anything that is not harmful to him and involves no wrongdoing....Permit him to do anything you can safely let him do without endangering his physical or moral welfare."[4]

Guidance on practical issues, however, is ineffective if parents have not learned the emotional control necessary to put Torah values into practice. It is not enough merely to tell parents to reprimand calmly and not get angry — they usually know that. They need to learn *how* to accomplish this. While the Torah contains specific advice on the problems of child-rearing, many people seem to have difficulty applying that advice in practice.

What is needed is a method of coping with emotions which reasserts Torah perspectives. Cognitive psychology, a recently developed system, answers this need. It teaches that we have the ability to change our basic outlook and behavior, and puts control into the hands of the individual.

Cognitive psychology maintains that it is not the events in our lives that disturb us, but the way we have learned to interpret and evaluate them. This approach aims to change our basic, problem-causing beliefs, enabling us to see our life's events in a more positive light. As a result, we function better and increase the satisfaction in our lives.

In the child-rearing situation, parents who wish to change the way they react to their child must first learn to *think* differently about the child's behavior. The natural result is that parents will then *feel* differently about that behavior. They will then be in better control of their own behavior and find it easier to alter it.

Once we begin to change our characteristic way of reacting to situations, we find that this in turn changes our feelings and way of thinking. Our Sages have taught: "A person is shaped by his actions; his heart and all his thoughts always [follow after] his activities."[5] When we work to change our customary behavior, we also establish new, more positive patterns of thinking and feeling. These, in turn, reinforce our new habits of behavior. Essentially, we reverse the vicious cycle wherein children misbehave, parents become upset and react nonconstructively, and the misbehavior continues.

In this book, we will draw on the educational teachings of Torah authorities throughout the generations. And we will use modern cognitive psychological findings as a tool for putting into practice the teachings of our Sages.

Chapter One

THE FOUNDATION: LEARNING TO COPE WITH OUR EMOTIONS

"My kids get me so *mad!*" said Rachel. "When they start fighting, before I know it I'm yelling and screaming at them. I know I shouldn't get angry, but what can I do?"

"Me, too," Rachel's friend, Devorah, admitted. "And the worst of it is, after I've lost my temper at my kids, their reproachful looks make me feel so *guilty*. Then I try to make it up to them by being overly permissive!"

Rachel and Devorah realize that by allowing their feelings to get in the way, they are reacting inappropriately to their children. If they, and we, want to be more effective parents, we must find a way to cope with our emotions, rather than remaining locked in an exhausting and never-ending struggle to keep them under control

— with the resulting difficulty in achieving our educational goals.

Where do these overpowering emotions come from? People often say, "*That* made me so mad!" or "*He* made me feel so guilty!" as if outside events produce our emotions. Yet according to the cognitive view of behavior,[1] we bring on emotions ourselves, with the *interpretations* we give to events. In other words, our emotions are not imposed on us. They result largely from the things we tell ourselves, from our thoughts. Thus, we feel the way we think.

According to this theory, our thinking takes the form of little inner conversations with ourselves. Sometimes we're aware of these "inner dialogues." At other times, they occur so swiftly and subtly that we don't sense them at all. Yet we know only too well the feelings and behaviors which result from these dialogues. With practice, we can learn to identify these upsetting thoughts which set off our emotions. We can challenge the beliefs on which they are based, and gradually change them. This will create a calmer emotional state. By learning to control and prevent emotions which cause self-defeating behavior, we can even alter long-established habits. Once we have brought our emotions under control, we'll be much better equipped to handle the problems of child–rearing.

In this chapter we will focus on two of the most troublesome emotions that parents encounter in dealing with children: anger and guilt.

WHAT MAKES US ANGRY?

Anger is a major problem for most parents, and is one of the most destructive forces within the family. "Anger in the home," states the Talmud, "is like worms in grain," destroying the home.[2] "All kinds of hell rule over the person who is constantly angry";[3] "His life is no life."[4] Most quick-tempered people are aware of the harmful effects of their anger, and of the misery it causes them. But they are generally helpless to do much about it, because they are unaware of the underlying causes of their anger.

The thought process beneath anger is usually the expectation that life should always go the way we want it to. The Talmud speaks of anger as a "false god within you."[5] This "god" decrees how everything must be. When people or situations contradict this decree, the person breaks out in angry condemnations. Perhaps this is what the Sages referred to when they said, "He who gets angry is as if he worships idols."[6]

Our demand that everything must be as *we* want it to be under- lies our anger toward our children as well. For example, Rachel fre- quently gets angry and screams at her children for leaving a messy room. But it is not the disorder which creates her anger; it's what she *tells* herself about that disorder. If she thought, "What a mess! I wish the kids wouldn't leave their room like this," Rachel's emo- tional reaction would be mild. She would feel unhappy, but proba- bly not unduly disturbed. However, Rachel is more likely to be telling herself, "Never in my life have I seen such a horrible mess! Why are my kids such slobs?! Why *can't* they keep their room in order?!" Implied in these complaints is a *demand:* "My children *must* keep their room in order!" We may not always be aware of the demand, but it is there nonetheless.

But what, one might ask, is wrong with that? After all, order- liness is important and all parents should try to teach it to their children. The trouble is that when we're angry, our own demands for perfection are at the center of our message. What we're really saying is, "My children should always behave as I want them to!" This demand is unrealistic and irrational. The intention to train our children in orderliness is praiseworthy, but the angry way we do this interferes with our goal of fostering good character traits in them.

Intolerance

While such demands underlie most anger, they are not the *direct* cause of it. What initially triggers our anger is our assessment of how intolerable the situation is. When we're angry, we don't just think it's inconvenient that our children don't behave as we want them to. We tell ourselves that it's "*terrible*" and that we "*can't stand it!*" When we insist that our children come immediately when called, regarding it as intolerable when they don't, or if we demand that they help out willingly and with pleasure, viewing it as unbearable when they grumble and make a fuss, we inevitably become angry. If, when her children quarrel, Rachel would think, "They shouldn't fight so much," yet accept the fighting as merely an unpleasant but normal aspect of sibling relations, she wouldn't be as upset. The problem is that she views it as "awful" and "unbearable."*

Negative Judging

But anger consists of more than intolerance of the situation. It also entails a judgment. When our children misbehave, we jump quickly from "I can't stand it!" to "They're bad kids!" For example, if we're furious with a child for not coming when called, we're not only upset about the "terrible" inconvenience we're being subjected to. We also blame and condemn the child for causing our inconvenience. We're probably thinking to ourselves, "He heard me; he knew he should come; why didn't he? Obviously, he doesn't want to listen. He's just a bad child!" By ascribing bad motives to the child, we see *him* as bad. Our anger intensifies if we believe that the child misbehaves on purpose just to make us angry, or that he could behave better if he really wanted to.

We're not always aware of this negative judgment behind our anger. But when we remember the thoughts which accompanied our anger, we can readily discover it. For example, we might think to ourselves, when our child speaks to us disrespectfully, "How dare he talk to me this way!" While there's no explicit negative evaluation of the child here, it is strongly implied. To reveal it, we only have to ask ourselves, "What kind of kid is he for daring to talk to me this way?" (A bad kid!) Similarly, if we think, "He *shouldn't* talk to me this way!" we can continue our trend of thought, (and because he *does* talk that way) "he's a bad boy!" We may not like to admit it, but the judgment is nearly always there.

---

* The words shouldn't be confused with the judgment they represent. It isn't the words in themselves that reveal our true view and determine our subsequent feelings. For example, we may use the words "awful" and "terrible" when what we really mean is that the situation is merely unpleasant. "I can't stand their fighting," expressed with a sigh, doesn't necessarily indicate intolerance. But when we furiously declare, "I can't stand their fighting!" anyone can tell that we really mean it. Similarly, we might say, in a neutral, matter-of-fact tone, "I don't like the way this room looks." Or we could say, "I don't like the way this room looks!" indicating great intolerance. Thus the tone in which we express ourselves reveals our true feelings, much more than the words we use.

Annoyance conveys the same negative judgments as does anger, but in a milder form. The evaluations are identical, but not nearly as extreme. On a scale of 0 to 10, we might put anger at a point between 6 and 10, depending on the intensity, whereas annoyance would be assigned a 1 or 2 if it's very mild, or 3 to 5 if it's stronger.

When we're annoyed, we tend to speak in a sharp tone of voice. We'll tell a child who's bothering his brother or sister, "Leave him alone!" or snap at a youngster who has ignored a request to remove the dishes from the table, "I thought I told you to clear the table!" Some parents resort to sarcasm when they're annoyed. They'll remark to a child playing with his cup at the table, "I see you won't be satisfied until that breaks."

Because the negative judgments in annoyance are milder than those in anger, we're apt to have greater difficulty identifying them.

Low Frustration Tolerance (LFT)

Parents who find themselves frequently getting angry at their children are probably suffering from low frustration tolerance (LFT). LFT is the belief that we cannot endure pain, discomfort, or frustration. Parents with LFT demand that their life must always be easy and comfortable; that they shouldn't have to undergo suffering or inconvenience. But children cause no end of inconvenience as they grow up. They deprive us of sleep; they tie us down to the house; they cause us extra work; they are a financial burden; and, because they have minds of their own, they don't always act exactly as we want them to.

Though we might sometimes wish things to be different, we can be reasonably happy as long as we learn to accept inconveniences and frustrations with equanimity. But if we think to ourselves, as we clean up a child's spilled milk on the floor, "Now I have this *terrible* mess to clean up. It's awful! I *shouldn't* have to work so hard!" we'll invariably get angry over the situation — and also at the child who caused all the extra and disagreeable work.

Thus, our demand that annoying and frustrating situations *should not* exist creates our wrath. We keep insisting that things must be different from the way they are, meaning, "Things should be the way *I* want them to be, and I can't *stand* it when they aren't!" Annoyance or inconvenience in themselves can't make us angry unless we tell ourselves, "I shouldn't be inconvenienced in this dreadful way!"

Observe the basic demand underlying anger: "I must have what I want!" When we don't get what we want, we are frustrated. The anger-producing thought is, "I can't *stand* the frustration of not having what I want!" Thus we get angry when we insist that we have quiet, yet have unbearable noise instead; or when we demand that our children be well mannered and obedient, yet they are rude and unruly.

ANGER DOESN'T GET US ANYWHERE

If anger were a way of making children change their behavior, we would have seen an end to misconduct long ago. Anger is one of the most counterproductive ways to deal with children's misbehavior. Naftali, Rachel's 5-year-old son, regularly teases and hits his younger sister Shifra, making her cry. Rachel has asked him many times to stop, but he keeps right on teasing. Finally she loses patience. "What's the matter with you?" she yells angrily. "Why are you so mean to Shifra? Why can't you treat her nicely?"

Will Naftali stop now? No. He is now even less motivated to change the way he treats his sister. If he accepts his mother's negative evaluation, he'll become preoccupied with thinking about how bad he is. If he rejects it, he'll attempt to defend himself. And his mother's attack will probably make him feel resentful and rebellious toward her — hardly the best mood for a child to be in when you are seeking his compliance.

Thus anger defeats our goals.

In fact, anger often reinforces the very behavior we wish to eliminate. In the child's eyes, our anger implies that he's bad. He then accepts this evaluation of himself, concluding, "This is the way I am. I guess I'll always act this way." So he continues in his negative behavior pattern.

Of course, anger can frighten children into obeying. But this is accomplished at great cost to our relationship with them, and the results are temporary at best. In all likelihood, we'll find ourselves resorting to anger continually to make our children comply.

Eventually we'll reach a point where we're forced to admit, "The only time they listen is when I get angry."

The well-known Torah scholar, Rabbi Simchah Wasserman, pointed out, "Parents should make up their minds what they want. If they want to vent anger, let them do so. But if they want to *achieve* something — they cannot do it by venting anger."[7]

Can controlling anger be harmful? Our Sages have always denounced short-temperedness as a destructive character trait. But modern psychology has taught that suppressing anger — "bottling it up inside" — is harmful, and has encouraged people to vent their anger instead. Some psychologists now challenge this ventilationist view of anger. As Dr. Carol Tavris writes, "It seems to me that the major effect of the ventilationist approach has been to raise the general noise level of our lives, not to lessen our problems. I notice that the people who are most prone to give vent to their rage get angrier, not less angry."[8]

In the cognitive approach, however, anger isn't held in. It is prevented from happening altogether. This is accomplished by dealing with the root cause of anger — our negative judgments. Notice the difference between the two approaches in this mother's account:

> My son would not dress himself, even though he was completely capable of doing so. Whenever I told him to dress himself, he would either ignore me or tell me I should do it. As I kept repeating myself, I found my tone of voice was getting sterner and sterner. I kept telling myself, "No, I will not lose control — I will not yell at him — I will not spank him." But with each time I had to repeat my request, I was getting angrier and angrier inside. Thinking over the situation later, I wondered where I was going wrong. I suddenly realized that the idea is not to remain in control while angry, but rather to remove the anger in the first place. What helps me most is telling myself, "I am not going to achieve my goal through anger!" Now that I am talking more calmly, my son is starting to get dressed on his own, without being told. He doesn't do it all the time, but those few times are certainly a beginning. It proves to me that you can accomplish so much more when you are calm.

Some parents get angry at their child when they try to force him to obey them. They justify this coercion on the basis of the child's Torah obligation to honor them. Children are indeed obliged (and must be taught) to obey their parents,[9] but we can't *force* them to do so, with any great success.

We must also keep in mind that the Torah forbids us to cause anguish to others.[10] Parents are not permitted to express pent-up resentment toward their children for failing to meet their demands, because they thereby cause them unnecessary anguish. In fact, children may well come to resent their parents for it.

Under special circumstances, parents may *act* angry toward their child in order to correct his behavior, even though it causes him anguish.[11] Such intentional "anger" is far different from the uncontrolled indignation which stems from not having our perfectionistic demands met. Deliberate shows of anger must be reserved for those rare occasions when it's necessary to forcefully impress a child with the gravity of his wrongdoing.[12] All traces of anger must be removed from the heart before this kind of reprimand is employed.

GETTING RID OF ANGER

Focus on the Child's Welfare

The first step in preventing anger is to give up our demands for perfection and convenience. We must begin to focus not on what *we* want but on our child's welfare. For example, if we want to stop getting angry at our children because of their messy rooms, we should stop focusing on our personal displeasure. Instead, we should think how orderliness would help our children function more effectively. From there we can start looking for solutions to the problem of the messy room.

Frustration

Remember, the anger we feel when we're inconvenienced or frustrated doesn't stem from the inconveniencing or frustrating situation itself, but from our *evaluation* of it as unbearable. A child's continuous whining is irritating, but it makes us angry only because we tell ourselves that we can't *stand* the irritation. The underlying cause of our anger is our *demand* for a trouble-free and comfortable life. We don't tell ourselves that we would *prefer* not being disturbed by the noise — viewing it as a tolerable nuisance. Rather, we tell ourselves that we *shouldn't* be disturbed in this awful way, that it's intolerable, and we can't stand it for another minute!

It is the escalation of a *preference* for a life free of trouble and frustration into a *demand* for it which causes our anger. Therefore, the first step towards eliminating the anger is to give up this demand, to stop insisting that because we prefer such an easy existence, we *must* have it. (It is, after all, a little foolish to expect that anyone could ever lead a trouble-free life!)

Relinquishing this demand isn't easy — especially if we've been accustomed to believing for years, that if we want something, we *must* have it. We need to get tough with ourselves and challenge this basic belief. Just because we'd like our children to get along well, *must* things therefore be as we would like? Because we'd prefer never to undergo inconvenience or frustration, does our life *have* to be like that?

It's pointless to tell ourselves, when something doesn't go our way, that we can't stand it. The fact that we continue to exist is obvious proof that we can very well stand it, though we may not like it.

Imagine someone at the window on a rainy day, looking out on the downpour and angrily declaring, "It shouldn't be raining; the sun must come out!" When we find ourselves becoming angry and thinking, "Things shouldn't be this way!" is what we're doing any different? Life will frequently be difficult and frustrating; we have to accept this fact and learn to live with it.

Rachel is exhausted and worried. A sick child has kept her up all night. How will she get her work done today? *Not* by making herself angry with such thoughts as, "It shouldn't be this way; I shouldn't have such a difficult life!" Instead, let her choose thoughts like, "I've had a rough night. I'll be tired and probably find it difficult to get my work done, but I guess I can cope." Coping doesn't necessarily mean functioning as usual. It means somehow getting through the day, albeit with lowered expectations.

The next time your children fight, don't become enraged by telling yourself, "They shouldn't be this way; they shouldn't cause me so much aggravation!" Tell yourself, instead, "It's a shame that they're acting like this, but let me see what I can do about the situation."

The essence is to avoid extreme or exaggerated appraisals. If a child has been crying for over an hour, it seems natural to scream, "I can't *stand* this horrible crying for another minute!" But it's more helpful to substitute a less extravagant complaint: "His crying gets on my nerves, but it's not unbearable. I can live through it." We can think to ourselves, as we clean up the spilled milk, "I don't like doing this, but it's not so awful. I'll survive." Telling ourselves that we shouldn't have this horrible mess to clean up is what makes the job so very disagreeable. We only add to our problems by getting upset over them. We might dislike mopping up the spilled milk. But when we get angry because we're thinking we shouldn't have this extra work, then, in addition to the work, we have our upset feelings to contend with. Thus we cause ourselves much additional and unnecessary suffering.

When we learn to accept whatever frustration and difficulties come our way, we eliminate a major cause of much needless anger and aggravation. And we find ourselves far better able to cope with troublesome situations when they arise.

Judging Favorably

Besides insisting that everything go our way, the other major source of anger toward our children is our habit of judging and condemning them for their deficiencies. If we want to avoid getting angry, we must learn to judge our children favorably, despite their obvious shortcomings.

In general, Judaism opposes negative judgments of others. The Sages teach, "Don't judge your fellow man until you are in his place."[13] The Meiri comments, "If you see someone transgress...don't judge him unfavorably...it is sometimes very difficult to resist temptation. If you had been similarly tempted, perhaps you would not have exercised [more] self-control." Since we can never put ourselves exactly in someone else's position, it follows that we really can't judge anyone. Our children are no exception. We must accept that judgment is God's domain alone, for only He can rate a person's merits against his sins.[14]

Not only should we refrain from negative judgment, we are also taught to judge our fellow man favorably and give him the benefit of the doubt whenever possible.[15] Rabbi Samson Raphael Hirsch writes:

> Even if you see him sin with your own eyes, or if credible witnesses testify to his guilt — you are not the judge; for you, justice in this case means love; and in this love he finds his most trusty advocate, who excuses his act wherever possible, or at least looks for mitigating circumstances.[16]

We should give our child the benefit of the doubt, whenever possible. Avi didn't come when called? Maybe he didn't hear. But if it's clear that he heard and is aware of his disobedience, we should speak to him about it. However, just because he has misbehaved, we don't have to evaluate *him* negatively as a person. Instead, we should look for extenuating circumstances for his behavior (e.g., he just didn't want to leave his friend, or his game). Still, this doesn't excuse the behavior. The child should be told, quietly but firmly, "I know it's hard to leave your friend while you're playing, but when I call you, you must come." Parents shouldn't hesitate to assert themselves, but they should do it without making negative judgments, without writing off the child as "just no good."

It's especially easy to judge a child unfavorably for misbehavior that has continued despite repeated reprimands. "He could behave differently if he really wanted to!" parents tell themselves. But remember that change is difficult; it takes time and effort. Rabbi Simcha Zissel Ziv once told the *mashgiach* (spiritual director) of his yeshiva that very often a teacher will become angry with a student who is corrected three or four times and still does not obey. Before losing patience, suggested Rabbi Simcha Zissel, the teacher should ask himself if he always corrects his *own* shortcomings by the third or fourth reminder.[17]

One of the most frequent negative judgments parents make when confronted with a misbehaving child is that he misbehaves only in order to annoy them. But even if it appears that the child is misbehaving on purpose, they should assume that there are some mitigating circumstances. For instance, instead of viewing the child's teasing of his younger sister as a deliberate attempt to be irritating, a favorable interpretation of his action might be: "He's not trying to annoy me; he does this because he's used to it." Instead of getting angry when our child shouts at us for not granting his wishes, we can tell ourselves, "I know he doesn't intend to hurt me. It's just that he hasn't yet learned to tolerate being frustrated. He hasn't yet developed self-control."

It helps check our anger if we also keep in mind that the child may sincerely regret his behavior and feel remorse over it afterwards.

Distinguishing Between the Child and His Behavior

To avoid getting angry at your child, don't think he himself is bad when he misbehaves. While his *behavior* may be bad, we shouldn't judge *him* badly because of it. We must learn to distinguish between the deed and the doer. Shanny argues with you about washing the dishes. If you think to yourself, "She always argues when I tell her to do something! She's so inconsiderate and spoiled!" you're bound to criticize her angrily. Instead, separate Shanny's behavior from Shanny by telling yourself, "She has a bad habit of arguing when asked to do something." You're then more likely to find yourself feeling calm, and in a much better position to handle the situation constructively. (For example, you can simply avoid responding to Shanny's arguments, and pleasantly but firmly repeat your request about doing the dishes.) Keep in mind: It's not her, it's her bad habit. *The child doesn't equal her behavior.*

One mother told how, by refraining from judging her child badly for his behavior and instead viewing his conduct objectively, she was able to control her anger and handle the situation more effectively:

> *We were on our way home and preparing to cross the street. Daniel was a bit ahead of us. He looked both ways carefully and crossed alone, something he knows I don't allow. In the past (this has happened before) this always got me so angry — my thoughts were basically, "He knows he's not allowed*

to do that — how could he?" Whereupon he got a good scolding and a smack. Afterwards he would make faces, stamp his feet, stick out his tongue, all to show that he didn't care about what I said.

This time I was able to look at the whole incident from a different vantage point — knowing what caused my anger and realizing that the anger was ineffectual. I remember thinking, "I guess Daniel has not learned yet that I don't want him crossing the street alone — I must remind him." When I finally crossed, I gently but firmly said that I simply do not allow him to cross alone, even if I am nearby and he is careful, and that in the future he is to wait. He accepted it. Interestingly enough, he seemed to have been anticipating the usual tongue–lashing. This time, after I had spoken to him, I took him by the hand and he came quietly and cooperatively to the house — with no retaliatory or resistant behavior.

Stress

Guarding against exaggerated and negative judgments can help prevent anger, but sometimes circumstances increase our emotional sensitivity. It's harder to cope with frustration when we're under strain — emotional or physical — or just having a hard day. We should keep in mind that pain, illness, trying experiences, lack of sleep, and fatigue are all likely to lower both our resistance and our frustration tolerance. We must expect and accept that we will have a harder time controlling anger under such circumstances. But we can maintain a degree of inner calm by recognizing that there are techniques we can use during trying times. (Remember to give yourself a well-earned pat on the back whenever you do succeed in controlling yourself while under stress.)

Many women find pregnancy an especially taxing time, emotionally, as this mother relates:

Generally, I've always been quiet and calm. But in the beginning of my fifth pregnancy (my oldest was 5), I was feeling awful and without realizing it, began losing my patience, snap-

ping more and more often at my kids. I wasn't screaming that loudly — I mean, the neighbors couldn't hear me — but it was enough. I was terribly dissatisfied with this kind of parenting.

After the birth, I noticed that I was no longer the same patient mother I had once been. I figured this must be because the kids were older now and that has to make things harder. Also, with a larger family, there's just no way to be a calm mother.

Then I started the parenting workshop. Baruch Hashem, I'm back to being a calm mother. What helped me was learning to pinpoint the cause of my anger. For example, I used to storm into the kids' room, which was a total wreck, and stand there thinking, "What a ghastly mess this house is! This is terrible! It's just awful! It's impossible to go on like this! What kind of kids are these that they don't know how to keep any semblance of order! I work and work and it doesn't help a bit!!" (Sound familiar?)

Underlying these thoughts were exaggerated evaluations such as: "It shouldn't be like this!" or, "It's unbearable!" I learned to change these evaluations and with time developed the habit of looking at the situation differently: "That's the way it is, and I can cope with it" or, "This isn't so awful." Now when I come into their messy room, I say to myself, "True, the room is really a mess, but I can deal with it."

I have also stopped judging the children negatively for their bad behavior, or to see myself as a failure because of it, or to get angry at myself about it. I just think, "What he did really isn't good; he has to improve, and I have to teach him how." I feel that I am on the right track, and I'm happy and grateful for it.

Mothers should be particularly careful after childbirth not to rush back into their regular routine. They must realize that they need to take care of themselves at this time, to ensure proper recuperation. It may be necessary to "let things go" for a while, make do with the simplest of meals (tuna fish or cheese sandwiches will do nicely) and just rest, rest, rest. To ensure the children's cooperation, the husband can assemble them and explain, "Mommies need a lot of rest after having a baby. What can we do to help?" Let each child volunteer his ideas.

A mother may be stressed under a workload that's just too much for one person. This is often the case when there are many children, all too young to help out. Outside help would be one solution. If the couple can't afford this, the husband can pitch in. Sometimes, the husband would be very willing to help, but the wife hesitates to ask. She sees it as her job to manage the children and the household, and believes she should be able to do it all by herself. Perhaps she's comparing herself to some exceptional "supermom" who seems to manage splendidly without any help. With this attitude she does herself, her husband, and her children an injustice, since everyone in the family is bound to suffer because of it. An exhausted, overworked mother cannot function very well. Better for the wife to accept herself as she is, refrain from judging and blaming herself because of her inability to manage without help, and graciously accept her husband's help.

Self-Induced Stress

Much of our stress, however, comes from pressure we put on ourselves. We all know that it's harder to stay calm when we're trying to meet many demands. This is why it's so important for parents to set their priorities in order. We're far more likely to snap angrily at our children when we're trying to get many things done in a hurry. We need to ask ourselves such questions as, "Which is more important, a spick-and-span house or a warm and easy relationship with my children?" "Must I really slave to prepare a host of special dishes for an elaborate Shabbos menu, or wouldn't it be better to settle for a simpler menu and buy cake at the bakery, as long as my children are young?"

Keeping our priorities in order in this way requires a certain amount of inner strength. We can't allow ourselves to worry about what visitors might think of us because our house isn't quite as clean as they think it should be, or because we haven't served them home-baked cake.

When a woman is under stress because of her many responsibilities, part of her problem may be her attitude toward her situation. She has little time now to tend to her own needs and desires, and may deeply resent this. She continues to function, but her thoughts run along the following lines: "I just go from one thing to the next — there's no letup. What about *me?* I have no time for myself at all!"

The mother needs to develop greater acceptance of her present situation. The reality is that when her children are young, there just isn't as much time for her own needs and desires. Coming to grips with this, reminding herself that surely there will come a time when she'll be able to do those things she wants to do, will ease her frustration and help her to overcome her resentment.

At the same time, she can do whatever possible to make her job more pleasurable. A baby-sitter coming in for several hours a week can give the mother a much needed and deserved break. Beyond this, investing effort in improving parenting skills can produce dividends in the form of better behaved, easier to manage, and more enjoyable children. She can focus on the rewarding aspects of child–rearing, seeing her children grow into "menschen" and not seeing them as nuisances who prevent her from getting her work done. She can take out time to be with them and just have fun. After all, this is a mother's lot for a substantial part of her life — why not throw herself into it and make these years fulfilling ones!

Another kind of parental outburst tends to follow a series of minor "disasters." It is typically brought on by the following thoughts: "This is just *too* much. I've held on to myself long enough now. I can't take it anymore." Underlying these thoughts we often find the following reasoning: "How long can I be expected to control myself and remain calm?" The assumption is that it's unreasonable for anyone to expect of us that we stay calm under such circumstances, and with one more "disaster" we'll have the right to explode!

When parents become aware of these thoughts, they can attempt to challenge their validity. It does get harder to remain in control with each successive mishap; it does require greater effort. But it can be done.

When parents feel they are on the verge of screaming, they should control that urge and instead give quiet expression to their feelings. Telling the children, "Kids, this is a little too much for me," does no harm; it's the screaming and anger which we should try our best to avoid.

Though every effort should be made to prevent anger, it's neither possible nor desirable to remain *completely* calm at all times. It is appropriate — even beneficial — for the child to see sometimes that a particular action of his has upset us. A well-placed comment can often create sincere regret. For instance, if two children who are involved in an argument begin to insult each other, we can say — but quietly — "It upsets me very much to see you kids being mean to one another." When we've left a clean and tidy kitchen, and come back half an hour later to find a shambles, we can let the child who left the mess know how much it distresses us. It is not emotional reaction that must be avoided, but raised voices and negative character judgments.

There is also a special frustration that develops out of the learning process itself. Parents who have worked hard at learning to control their anger and have made good progress are likely to feel intensely disappointed whenever they slide back into old habits. *But regression is a normal part of improvement.* It will inevitably occur, sooner or later. Just remember that each time we regress and become angry yet again, we have the opportunity to study what went wrong, and thus to become more aware of the dysfunctional beliefs which underlie our anger. That awareness will produce ever greater growth and change.

Accepting Our Lot

By using the approach outlined in this book, we can reduce and even eliminate our anger. But there is an even higher level of coping with frustration; a serene acceptance of what life brings us. Acceptance is the secure feeling that we are in God's hands. We trust that whatever He decrees as our fate is for the good, for the very best. Achieving this lofty level of complete, simple trust (*bitachon*) is a lifetime job; our efforts should focus on striving continuously to come closer to it. We don't have to despair if we lack this quality as yet, for we can always be working to develop and strengthen it.

Of course, we should make every reasonable effort to improve our lives, changing those things which can be changed. Trust in God enables us to accept with serenity that which cannot be changed. Armed with *bitachon*, we will have the courage and strength to endure whatever befalls us. We know that God directs the whole world, not only for the good, but in the best possible way. Perhaps we're being tested. Perhaps suffering is intended to develop in us new depth of character, new strengths or insights. The good in our suffering is rarely evident to our shortsighted view; we cannot expect to comprehend God's plan. But we must try to accept it without question. Thus we come to accept our portion in life — whatever comes our way (certainly the spilled–milk moments!), ultimately achieving what we so much wish for — true inner peace.

GUILT

Some of us are trying to be perfect. We see any imperfection on our part as a sign of failure, and a proof of worthlessness. Frequently, we are as critical of ourselves as we are of our children, showing no more tolerance toward our own shortcomings than toward theirs. Our habit of self-criticism may be so ingrained that we are, literally, at it all day, subjecting ourselves to a continuous harangue of accusation and abuse, ending up feeling spent and miserable. "Why am I always yelling at my children? I shouldn't be so demanding! Why can't I be more patient and reasonable? Why am I so easily frustrated? Why do I get annoyed so quickly? I shouldn't be so critical! I should give my children more attention." It's as if we harbor within us a critic who won't be stilled. He stands by, waiting to catch us at some wrongdoing or error, ready to pounce on us at any moment: "Look how bad you are! You did it again! You made a mistake! You shouldn't have done it! You'll *never* change!"

When parents become aware of the harmful effects of their anger and other failings, their remorse often only worsens. "Why do I continue in this destructive pattern?" they ask themselves in anguish. "Why do I spoil my relations with my children in this way?"

The wisest of men said, "There is no righteous man on earth that does good and never sins."[18] No one can achieve perfection. Yet many of us insist that, as parents, we must never make mistakes or do anything wrong.

It's interesting that nowhere in the Torah do we find a requirement for perfection. Indeed, our Sages teach us just the opposite.

"It is not your obligation to complete the work, yet neither are you free to leave it."[19] We are required to invest the necessary effort to fulfill our obligations, but success is not a requirement. When we condemn our children because they are not the perfect beings we demand that they be, we become angry. When we condemn ourselves because *we* are not the perfect parents we insist we must be, we feel guilty. Thus, guilt is anger turned inward. We are stricken with excessive remorse and anguish over our faulty behavior.

TESHUVAH: The Torah Method of Dealing With Imperfection

Regret and remorse do have their place in our lives. They are healthy and constructive if they 1) arise from actual wrongdoing, and 2) lead to a resolve to avoid repetition of the faulty deed. This constitutes *teshuvah*, the Torah mechanism for behavior correction.

Rabbi Simchah Wasserman has compared *teshuvah* to a cleaning establishment: "If there were no cleaners, I would wear my suit until it became soiled, and then I would have to throw it out." Self-condemnation is like throwing out the suit; *teshuvah* takes out the spots.

Many people think we're required to repent only for active transgressions, such as stealing. This is a mistake, says Rambam. We have to do *teshuvah* for anger, jealousy, and other negative character traits as well. These traits, once ingrained, are far more difficult to eradicate.[20]

The implementation of *teshuvah* depends on the ability to make choices.[21] This concept of a God-given *bechirah* (free will) is basic to Judaism. However, many people subscribe to the principle of *bechirah* in theory only, considering themselves incapable of it in practice. They believe that past hereditary or environmental influences make change virtually impossible. There's no denying the crucial role of such influences in shaping our past behavior. But, according to the cognitive view, they continue to affect our behavior today only because we keep reindoctrinating ourselves with the very same beliefs and thought patterns which formed our behavior originally. These beliefs and thought patterns are often highly irrational. They were developed during our childhood from our *interpretations* of the events in our lives *at that time.* Today, however, we can adopt new and more rational interpretations. In this way we can release ourselves from the influences of the past.

To be sure, this isn't easy. Our thoughts, our "inner dialogues," are usually rapid and automatic. Effort and practice are required merely to become aware of them and identify them. We may work hard and consistently to alter our way of thinking, but habitual patterns will often take over, undermining our best efforts. These patterns make it difficult to erase the influences of the past. While in truth we are in control of our behavior and can change it freely at all times, in practice, this freedom is often limited.

In an article on *teshuvah,* the late Rabbi Yechiel M. Schlessinger describes the proper sequence for correcting ingrained negative character traits. The reason we have such difficulty doing *teshuvah* for them, he explains, is that we go about it the wrong way. In *teshuvah* for a single act of wrongdoing, regret should precede correction. But when changing long-established habits, correction should precede regret. This is the order described by the prophet — "After I return, I regret"[22] — and outlined in the writings of both Rambam and Rabbeinu Yonah. If one does *teshuvah* in the wrong order, he can become so engulfed in remorse and self-castigation over his behavior that he despairs, and concludes that change is impossible.[23] In other words, when a person has a longstanding bad habit, he will never believe that he is actually capable of change until he sees himself improve.

The founder of the Mussar movement, Rabbi Yisrael of Salant, describes the road to character change as long, difficult, and full of obstacles. He is well known for saying, "It is easier to review the entire Talmud than to correct one trait." He teaches that it's important to realize that progress is inevitably fraught with setbacks. Character improvement is by nature slow. If we try to *force* change with our will, we can easily end up discouraged and even discontinue our effort.[24]

Self-Denigration Prevents Change

When we realize that we've displayed a negative character trait, we must do *teshuvah.* But this doesn't call for vicious attacks on ourselves. The Mishnah teaches, "Don't see yourself as wicked."[25] *Teshuvah*, properly executed, can allow for healthy and beneficial guilt, but it has no place for unhealthy and destructive guilt.

Underlying self-condemnation is a belief that because we've done something wrong, we must punish ourselves for it. Such self-imposed suffering serves no useful purpose whatsoever. Indeed, self-denigration is often a major factor in perpetuating the very behavior we wish to change. Rambam comments on the Mishnah quoted above that if one has a low self-image, one learns to expect less of oneself and is bound to behave in a manner that meets these low expectations.[26]

Moreover, *teshuvah* demands a fairly high level of energy. Castigating ourselves diverts our energy into nonconstructive channels, making change all the more difficult. As Rabbeinu Yonah points out, a poor self-image leads to hopelessness, and is a major obstacle to proper repentance.[27] Therefore, any attempts to improve our behavior must begin with avoiding self-disparagement.

Rate Only Behavior

Self-disparagement begins with telling ourselves that, because we behaved badly, *we* are bad. Thus, if we wish to succeed at *teshuvah*, we must stop evaluating ourselves poorly because of our poor conduct.

We assess ourselves out of a need to prove our worth, both to ourselves and to others. We strive mightily to avoid making any errors, to maintain a good rating. If we manage our children well, we rate ourselves highly. When we cope poorly, however, we give ourselves a low rating. Our children's misconduct will also trigger negative evaluation. We reason, "If I did everything right, my children would always behave perfectly." Therefore we judge ourselves as bad parents whenever our children misbehave.

Such striving for perfection to prove our worth is wasteful and uncalled for. Perfection is not a requirement. While we might well prefer to be perfect, it's simply impossible. As the Torah observes, no one can be perfectly righteous.

Above all, judgment is God's domain and not our business. It's best to give up global evaluation of ourselves, and concentrate instead on particular traits and behavior. "I acted badly," not "I'm a bad mother"; "I have a bad habit of getting angry," not "I'm bad because I get angry." Again, we must separate the deed from the doer. When we've learned to stop thinking of ourselves as bad people because of our faulty behavior, we'll no longer feel destructively guilty.

Changing those inner messages is a major factor in eliminating harmful self-disparagement. Reproaches such as "I was such a stupid idiot when I...." or "No one else would have been so selfish as to...." are intolerant and negative self-evaluations. A negative view of ourselves leads us to believe that we'll always fail in this manner, and reinforces the very behavior we're trying so hard to change. By substituting more objective and less accusatory language, such as "It was improper to...." or "It would have been better to...." or "I haven't been very...." we're less likely to judge ourselves. Our emphasis should be on self-acceptance, along with an acknowledgment that we could do better. Instead of "How terrible of me to get so angry!" tell yourself, "It wasn't proper to get angry; I'll try to control myself better next time." Rather than "I should be more patient!" think, "I haven't been very patient, but I'll try to improve."

Once we've taken this step, we should focus on any irrationality in our statements. For example, "I should be more patient!" often implies an exaggerated expectation. We'd have to be angels to be perfectly patient all the time.

We might also question the validity of our descriptions. "Why am I *always* yelling at my children?" is an obvious exaggeration; it's unlikely that any parent yells at his children *all* the time.

Often, however, we criticize ourselves when in truth we've done nothing wrong at all! For instance, we call ourselves "mean" when, in fact, we acted in our child's best interest. Some of us manage to find fault with ourselves all the time. Nothing we do seems to be right or enough. If we were strict, we think we should have been more lenient. If we've been lenient, we tell ourselves we should have been stricter. If you have this habit, ask yourself, the next time you feel guilty: Did I really do anything wrong? If you did, do *teshuvah* for it. But if you didn't, why in the world are you feeling guilty?

Another insidious source of guilt and self-denigration is comparison. Many mothers constantly compare their performance with that of other mothers to see how they measure up. When they see a neighbor succeed better in some area, they conclude, "She's a better mother than I am."

Of course, it's possible to learn from others' exemplary behavior, but comparison of ourselves to others in terms of *worth* is harmful. If I notice that my neighbor is especially patient with her children, I can learn this skill from observing her. But such modeling of behavior is only effective after first eliminating all comparison of our essential worth as people.

Even rating ourselves highly is counterproductive; it implies the possibility of rating ourselves poorly as well. While our self-image may get a boost from a high rating for good actions, it inevitably takes a beating when our rating falls because of poor performance. The only permanent solution to the problem of our low self-image is to stop rating ourselves altogether.

Our ultimate worth is not our concern. No one is capable of determining his own, or anyone else's true worth; this must be left to God. It's sufficient for us to know that every individual possesses infinite potential worth, by virtue of having been created in God's image.[28] Indeed, our Sages teach that a person should always tell himself: "The world was created for my sake."[29]

Implementing Teshuvah

Once we've given up nonconstructive self-criticism and self-denigration, we can begin the difficult task of correcting our bad habits. Remember, when we do *teshuvah* for bad habits, regret should *follow* correction. First, we must concentrate on concrete efforts to change.

The first step is to recognize that most bad habits stem from lack of self-control. The essential root of this problem is our demand to have everything our way. Whenever we display some destructive trait, it can be traced to this demand. For example, when we get angry at a child for disobedience, underlying the anger is our demand, "My children *must* obey me (and I can't stand it when they don't)!" When we make selfish choices, we act from the belief that we *must* have comfort and convenience (and can't bear it when we don't!). Therefore, we elevate our needs above those of others. Once we realize this, we can gradually give up such demands. The key word is "gradual." We're dealing here with fundamental character change, and that takes time.

Only after we've measurably diminished our faulty traits should we begin to regret our past. Regret at this point, writes Rabbi Schlessinger, will not depress us. On the contrary, it develops and elevates the soul by cleansing it of the harmful aftereffects of our transgression. The extent of regret that this requires is a matter of individual judgment. In any event, after spending Yom Kippur in sincere regret, we may be confident that our transgressions will be forgiven.[30] Indeed, if we confess and repent a transgression on Yom Kippur and then continue to worry about it, this implies a lack of faith in God's promise to grant us atonement.[31] Moreover, such continued preoccupation with our guilt may interfere with our functioning.[32]

Reminding ourselves of our earlier transgressions and reexperiencing the pain of regret over them can reinforce our resolve not to repeat them. This is therefore recommended for subsequent Days of Atonement. However, it's inadvisable to let this interfere with the joy and optimism of our daily life.[33]

Apologizing to Children

Parents often wonder whether it's wise or proper to apologize to their own child when they've hurt him unnecessarily. Part of the *teshuvah* process, after all, is to ask for forgiveness from those we have wronged.[34]

Rabbi Wasserman says that parents definitely should apologize to their child in such situations, and that it will improve their relationship with him. However, one must know how to apologize. It should not be done guiltily; it's best to say something like, "I shouldn't have screamed at (hit) you before. I'm sorry about it." The child must know that anger is wrong. If our inappropriate anger toward him is overlooked, we're in effect teaching him that it's all right for him to get angry too.

When we apologize to our children, we're also modeling how to be *modeh al ha'emes* (admitting wrongdoing). This is a most effective method of teaching our children how to recognize their own mistakes and apologize. It sets an example for them to remember and follow.

Interactions of Guilt and Anger

Guilt is often a reaction to anger, but it can also trigger it. For example, when we see perpetual disorder in our children's room, we may jump to the conclusion that we are failures for not getting them to be neat. We then turn on the children in anger, blaming them for making us into failures.

We have to recognize that the source of such anger is our guilt feelings. What sets the anger off is thinking, "They make me feel like such a failure! (*I* am a failure.)" The only way to eliminate this kind of anger is to stop blaming ourselves for our poor parenting skills. Instead, we should do what we can to improve, and in the meantime be patient with both ourselves and our children.

Some parents find themselves in a vicious cycle of anger and guilt. When they feel guilty for getting angry at their child, they react by blaming the child for their anger *and* their guilt and become even angrier at the child. "It's all his fault!" they tell themselves. "If *he* hadn't behaved so badly, *I* wouldn't have had to get angry, and wouldn't be suffering these terrible guilt feelings now!" What fuels the anger in this situation is an inability to tolerate guilt feelings and the demand that they go away. It's another example of low frustration tolerance. In this cycle, anger triggers guilt, which triggers further anger, the cycle rising in crescendo. To stop the process, we must learn to tolerate the pain of our guilt feelings, as long as they still plague us.

Guilt Over Guilt

There are parents who are fully aware of their useless habit of constantly telling themselves off, and realize that they cause themselves senseless misery this way. But they then proceed to berate themselves even more mercilessly for behaving so stupidly, making themselves still more miserable. "Why do I torture myself with this constant self-criticism? Why don't I stop it, and change my behavior instead?" Such secondary guilt feelings are even more pernicious and difficult to uproot than the original guilt.

These parents should keep in mind that this habit, like any other, is difficult to change. If they want to succeed at behavior change, they must first learn to stop telling themselves off for substituting guilt for self-improvement.

Guilt About Not Giving Enough Attention

Because so much has been written about giving children sufficient attention, many parents have become anxious about it. Mothers in particular tend to suffer from guilt on this score.

Severe neglect is of course harmful. Yet children do not require nearly as much attention as some professionals would have us believe. In fact, giving a child constant, excessive attention can lead to a demanding child. If told quietly and pleasantly, "I'm busy now — in a few minutes I'll have time for you," children can learn to wait until the parent is free to tend to their needs. A child who keeps calling from another room, "Mommy, Mommy!" can be answered with, "I can't come right now — I'm busy with...." Thus the child learns to accept with equanimity that he can't always have your attention.

Mothers are sometimes told that they must give each child some "special" time when he has his mother's undivided attention. A mother who makes her child feel that he's accepted and loved, and who, when she listens to him, does so attentively, needn't go out of her way to give him such special time; these moments will arise naturally.

Guilt of the Working Mother

A mother who works outside the home may worry that she harms her children by being away from them for substantial parts of the day. She might even judge herself a bad mother and feel guilty.

The mother's plight is real. She would like to spend more time with her children, but — for whatever reasons, such as financial necessity, boredom, or, as some women have put it, "I'd go nuts if I had to be with my kids all day!" — she feels that she can't. However, her guilt is out of place. Judging ourselves, whether for real or imagined harm we cause our children, is always destructive.

Once the mother has made the decision to seek employment outside of the house, the best thing she can do for herself and her children is to make peace with her decision.

Accepting Ourselves

Parents who've read about the harmful effects of parental mismanagement may exaggerate the "awfulness" of it. They may believe that whenever they lose control, they inflict irreparable damage on their child. After a display of anger, they're likely to think in horror, "How awful! Look what I'm doing to my children!" Parents who suffered as children from *their* parents' anger, and who resolved never to cause their own children similar suffering, tend to feel particularly guilty about their anger. They tell themselves, "I said I would never do this to my children, yet here I am doing it anyway!"

There's no denying the possibility of harmful consequences to children when parents are in poor control — especially if their lack of control is constant and intense. But "awfulizing" and feeling guilty about this is destructive and does nothing to improve the situation. A noted psychologist comments:

> We have been subjected to abuses by parents throughout the ages and if human nature were not so strong as it is, what would have become of all of us? It is true that we could have been better and that we should try to help our children to become better and happier human beings. But one factor in helping them is to recognize their ability to withstand so many of the bad influences which we exert on them, unwillingly and unconsciously.[35]

It may help us better to accept ourselves if we downgrade the "awfulness" of what we ourselves suffered from our parents' anger. Our pain did not stem from their anger, but from our *evaluation* of it. As young children, we didn't know how to protect ourselves from our parents' anger. When they became angry at us, we jumped to the conclusion that we were bad. Our thinking was: "Mommy (Daddy) is angry at me. She thinks I'm bad. I am bad." We failed to make the necessary distinction between our basic nature and our behavior. So we concluded that we were bad and unworthy of being loved. This was the true source of our suffering at that time.

Though it's very discouraging to repeat the same mistakes our parents made, it's normal during a stressful situation to automatically revert to the patterns we saw acted out when we were children. It's no easy matter to change these automatic reactions.

For some of us, change may be so exceptionally difficult that we become convinced we're truly incapable of it. This is *never* true. People can and do learn new ways of reacting. But we'll continue to feel sure that we can't change as long as we keep telling ourselves so. The message repeats itself in our head like a tape being played over and over: "I *can't* change; it's *too* hard; it's *too* much work; I *won't* be able to do it; I give up." We must replace this recording with a new one; one that is more encouraging in its message. "I *can* change. It's difficult, but I'll keep trying and I *won't* give up. It may be hard work, but I'm prepared for it."

Thus, in order to change, we must believe in our ability to do it. We must also be sufficiently motivated to undertake the hard work necessary to succeed. We can draw strength from our belief in the God-given capacity for change, and from our faith that He who endowed us with this Divine attribute will grant us the wisdom and strength to exercise it as well.[36]

In the meantime, remember that the minute we become aware of our mistakes, they are no longer failures in parenting. They become steps in the process of becoming better parents. *Good judgment comes from experience, and experience comes from poor judgment.* So we can profit from our mistakes, rather than criticize ourselves for them.

Chapter Two

THE MITZVOS OF HONOR
AND REVERENCE FOR PARENTS

NATURE OF THE MITZVAH

he obligation to honor and revere one's father and mother is included among the first five of the Ten Commandments — those which deal with man's relationship to God — rather than among the last five, which have to do with man's relationship to his fellow man. From this we learn, say our Sages, that honoring one's parents is comparable to honoring God Himself.[1]

Honor of parents is linked to honor of God in another way: "There are three partners to [the creation of] a person: God, his father, and his mother. When a person honors his father and his mother, God says, 'It is as if I dwelt among them and they honored Me.'"[2]

A child's debt to his parents isn't only physical, but spiritual as well. It is the parents who transmit the Torah heritage to their children. They become the child's link to the Divine source of revelation.

Thus, a child's parents are the roots of both his physical and his spiritual existence. Therefore, he is commanded to honor and revere them.

GRATITUDE

At the heart of the commandments to honor and revere parents is gratitude. For the child, this involves a sense of appreciation for his parents' share in bringing him into the world, and for their love, concern, and self-sacrifice in caring for him. Children must learn to recognize the good they receive from their parents in order to properly revere and honor them. This gratitude will extend eventually to God Himself.

> It is only fitting that he render them all the honor and do them all the service he can. For they brought him into the world and they labored greatly on his behalf during his childhood. Once a person has acquired this trait, he will ascend from it to be grateful for the good done him by God, who is the Cause of his being and the Cause of the existence of all his forefathers, reaching back to Adam.[3]

Thus, teaching a child to show gratitude to his parents becomes the foundation not only of honor and reverence, but also of love of God which is central to religious life. This is why gratitude is so emphasized in Jewish ethical writings. It lends additional weight to the parents' obligation to initiate their children into the mitzvos of honor and reverence.

THE DIFFICULTIES

Teaching gratitude isn't easy. Children are naturally self-centered and it's difficult to instill in them any awareness of their parents' efforts. Since they're accustomed to enjoying their parents' favors and devotion from their earliest years, they take it all for granted, failing to appreciate to what extent their parents have taken pains for them. Consequently, children usually lack that gratitude which would motivate them to honor their parents.

Even if children are aware of all the things their mothers and fathers do for them, they may attribute this behavior to paternal and maternal instincts and deny that there's any real dedication and sacrifice for which to be thankful.

In addition, every child has a developing desire for independence, and may perceive his parents' educational efforts as an attempt at domination. He may resent and resist parental authority, the restrictions and requirements which parents impose.

Because of the difficulties in teaching honor and reverence, it's especially important to emphasize to our children that we require them to honor and revere us *for their own benefit.* We must try to avoid reacting with anger or hurt feelings when they don't show respect or fail to obey us. We want the welfare of our child, not our own feelings, to be the focus of attention.

When we reprimand our children about disrespectful conduct, we should be careful not to give the impression that we're merely promoting our personal honor. One way of avoiding this is for one parent to speak to the child about improper behavior toward the other parent.[4] Requests for apologies can also be handled in this way. For example, the father might gently urge the child, "Go tell your mother you're sorry and ask her to forgive you."

Keep in mind that while children have an obligation to revere and honor their parents, it's up to the parents to create an atmosphere where reverence and honor come easily. As the *Shulchan Aruch* states:

> The father is forbidden to impose too heavy a yoke on his children, to be too exacting with them in matters pertaining to his honor, lest he cause them to stumble. Rather he should forgive them and shut his eyes; for a father has a right to forgo the honor due him.[5]

Rabbi Aryeh Leib, eldest son of the Chafetz Chaim, writes of his father's educational approach: "We were cautioned little about the honor due our parents....He related to us as a friend and brother."[6] Parents who don't respect their children create a great obstacle to their children's respecting them. Parents who do respect their children are paving the pathway for their children to observe the mitzvos of honoring and revering them. The atmosphere in the home is most influential. Modeling the way to act will always be the most powerful form of education.

The way parents behave toward each other is also a model. That husband and wife must talk to each other respectfully is a mitzvah in itself, of course. But it also sets the tone for family interaction. Snide or sarcastic remarks, criticism, yelling, joking at each other's expense, interrupting each other, and other forms of disrespect between the parents usually reappear in the behavior of their children. Children are very observant and learn by imitation; give them something worth imitating!

Occasional disagreement on child-rearing issues is normal, but it's not for the children's ears. Never criticize your spouse's handling of discipline (or anything else) in your children's presence; all differences should be worked out in private. Husband and wife are partners in child-rearing. They should cooperate at all times, giving each other support and advice.

DEFINING THE MITZVAH

The mitzvos of honor and reverence for parents are based on two Biblical verses:

1. Honor your father and mother....[7]
2. You shall revere every man his mother and father....[8]

The Gemara defines honor and reverence as follows:

Our Rabbis taught: What is reverence and what is honor? Reverence means that [the son] must neither stand nor sit in his [father's] place nor contradict his words, nor express an evaluation of his opinions.

Honor means that he must give him food and drink, clothe and cover him, and accompany him when he enters and leaves.[9]*

---

* No significance should be attached to the use of the masculine singular in this and other passages. The obligations of reverence and honor apply to daughters as well as to sons,[10] and mothers are to be accorded the same honor and reverence due to fathers.[11] The Mishnah deduces this from the above-quoted verses.[12]

These descriptions should be taken as illustrations rather than comprehensive definitions. Honor and reverence are attitudes and the above are manifestations of these attitudes, reflections of an inner feeling. The specific examples given in the Talmud are certainly meaningful, but proper fulfillment of the mitzvos consists of far more. The actual obligations are "too numerous to list and discussions of them would be overly long."[13] Our Sages view honor and reverence for parents as knowing no limits.[14]

We'll confine ourselves here to those aspects of the mitzvos with which parents must be familiar in order to teach them to their child.

WHAT IS REVERENCE?

Reverence means that the child is conscious of his parents' elevated status and dignity, and is careful never to dishonor them in any way.[15] The mitzvah of reverence requires him to see his parents as a "king and queen" whom he must be very careful not to offend.[16]

The halachic authorities stress several formal expressions of reverence:

1. *Occupying the parents' place.* A child should not stand or sit in the place habitually occupied by his parents, either in the home or outside of it, such as in the synagogue.[17]

2. *Contradicting the parents' words.* A child may not contradict his parents, either in discussions on Torah or in general conversation. This applies only to explicitly contradictory statements; it's permissible for children to engage in debates with their parents on general topics, as well as Torah law. Children are allowed to present arguments which contest a parent's position as long as it's done respectfully.[18] Thus, for example, if the father says that it is permissible to read a newspaper on Shabbos, the son may not say that it's forbidden. He may, however, cite opinions which disallow it.

Even where a child has been rebuked by mistake, he may not contradict the parent by saying, "That's not true." Rather, he should try to set things straight by expressing himself in a noncontradictory way such as, "I can explain myself."19

3. *Evaluating the parents' opinions.* If a parent has a disagreement

with someone else, the child may not decide in favor of either side. He may not even express endorsement for his parent's point of view by saying, for example, "My father is right."[20] It is arrogant for a child to set himself up as a judge of his parents' opinions.

4. *Calling parents by their name.* A child must not call his parent by name.[21] However, if someone asks him, "Whose son are you?" he is permitted to state his parent's name.[22] It's also permissible for a child to write his parent's name.[23]

5. *Waking parents.* A child is generally forbidden to wake his parents. But if he knows his father would want to be woken, for example, to prevent a financial loss, then he fulfills a mitzvah by waking him. Likewise, a child should wake his parents when it's necessary for the performance of a mitzvah, such as synagogue worship.[24]

The Bible pronounces a curse on anyone who treats his parents lightly or shows them contempt in any way.[25] In the words of Rambam:

> Anyone who treats his father or mother with contempt, even if by mere word or gesture, is cursed from the mouth of God.[26]

Included in this category is one who causes his parents distress.[27]

WHAT IS HONOR?

The essence of honor is that a child hold his parents in the highest esteem and regard them as persons of great worth and importance. Honor expresses itself in thought, word, and deed.[28] It obligates the child to serve his parents personally, as befits persons of great worth and importance. He should tend to their needs and serve them in all the ways a servant serves his master.[29]

The obligation to provide for parents' basic needs applies even when they don't make an explicit request. For example, if a child knows that his mother is thirsty he must bring her a drink. However, if something isn't a basic need, the child is required to provide it only if the parent has actually asked for it.[30]

From the Talmud's definition of honor quoted earlier, we see that it includes both the satisfaction of physical needs — such as food, drink, and clothing — and symbolic gestures of attentiveness, such as accompanying parents when they come and leave.

We also find a revealing reference in the Talmud to the manner of service:

> Rabbi Shimon ben Gamliel said, "I served my father all my life, but I did not extend to him even one-hundredth of the honor given Isaac by [his son] Esau. For I would serve my father dressed in dirty clothes, and when I would go to my affairs, would change into clean clothes. But Esau always dressed as royalty to serve his father."[31]

Clearly, true honor goes beyond physical acts of personal service. It also involves the manner of performing the service: the positive and caring attitude and the extra thoughtfulness.

OBEDIENCE

Though there is no statement making obedience part of the mitzvos of honor and reverence, it's implied. A disobedient child who acts contrary to his parents' expressed wish, or fails to do as he's asked, is being disrespectful and thus transgresses the mitzvah of reverence: "If the son does not obey his father, it is the same as if he contradicted him."[32] Others see the fear of transgressing the parents' requests as part of reverence.[33]

Many of the things which parents ask of a child, such as helping with housework or going on an errand, are acts of service from which the parent benefits. Such acts of obedience are a form of honor. Rabbi Akiva Eiger points out that even when the request doesn't relate to personal service, the pleasure which the child causes his parents by his obedience is a fulfillment of the mitzvah of honor.[34]

TEACHING THE MITZVAH

If children are to honor and revere their parents, they must be taught how to do so. Ideally, the laws pertaining to these mitzvos should be taught in school. This is because no matter how much parents emphasize their concern for their child, and no matter how careful they are to be objective, the child may still think they are asking for respect and honor out of their own self-interest. It will always be somewhat awkward for a parent to say, "This is how you have to treat me." It is simply easier for outsiders to teach these attitudes. Still, parents must explain aspects of the mitzvos when necessary.

TEACHING REVERENCE

Parents should make sure that even their very young children show respect toward them. This is important not only for the parent-child relationship but also for the child's developing attitude toward others. It is in his dealings with his parents that he learns how to behave toward people in general. Besides, if parents let their children acquire habits of disrespect toward them while young, they may find it extremely difficult to change this behavior pattern as their children grow older.

Careful as we may be in modeling respectful behavior for our children, there still will be times when they show disrespect toward us. Sadly, Western society provides them with plentiful role models of disrespectful behavior. Besides, all children will be displeased with their parents on occasion; perhaps due to some imposed restriction, or requirement of something they don't want to do. At such times, they are likely to act disrespectfully.

To deal with such behavior, we must try to view the situation objectively. This means avoiding reacting with anger ("How dare he talk to me this way!"); hurt ("How awful that *my own child* talks to me like this!"); or guilt ("Where have *I* failed that my child speaks to me with such disrespect?"). Instead, our reaction should be one of concern: "My child's behavior is bad for *him*. Let me see how I can best handle the problem." But parents don't have to keep their feelings completely neutral. Sometimes, a show of mild hurt can move children toward regret. Merely saying the child's name softly with a slightly disappointed facial expression can be enough — or a serious look while slowly shaking the head from side to side. Telling him (but not often) that we feel hurt because of the way he spoke to us can help.

For the very young child, a mild reprimand, delivered quietly and lovingly, is usually sufficient. Taking the child's hand in his, the parent might say, "You're not allowed to talk to Daddy (Mommy) this way."

If despite such reprimands a child continues to speak disrespectfully, try telling him, "The next time you speak to me disrespectfully, I'm not going to say anything to you about it again. I'm just going to walk away and not talk to you for a while." Then, follow through on this. Of course, explain to your child, afterwards, the reason for your action. "Remember I said I wasn't going to tell you again? I was just going to walk away."

Young children sometimes hit or bite their mother. Usually the child is playing, or testing to see his mother's reaction; sometimes he may be expressing anger or frustration. Remember, he can't yet express his feelings very well with speech, or even sort them out in his own mind. But whatever the reason for the child's behavior, do not allow it. Don't hit or bite back (even if only to show what it feels like). Instead, say quietly, "No," holding up a finger for emphasis. If he persists, hold his hand or gently take hold of his mouth as you tell him with great seriousness, "You are *not* allowed to hit your mother" ("You are *not* allowed to bite"). Children don't usually keep up such behavior for long.

But what about an older child who acts with impertinence? A good initial reaction is to ignore him. For instance, Ze'evi demands, "How come I don't have any clean socks?!" Don't answer, but turn away and continue going about your business. "Hey!" Ze'evi continues. "Don't you hear me? I said I don't have socks!" Eventually, ask quietly, "Do you know why I'm not answering you? Maybe you don't realize it, Ze'evi, but the way you spoke to me was disrespectful. You're not allowed to complain to your parents that way. Now, if you need clean socks and there aren't any in the drawer, how could you come and tell me about this in a pleasant way?" (If you've overlooked such disrespect in the past, you might add, "I know I haven't corrected you on this before but from now on I'll point it out to you.")

Similarly, a child who screams at his parents should be ignored for the moment. When he's calmed down somewhat, you might say, making sure to keep your voice low, "I know you were upset before, but you know, you're not allowed to scream at me. You can tell me you're upset and that something is bothering you, but you must tell it to me quietly."

Be careful not to defend yourself or offer explanations when your child complains to you disrespectfully. Parents often forget themselves in such situations and start arguing with their child. But by overlooking his disrespect they're sanctioning it. Set aside, for the moment, the issue raised by the child, and deal first with the more important issue of his disrespect, as in these examples:

D'vory complains at mealtime, "Hey! You always give Deeny first!" Try answering, "I can see you're unhappy, but that's no way to tell it to me. What could you say instead?" (pause) "Mommy, could you give me first sometimes too?"

Shlomy grumbles, "How come Ilan's parents let him buy himself something when he goes to the grocer for them, and you don't?!" Don't let your first response be a defensive explanation such as, "This is the way things are done in our house." Rather, point out quietly to Shlomy that he's not allowed to complain about his parents' decisions in this way.

The issues of fairness and comparison should be dealt with only *after* the issue of speaking respectfully. It's acceptable for children to ask for something, but not to imply that their parents are acting incorrectly or unfairly.

Parents also often unwittingly contribute to the problem of disrespect by arguing back when their child contradicts them. Remember, a child isn't allowed to directly contradict his parents. Be careful not to push him into further transgression. For example, you say something and your daughter responds with, "That's not true." Don't argue with her. Don't enter into a debate where you and she take turns defending your positions. But don't correct her on the spot either. Saying, "You're contradicting me!" will most likely only result in sullen resentment. Instead tell her, "I can't talk to you now. We'll continue soon."

A little later, when emotions have cooled and defensiveness is at a minimum, you can correct your daughter for contradicting you. Try to do so lovingly and without any hint of criticism or reproach. Now is your opportunity to explain how she can express dissent: "Here is how you can tell me if I said something which appears to you to be incorrect — 'Mommy, you said Aunt Rivkah is coming to visit on Monday. I thought I heard her say that she'd come on Tuesday.'"

Be careful also not to ignore seemingly minor shows of annoyance, such as, "Okay, okay, I heard you." This kind of impertinent behavior is frequently overlooked: The Schwartz family, including 5-year-old twins Ruth and Naomi, went for a Shabbos walk. Mr. and Mrs. Schwartz met some friends and stopped to chat, but the twins wanted to go on. "Let's go!" Naomi yelled, tugging at her mother's skirt. "You can go ahead," Mrs. Schwartz answered, and off ran Naomi. But then Ruth began trying to drag her mother yelling, "Come, Mommy, come!" "Stop that now," Mrs. Schwartz said, rather sharply. "That's enough!"

This kind of handling is a mistake. Mrs. Schwartz shouldn't have given in to her twins' nagging and tugging. She should have told them, calmly, that it isn't proper behavior to yell or to pull at their mother. In this way Ruth and Naomi would learn to restrain themselves in the future, and Mrs. Schwartz's task of managing them would become easier as well.

One mother describes the effects of developing a clear but loving way of correcting her impertinent 11-year-old:

> Esther was getting more and more "chutzpadik." She was really talking to me like I was a child — or worse, like I just didn't count! I found myself getting angrier and angrier. She complained about my cooking, about my asking her to help with chores, about having to keep her room in order — everything. Whenever anything like this happened, I would yell at her, she would yell back, and then act even worse. Once I really hit her hard across the face, after which I felt just awful! It was so unpleasant to be around her.
>
> At our parenting workshop it was suggested that I hold her hand and say things like, "You know, you have a very bad habit of talking to your parents in an unkind and disrespectful manner. I know you can control yourself. I'm sure you don't like being like this." It really worked — especially the hand-holding. Esther was very much affected by that. She would become very contrite and apologize. She told me that

she knew that what she was doing was wrong, but that "I just couldn't control myself." I assured her that though it might be difficult, she could learn to control herself. It was just a matter of changing a bad habit. Esther was really sorry. This new way of handling Esther's impertinent behavior proved much more effective and has helped maintain a loving relationship between Esther and me.

Once children learn about the mitzvah of respect, they often feel unhappy and regretful after having shown disrespect. Then reprimands aren't necessary. It's enough to say, "I know you're sorry about the way you talked to me before." Children are likely to tell us they're sorry on their own more and more often, as they become more aware of their disrespectful behavior.

Remember, when correcting a child, it's essential to speak in low, gentle tones. This conveys your love and concern, most powerful tools for changing behavior. (If impertinent behavior becomes more serious or persistent, it may be necessary to resort to punishment. See Chapter 5, "Punishment for Disrespect.")

TEACHING HONOR

Parents should encourage their children to serve them, and should provide opportunities for this — asking, for example, for a glass of water, or sending them on errands. It's a nice practice for the father to ask the child to do things for the mother, and vice versa. Thus, the mother might say, "Please take Daddy this cup of tea I prepared for him."

Mealtimes are a natural opportunity to train children in this — the leisurely Shabbos meals especially. My family and I were guests recently at a home where we had the pleasure of watching two small children, a boy of 4 and a girl of 6, serve nearly the entire Shabbos lunch meal with obvious pride and pleasure, virtually unaided by their mother. Most impressive of all, the children did what was necessary without being told; this included clearing the table after each course. Obviously, some perseverance is needed to bring children to such a level. But in the long run, don't such beautiful results make it worth our while?

TEACHING OBEDIENCE

As mentioned, obedience is an aspect of the mitzvah to honor and revere parents. It is also the tool that enables parents to train their children, helping them to acquire the self-control they need in order to develop all other good character traits. Finally, obedience to parents prepares the child to obey God, which is the foundation of Jewish life.

But, important as it is, obedience can't be forced on children. Parents who keep insisting, "You *have* to do it!" are bound to encounter resistance, sooner or later. Though obedience to parents is required by Torah law, parents who demand it of their children — reminding them frequently of their duty — will only arouse resentment. Continual use of punishment to force children to obey is also sure to backfire.

How, then, can we make our children obey? Rabbi Simchah Wasserman points out, "We cannot make people do what we want them to do, but we can make people *want* to do what we want."[35] That's the answer. We must concentrate our efforts on instilling in our children the *desire* to obey us. This willing cooperation can only evolve if the parents' demands are based on loving concern, sincere respect, patience, and moderation.

LOVING CONCERN

Children are quick to sense if their parents are demanding obedience for their personal convenience. They'll learn from their parents' example to put their own interests first, too. Parents' primary motivation must be genuine concern for their children's welfare. When children sense such loving concern, it encourages them to obey; they know that to do so is for their own good. They will have confidence that caring and consideration for them underlies all of their parents' demands.

SINCERE RESPECT

Parents must treat their child with the same respect they want for themselves. The Sages teach, "Let the honor of your pupil be as dear to you as your own."[36] Rabbi Samson Raphael Hirsch comments on this that parents will get their child to do their bidding much more readily if they acknowledge and respect the unique nature and the human dignity of this person entrusted to their guidance.[37]

Patience

Sometimes, a child's obstinance stems from his resentment over our obvious annoyance when he doesn't comply with our wishes. Learning to keep our negative reactions under control is an important part of teaching children.

In particular, nothing gains a child's cooperation as well as a soft and gentle voice. In the classic *Igeres HaRamban*, Ramban wrote to his son, "Always speak to people in a low tone of voice," adding that this will stop us from growing angry. A quiet voice is soothing; it creates that relaxed atmosphere which is so reassuring to our child and makes him feel much more inclined to do as we ask. When we speak quietly, we also convey strength; it is obvious that we are in control of ourselves and the situation. Parents who have worked on reducing the volume of their voice report dramatic changes in their children's behavior. As one mother relates:

> Now that I have been trying out and using my newly learned skills in talking to my 3-year-old son, I feel so much more in control because I can get him to do (or not to do) just about anything I want. All I do is just softly repeat my request (a few times if necessary) and he eventually comes through.

Moderate Demands

If parents' demands are excessive, children are unlikely to cooperate. Impositions should be made thoughtfully and kept within reasonable limits. Otherwise, parents become dictators rather than educators. Rabbi Hirsch writes:

> Never ask a child to do something unnecessary and unimportant; similarly, don't refuse a harmless and trivial request. But if you give an instruction, you must insist on its fulfillment, and if you have refused a request, you must stand by your

refusal, despite all pleading and pressure on the part of the child....Be careful with the word "No!" Let your child do and have whatever you can permit him, on the condition that it won't endanger his physical and moral well-being....

The manner in which we prohibit or permit, and the joy with which we grant the child the freedom to do as he pleases, make it obvious to him that prohibiting and permitting are not the expression of an arbitrary mood, a desire to dominate, or simple stubbornness; but rather result from serious considerations.[38]

Children balk and resist when we place excessive restrictions and requirements upon them. Getting them to be more obedient often involves reducing our demands. This means learning to stay calm and not worrying about having everything be "just so." It means learning to think mainly of our child's welfare rather than of our own immediate needs. Once we develop more inner calm and expect less perfection, we can overlook many more things. It becomes less necessary to impose so many burdens on our children. Again, we can help ourselves stay calm by learning to speak gently.

Following Through

Still, as Rabbi Hirsch advises, whenever we do ask something of our child we must make sure that he does it, and whenever we do refuse him something we must not let him have it, no matter how hard he tries to make us change our mind. It's often tempting to overlook disobedience as a way of avoiding conflict, but in the end, this undermines our authority. For example, if we tell our child, "No standing on the bus seats," and then ignore him when he stands on the bus seats anyway, we teach him that he doesn't have to listen to us. If we want our child to take what we say seriously, we must follow through at all times.

We minimize our demands not in order to be permissive, but to render more potent and meaningful the demands that we do make.

Though it requires some persistence and firmness, parents will find it easier to gain obedience once they become more consistent about following through — as this next story illustrates:

I was out with my 4-year-old who was riding his tricycle, when he accidentally bumped into a baby carriage. I told him to say "I'm sorry" to the mother who was pushing the carriage, but he refused and started to go off with his tricycle. Formerly I would have let him go, but this time I decided to follow through. I held on to the tricycle saying, "No, you can't ride until you say 'I'm sorry.'" He began hitting me. I said, "No, you cannot hit me," and held his hand. He started hitting with the other hand, and I held on to that hand too. I kept repeating, quietly but firmly, "No, I won't let you go until you say 'I'm sorry.'" Finally he yelled out, "I'm sorry!" I said to him, "Please say it nicely." He thought it over a bit, and then said it again, this time without yelling. "That's nice," I said, "now you can go."

To set limits, we must know what can be expected of our children, at their age and level of development. Parents who are unsure about this ought to discuss it with other, more experienced parents.

Beginning With Babies

Wise parents will childproof their home when their baby first begins to crawl, putting dangerous objects and breakables well out of the infant's reach. But sooner or later, we must teach him that there are some things he must leave alone.

We can't stop a baby by merely saying "No" — at least, not at first. He must learn what the word means. As soon as baby Rivky crawls toward some forbidden object, whisk her to another part of the room, saying "No" in a serious but nonthreatening voice. Give her something interesting to distract her. If she persists in her determined quest, take her out of the room, while saying quietly, "Mommy (Daddy) said 'No'." Don't threaten, scold, or hit. Quiet, firm action is all that's called for. Baby Rivky should be confined to her playpen or to some other part of the house for at least 10 minutes. A children's gate at the door is good for this, and enables you to keep an eye on her. You may have to repeat this procedure several times, but if you can remain patient and calm during this training period, Rivky will eventually learn to obey your "No."

Parents often think their child disregards them deliberately. They notice his glances in their direction and conclude that he's fully aware of what he's doing, but it's more likely that he's testing his parents to see how they'll react. Consistent handling is essential; then there will be no more reason for such testing.

We have to expect some damage to our possessions while children are young. Our reaction at such times is crucial. A serious and regretful expression makes the deepest impression on our child. We might say, rather sadly, for instance, "Daddy's book is torn — now he can't read it," or "The plate is broken — now we have to buy a new one."

Little children often enjoy coloring on the walls, much to their parents' consternation. Putting crayons out of reach is usually not enough to deter the budding artist; he'll express his "creativity" with pencils, pens, or ketchup. Everything can't be put out of his reach, indefinitely. Even if it could, what happens when you go visiting with him?

A scribbled-up living room wall can arouse great anger. Nevertheless, parents should try to control themselves. As mentioned in the previous chapter, on the rare occasions when anger is displayed, it should be a deliberate, feigned anger only — that which the parents deem necessary to impress a child with the gravity of his wrongdoing. If we show anger over a crayoned wall, which isn't a serious wrongdoing or character flaw, it teaches children the wrong values.

Take hold of your child's hand and say, very firmly, "Walls are *not* for coloring." Then, immediately produce paper and, placing a crayon (or pencil) in his hand, color with it on the paper, saying, "*Paper* is for coloring."

When you have to take some forbidden object away from a young child, try to find something else to offer him as an alternative. Tell him, "You can't play with that but you can have this instead."

Regarding potentially dangerous situations, a much stricter standard is necessary. This requires immediate and decisive handling. A sharp word and even physical punishment, properly administered, may be appropriate. A toddler has just run out into the street. The parent might shout "No!" and give him one sharp spank as he retrieves him. It's best not to show anger or hysteria but only great concern for the child's safety. Back safely on the sidewalk, the parent can tell the child in a serious, very emphatic voice, "The street is dangerous! Cars can hurt you! Don't *ever* do that again!!"

It's relatively easy to teach a child to stay away from hot objects. The first time he approaches anything hot, take his hand and very quickly and lightly touch it to the hot object, saying emphatically, "Hot, hot, hot!" One or two such demonstrations are usually enough to result in a quick retreat whenever we only call out "Hot!"

Excursions and shopping errands are another problem area. As long as the toddler is kept in his stroller, he's fine. But as soon as he's taken out, he begins to wander all over. Often, calling him doesn't help. This situation calls for resolute handling: Firmly place your child's hand on the side of stroller handle and put yours over it. If he keeps breaking away, quietly strap him into the stroller for a few minutes. He can be given another chance after 10 minutes or so. Ignore his crying completely, except perhaps for a brief "I'm sorry, but now you have to stay in the stroller for a while."

There's no need for raised voices or arguments if your child doesn't want to leave the playground when it's time to go home. So that your child will have time to get used to the idea, give him some prior warning: "We'll be going home soon, in a few more minutes." After the time has passed, tell your child in a friendly way, "We have to go home now." He may scream and thrash about in protest, but don't let his carrying on shake your resolve. Pick him up and carry him away, or place him firmly in his stroller, and go off without further ado.

When Children Say "No"

Parents should be careful not to overreact to their child's "No." Very young children sometimes use this word for the shock effect it has on their parents. Don't explain. Don't try to reason with your child. Ignore him completely and act as if he'd never said it. For instance, if you tell your child, "Come, it's time for your bath," and he says, "No," just undress him and put him into the tub.

You can make things easier for your child (and for yourself) by not asking questions such as, "Do you want to (have your supper) (get dressed)?" Instead, steer him through his routines in a matter-of-fact way. It also helps to be tactful. If your 20-month-old is busy assembling a necklace of pop-it beads at lunchtime, you can let him carry some beads to the table, taking them away only as you hand him his spoon. With older, less distractable children, try to give a little friendly advance notice when possible, so that you don't have to pull him away suddenly from some exciting activity.

What if your young child refuses to do something he was told to do, such as picking up an item from the floor? Basic guidelines for handling the situation are as follows: At the first refusal, repeat your request calmly but firmly, several times if necessary. If he still doesn't comply, ignore it for a minute or two. Then get back to him, reminding him of what he was requested to do. The trick is, on the one hand not to be on top of the child — but on the other hand, not to let go either. Keep your voice low, to convey that you're in control of the situation and expect eventual compliance. With this approach, the child generally does come around sooner or later.

Showing your child that you're unhappy with him can be effective. Lower your head slightly, and say, "Mommy (Daddy) is unhappy because you didn't listen." To heighten the effect, keep up this show of unhappiness for a while, maintaining a serious and somewhat sad tone when you speak to him.

As you develop confidence in your ability to handle your child, you'll no longer panic at his "No." You'll convey your authority, while maintaining a calm manner. (For more on this subject, see Chapter 3.)

Accustoming Children to Obedience

Beyond the toddler stage, our expectations of our children become more complex. Our methods of enforcing those expectations also become more subtle. A simple "No!" and bodily transfer of the child to another room is no longer appropriate. The challenge for the parent is to exercise full authority without subjugating the child.

To become accustomed to obedience, children must be given a chance to practice it on their own. Forced obedience, induced by coercive methods, teaches very little and should be used only as a last resort. For example, your little one helps herself to cookies, candies, and other snack foods which she knows she's not allowed to take. Don't immediately put these out of her reach. Children can learn obedience only when they have a choice. Allow her to choose between sneaking the sweets or controlling herself. This choice should be taken away only after she's repeatedly disregarded your rules. Even then, she should be given fresh opportunities, from time to time, to behave appropriately. Thus you might say, "I'm putting the cookies back in the drawer. Let's see how well you're able to control yourself."

When your child doesn't want to do as he's told, try saying, "I expect this to get done," and then leaving him alone for a while. This can be effective.

Withholding Privileges

Parents shouldn't hesitate to withhold privileges if necessary. For instance, when a child who's neglected to do some chore asks for a snack, he can be told, "You may have crackers as soon as you've (emptied the garbage)." Other privileges which can be withheld might be: listening to music, going to visit a friend, or choosing the bedtime story. Some forcefulness and perseverance may be called for at times, but the results are well worth it. One mother, who in the past had either resorted to screaming or had given in to her child, told about her experiences when she began acting more firmly and consistently:

> We were just finishing lunch. Three-year-old Menachem was throwing the remains of his tuna fish on the floor. The other children took oranges and went outside. As Menachem went to get his orange, I decided that this would be a good time to try the "new approach." "As soon as you pick up your tuna fish from the floor, Menachem, you may have an orange," I said, closing the refrigerator. Menachem gave me one of his daring looks and walked over to the refrigerator, opened it, and took out an orange. "As soon as you pick up the tuna fish you may have an orange," I repeated, taking the orange from him. I was determined to keep my cool this time and not scream at him or pick up the tuna fish myself, as I had been doing in the past. One more try from Menachem and one more repetition of my firm decision, and Menachem gave me the funniest look,

picked up the tuna fish and said, "Okay, now can I have an orange?" This was quite an encouraging beginning!

Giving Directions

Many of the dos and don'ts which we issue during the course of the day can be avoided by giving our children information which allows them to figure out for themselves what they should do. For example:

> "Muddy boots belong outside."
> "Clothes which are thrown on the chair get crumpled."
> "Your hands are dirty."

Point out what has to be done, without placing yourself at the center of the request. For example: Instead of "I want you to go to bed" — "Time for bed." Rather than "I want this room cleaned up" — "The room has to be cleaned up." Speak quietly but unhesitatingly, using a minimum of words. Let your manner of speaking convey to your child that you expect compliance.

When restricting children, it isn't necessary to warn or threaten them. State the limitation quietly but firmly; whenever possible, give a brief reason for it. Here are examples:

> "No jumping on the sofa — it ruins the material."
> "I can't let you run around here at the bus stop — it disturbs the other people."
> "No sand throwing — it can get into someone's eyes."

If children don't obey, take action to restrain them. For example, your child running around at the bus stop must now sit down with you or hold your hand. The toddler throwing sand is whisked out of the sandbox and quietly told, "Come, you'd better sit down next to me on the bench for a while." If necessary, hold on to him to prevent him from going back.

Teaching Children to Come When Called

Many parents have trouble teaching their children to come when called. If a child doesn't come by the third time, they go after him, scolding, "How many times do I have to call you before you come?!" Be aware that this is a complaint, a rhetorical question to which, in truth, we expect no response. (What should he say — "How do I know, Mommy?") It may get temporary results, but unfortunately, the child will learn to ignore his parents until they yell.

To teach children to come when called, we must learn to control our angry reactions. We can do this by identifying and changing the thoughts which produce our anger, namely, "I shouldn't have to call him so many times! He should come right away!" We must be tolerant of our child's behavior, while at the same time working to change it.

Make it a practice not to call your child more than once. If he doesn't come, don't keep calling him. *Go* to him and tell him quietly, "When I call you, you have to come right away," or, "You know, I called you." A mild rebuke such as, "It's not right for you to ignore me when I call," might sometimes be in order.

Don't expect a child to come the instant you call; give him a minute or so. Explain to him that when it's difficult for him to come right away, he can call out, "Just a minute, please."

Even when a child is playing outside, we shouldn't keep calling him. It may be inconvenient to have to leave the house, but we must be prepared to suffer some inconvenience in order to achieve our educational goals.

Getting a Child's Attention

Parents should avoid shouting instructions from one end of the house to the other. Many children have developed the habit of tuning out their parents' voices. If we want to be sure a child is attentive, we have to take the time to talk to him face to face. That way, we're less likely to have to repeat what we say.

When a child acts as if he hasn't heard us, it isn't always necessary to repeat what we said. Instead, we can find out whether he got our message. For example:

MOTHER: Menuchah, please take the laundry out of the washing machine and put it into the dryer.
MENUCHAH: (doesn't answer and continues reading)
MOTHER: (quietly) Menuchah, what did I just say?

MENUCHAH: (looking up) Oh, you asked me to put the laundry into the dryer.

MOTHER: Right. So please do it now.

Reminders

Another way to encourage obedience is by well-placed reminders. For instance, we might tell a daughter who habitually postpones doing what she was asked, "Rebecca, would you set the table, and please remember what I said about not putting off jobs that need to be done right away." Similarly, instead of always telling our children that if they're tired from not sleeping during naptime then we won't take them to the park, we can say, "Remember what we said about children who don't sleep during naptime." This way we avoid constantly having to repeat ourselves.

Correction and Punishment

Appropriate correction is a major factor in gaining obedience. For example, if a child frequently neglects to do what's required of him, we might discuss with him the importance of complying promptly, explaining that this is part of the mitzvah of honoring parents, and that he gives his parents pleasure by fulfilling their requests eagerly. When a child responds to a request by saying, "I don't want to," he can be told, very quietly, "You know, children have to do what their Mommy and Daddy tell them to do."

We may also need to use punishment at times. (For more on this, see Chapter 5.)

A Final Word

Keep in mind that it takes time and patience to teach a child obedience. It's important to have realistic expectations. Remember that children aren't angels. Even the best behaved youngster will disobey his parents at times. Don't generate anger in yourself by thinking, "Why can't he listen!" On the other hand, don't focus on thoughts of personal failure ("What's wrong with me that I can't get him to listen?"). We need to maintain emotional control in order to decide calmly how best to handle the situation.

Chapter Three

MAINTAINING
A FIRM POSITION

To teach children good conduct and good character traits, parents must be firm and consistent. But this is easier said than done. Parents may well understand the importance of being firm and consistent, yet have great difficulty putting this theoretical knowledge into practice. For example, they may realize that it isn't sensible to yield when a child cries about a refused request. Why, then, do they give in? Certain common fears and attitudes usually create the parents' difficulties. In this chapter we will try to understand these fears and attitudes, and the misconceptions on which they are based. By thinking more precisely about the way they're dealing with their children, parents can begin to maintain a firmer and more consistent position.

CONCERN ABOUT THE CHILD'S HAPPINESS

Often, parents aren't firm because they are afraid their child won't be happy if he doesn't have things his way. This fear stems from three false beliefs: 1) The goal of life is happiness; 2) It's the parents' job to make the child happy (expressed in the oft-heard, "...as long as he's happy"); 3) The child must have what he wants in order to be happy.

Happiness

Of course we want our children to be happy. But it is a mistake to believe that it's our job to *make* them happy. The Torah requires a father to teach his son three things: Torah, a trade, and good character traits.[1] Nowhere does it say that he must make him happy. Why? Perhaps because by teaching him these three things, he's giving his child all the tools needed for happiness.*

Even if happiness were the most important thing in life, parents who try to make their child happy are bound to fail. Here is what the great 19th-century English philosopher, John Stuart Mill had to say on happiness:

> I have always felt that happiness is the touchstone for all rules of behavior, and the purpose of life. But I think now that the only way to be happy is *not* to make of it the purpose of our activity. There is only one way to be happy; it consists of striving to any aim but that of happiness itself. As to where pure pursuit of happiness, without moral moderation, leads the entire collective society — our generation has the unfortunate opportunity to witness it.

Modern educators emphasize the same basic idea:

> The goal of keeping a child happy will keep him from being a happy child....So many mothers make the same mistake. They think the most important thing in raising children is to make them happy. It's not. If you raise your children to be

---

* Perhaps it's significant that there is no word for "happiness" in classical Hebrew. The term *osher*, translated as "happiness" in modern Hebrew, means "progress" in classical Hebrew. The closest term in classical Hebrew is *nachas ruach*, which literally means "rest of the spirit" and denotes peace of mind. Another term is *samei'ach b'chelko*, "rejoicing in his lot." Both of these terms indicate a harmony between the individual's striving and reality. This, apparently, is how the Torah sees happiness.

dependable, industrious, honest, and considerate of others, they will make themselves happy.[2]

Satisfaction of Desires

Now to the false belief — that in order to be happy, a child must have what he wants. Our ages taught that "No one dies with half his wishes fulfilled. When he has 100, he wants to turn them into 200, and if he has two, he wants to turn them into 400."[3] And King Solomon said, "One who loves money will never be satisfied with money."[4] A person can never have all he wants; the child needs to learn this early in life.

Parents who satisfy their child's every wish to ensure his happiness accomplish just the opposite, because the child who's used to getting what he wants comes to believe things must always be this way. His need to have every wish fulfilled leads to frequent unhappiness, since his parents will eventually become irritated over such demanding behavior. Moreover, later in life, he will feel unhappy whenever he doesn't have what he wants. The happiness he experiences each time a desire is satisfied will be relatively short lived; it won't be long before the next as-yet-unfulfilled desire causes renewed unhappiness.

There's still another reason not to overindulge children:

> Although it sounds paradoxical, you actually cheat [your child] of pleasure when you give him too much. Pleasure occurs when an intense need is satisfied. If there is no need, there is no pleasure....There are few conditions that inhibit a sense of appreciation more than for a child to feel he is entitled to whatever he wants, whenever he wants it.[5]

Indulgence doesn't equal love. Modern psychology has gone to great lengths to stress the importance of parents showing love for their children, and has thereby done everyone a real service. But when we equate love with the granting of all desires, we pervert this lesson. We demonstrate *true* love when we do what's good for the child. Restricting children when necessary is an important part of love, and it won't damage their affection for their parents if it is done in a caring, loving manner.

When one of a child's wishes is denied by a loving parent and the child sees later that he is still happy, he learns a most fundamental lesson for life — that his happiness doesn't depend on getting what he wants. In the end, he'll love and respect his parents for having taught him this wisdom.

To be sure, children may feel quite miserable when they aren't allowed to have their way, especially if they've been indulged in the past. We can help them over their unhappiness by conveying genuine empathy — a smiling face, gentle voice, and loving manner. The message to the child should be, "We limit you because we care about you. We're sorry that it causes you unhappiness."

AVOIDANCE OF CONFLICT

Children frequently show their unhappiness over an unfavorable decision by complaining, pouting, crying, throwing accusing looks, and so on. Parents must be able to stand firm in the face of such behavior, no matter how unpleasant it may be. If they tell themselves that they "can't stand" the child's carrying on, they'll find themselves giving in to him, against their better judgment, just to have some peace and quiet. This encourages the child to continue these strategies — crying, nagging, and the like — since they get him what he wants.

To avoid all unpleasant fuss, parents will also say "yes" to their child when they really want to say "no." They may succeed in avoiding immediate conflict, but the child learns that his parents will give him whatever he demands. In the long run, he becomes more and more demanding, forcing his parents to go to ridiculous lengths in order to avoid conflict.

We need to be aware of this problem so that we can combat it. Rabbi Samson Raphael Hirsch advises:

> You must get used to suffering from a child's expressions of aggression, and not surrender in the face of screams. Don't give a child, because of self-love (so that he won't disturb your peace), what you wouldn't give him because of your love for him.[6]

When we give in to our children, we deprive them of training in building up tolerance for the many frustrations they're bound to experience throughout life. It's worth learning to tolerate some unpleasantness now because in the long run, this will make things easier for everyone. When we stop giving in to children because of their disagreeable carryings–on, we may sometimes be quite surprised at the results, as the following stories illustrate:

Every evening, I prepare the lunchboxes for my six children. Since by then I am usually very tired, I don't look forward to this job. In the past I'd asked my children to make the lunches, but they always argued and made such a fuss over the job that I would end up giving in.

Armed with incentive from my parenting workshop, I decided to try again. Each evening, one of my four older children has the job of clearing the supper table and tidying up the kitchen. On Monday night at suppertime I made this announcement: "From now on, children, we're going to take turns making lunches. The one whose turn it is to clear the table and tidy up will also make lunches for everyone."

Immediately my 10-year-old Avram, whose turn it was that evening to do the kitchen chores, began complaining in his usual manner. "Oh no, we can't do it — it takes too long — it's too hard! Especially not the night I clear the table, then I won't have time to play!"

"Avram," I said, "tonight is your turn. I know it's not an easy job, but do it anyway." He continued to complain but I did not permit it to weaken my resolve. "Avram, I know you don't like to. If it's too hard, I'll help. But please do it anyway."

Grumbling a little, he started the lunches. I pitched in, and sent everyone else out of the kitchen so only he and I could work together. He completed his job quite nicely.

The next night it was my daughter's turn. I didn't have to say a word. She began preparing lunches and needed almost no help.

The third night it was the turn of my 8-year-old son, who generally grumbles a lot. He had a class at yeshiva that evening which he was eager to attend. Right after supper he asked, "What should I make for sandwiches 'cause I have to leave soon?"

I'd caused a minor miracle with only a small change in tactics!

It was evening. I had given my 5-year-old son a teaspoon of medicine and immediately after that a glass of water. He started crying, "The water's warm — give me cold water." I said, in a calm voice, without any anger, "You're a big boy — you can reach the sink yourself, take a cup and fill it with cold water from the faucet." "No," he cried more loudly than before, and demanded, "You give it to me."

This time I decided to remain firm. The exchange was continuing for a while. He was screaming and crying, and I kept on saying, "You're a big boy — get yourself some cold water." I wasn't getting anywhere. I turned the lights off and said, "I'm very tired — I'm going to bed." He followed me and sat on my bed, still demanding hysterically that I give him a glass of cold water. Then I said, "You know, I'm so tired — you are such a big boy — could you please bring me a cup of cold water? I'm also thirsty." And then I added, "And when you do that I'll give you a big hug and carry you to your bed."

Lo and behold, with tears streaming down his cheeks and still whining miserably, he got off the bed and brought two cups of water into the room. I praised him and said, "Now get your yarmulke and say the berachah." He was still crying but he got the yarmulke, which always falls off, and, half choking from the tears, said the berachah. I kept on praising him, and then my 3-year-old daughter started, "I want a glass of milk." "Uh-oh," I thought to myself, "if I give her, after refusing him...." So I turned to him and said, "You're such a big boy — could you open the refrigerator yourself and give Chavi a glass of milk?" He went without a word to do this too. On his return, he reminded me, "You said you'll give me a hug and carry me to bed." I gave him the hug he earned and carried him to bed.

He had a wonderfully contented look on his face. It was well worth it.

Shopping Trips

It's particularly difficult to remain firm and not give in when children ask us to buy them things on shopping trips. "Buy me (candy, potato chips, a toy)," says the child. And "No, you can't have any" or "No, I'm not buying you anything now," answers the parent. But the child continues nagging, relentlessly. Sometimes parents manage to stand firm, but at other times they relent just to have some peace. Of course, this reinforces the child's "buy me" habit. To break this behavior pattern, parents must *consistently* refuse to give in, making absolutely *no exceptions.*

Before going shopping with your children, say, "Children, we're going to buy things we need for the house. Please don't ask me to buy you anything special." Then, if anyone forgets, remind him: "Remember what I said about not buying you things." Give no other answers or explanations. If the child pleads with you, ignore him. Of course, the children won't give up their habit right away. But if you stick to this approach, *never* responding at all to any requests except to say, "Remember, we're buying things for the house now, and not special things for you," they'll eventually stop. When you do want to give your child some small treat or toy, buy it when the child isn't along and give it to him at home.

Tantrums

If your child has learned to get what he wants by crying or screaming, it may be necessary to ignore his temper tantrums for some time, to teach him that this method will no longer work. You'll need strong will-power and considerable patience to resist a lengthy period of unpleasant racket, accompanied by kicking and thrashing. Even a parent who is usually firm may be tempted to give in to a child who persists in crying for a long time. *Don't!* Yielding after a while will teach him that if he just keeps up his efforts long enough, he'll get what he wants. "They gave in before when I kept crying," he'll reason, "I bet this time they'll give in again if I just keep crying long enough!" Therefore, the longer the crying has lasted, the more important it is not to give in to it.

However, you don't have to be indifferent to your child's (self-imposed) suffering. You can say, gently, "I'm very sorry, but I can't let you have what you want." For a young child, a soothing hug given at the onset of a tantrum can often help him to get over it quickly.

Keep in mind that the child who has tantrums often, in order to get what he wants, may well have been born with a predisposition to LFT (low frustration tolerance). By reacting calmly to his outbursts, and being a good role-model in terms of your own reactions to the everyday frustrations of life, you can teach him that frustration needn't be viewed as catastrophic. Ultimately, he'll learn to take it in his stride, realizing that he can be reasonably happy even when things don't go his way.

Abusive Behavior

A child who is very angry and frustrated may, in order to get his way, scold and criticize his parents, throw objects, bang doors, curse, and even become physically abusive. Such behavior can frighten his parents into submitting to all kinds of unreasonable demands. Of course, this only reinforces the child's low frustration tolerance and encourages further aggression.

Again, though it may be difficult, parents must learn to stand firm and remain unaffected by their child's behavior. If he abuses his parents verbally, they should calmly explain that they won't listen to him if he speaks disrespectfully — and then ignore him until he calms down. If he damages objects, he should be quietly told to leave the room, or even the house if necessary, until he can control himself.

Physical attacks on parents are another matter. Since they are a serious transgression, the parents must stop the child by restraining him physically — with the help of other adults if necessary. This must be done without hostility; it should be made clear that the parents are acting out of concern for the child's welfare. If parents focus on what needs to be done rather than on their feelings of hurt or anger, they'll be able to maintain the calm but firm manner required.

Remember, the child is undoubtedly frightened by his own violence. It is also likely that he fears parental rejection because of his behavior. Therefore, it is vital to demonstrate that you still love him, and that it's only his behavior which can't be tolerated — but you don't reject *him* because of it.

WHAT WILL PEOPLE THINK?

When a child carries on in the presence of guests or in a public place, parents sometimes worry, "What will these people think of me?" or "I can't let him bother all these people!" The first of these worries stems from an exaggerated concern about the opinion of others. The second worry places concern for other people's inconvenience above the very fundamental educational needs of the child. In either case, the parent capitulates to the child's demands, which temporarily stops the fussing and crying. And the child learns that fussing in public gets him whatever he wants! He'll make more and more demands, knowing that his parents fear the public disturbances he makes when his demands aren't met.

Parents who are concerned about "what others will think" may find themselves overlooking all sorts of bad behavior, just to prevent a temper tantrum. When we depend on the approval of others, we undermine ourselves; there will always be someone who disapproves or disagrees with whatever we're doing. At some point, we must turn a deaf ear to what anyone else is saying and hold to our own priorities.

If your child throws a tantrum in public, it challenges you to exercise judgment. You must give due consideration to the needs of others, but without sacrificing the educational welfare of your child. One good solution is to pick the child up and quickly move to a more secluded spot. If this isn't practical or possible, try hard not to feel embarrassed as you wait out the child's tantrum, without appeasing him. To any disapproving or annoyed onlookers, explain, "I'm really sorry that my daughter's (son's) crying is annoying you, but she needs to learn that she can't have everything she wants."

When your child fusses at home in the presence of guests, it's usually best to take him to another room immediately, and talk to him there.

GUILT FEELINGS

Some parents automatically blame themselves whenever anything unpleasant happens. When there is conflict with their child, they assume it's they who are in the wrong. For example, a child is upset because he was denied permission to stay up late. The parent now begins to think, guiltily, "I was mean, I made him feel bad, I should have let him stay up." The classic accusation "It's not fair!" triggers similar feelings. Children sense their parents' doubts and learn to exaggerate their hurt feelings even more in order to get their own way.

Parents need to remind themselves that they are remaining firm for the benefit of the child, and stop such nonproductive self-criticism.

Part of the problem is our distress at causing pain to another person. Certainly, this is praiseworthy. But as parents, we have a special obligation to educate our children.[7] The commandment to avoid causing pain refers only to unnecessary pain. When necessary for their benefit, we must restrict our children — even if we cause them anguish by doing so. We might well sympathize with the child's plight: "David, I know you'd like to stay up..." — but we can't let his suffering influence us to change our minds — "...but you still have to go to bed now." (Remember, the child's true suffering results from his unwillingness to tolerate frustration.)

What if a parent has valid second thoughts about the position he's taking? Usually it's best to stick to the original decision. Still, this doesn't have to be a hard and fast rule. If we occasionally regret a particular decision, we can certainly choose to reverse it or decide to handle the situation differently in the future. But the reversal of a decision shouldn't immediately follow the child's complaining; that reinforces unpleasant behavior.

Neither should we take too much to heart our child's accusations of "It's not fair!" It's not always possible to be perfectly fair. If we demand it of ourselves, we're likely to instill a similar, unrealistic demand in our children. But they must learn, as a necessary preparation for life, to endure some injustice.

The following was told by a mother who felt guilty about having taken a job:

> When I started my job three weeks ago, Hadassah, my 4-year-old, began literally stepping all over me. I was feeling guilty and I think my daughter sensed this and saw it as an opportunity to test me. Her demands were never ending. There was never enough I could do for her, and the frustration of dealing with her brought on frequent explosions.
>
> Then I started attending the workshop. Well, the following morning I woke up at 6 to a "Mommy, Daddy, make me a peanut-butter sandwich!" She kept repeating this, whining on and on. My husband was about to get up and serve her, but I told him not to. "I'll handle this," I said. "Hadassah," I told her, "you're a big girl now. You're 4 years old. You know about the mitzvah of kibud av va'eim (honoring parents). See how everybody is sleeping now? Go help yourself. The spreader is in the drawer, the peanut butter is in the pantry, and the bread is on the shelf."
>
> Hadassah wasn't interested. She kept crying and complaining that Daddy always gives it to her and she doesn't care who's sleeping, and so on and so on. I repeated my instructions three times, in the calmest manner (and lovingly as well). I then asked her twice to leave the room if she persisted in complaining and crying. When she still did not stop, I was about to walk her out of the room and go back to sleep. But suddenly Hadassah just walked out by herself, went into the kitchen and made her own peanut butter sandwich!! Later my two boys (ages $1\frac{1}{2}$ and $2\frac{1}{2}$) woke up. Hadassah also made them peanut-butter sandwiches, and gave them each a banana. Beaming with pride she announced that she'd made her own sandwich, and also dressed herself (for the first time in three weeks). She didn't complain for the rest of the morning.
>
> If I had not experienced this myself, I never would have believed it! I have really learned from this to be firm, not guilty, and to act with love, not anger.

Am I Being Selfish?

Sometimes parents feel guilty about asking their children to do things for them. For instance, they may want to ask a child to wash the dishes, but then hesitate. "Is it all right for me to make this request? Maybe I'm being selfish. Brachy has a lot of homework (wants to play). Maybe I should be more considerate." They may also hesitate when they find it necessary to limit their child for reasons of convenience or economy.

Parents with this problem seem to think that their needs must *always* be secondary to their children's needs. They mistakenly think they are selfish if they don't always give their children's desires precedence.

A hesitant manner subtly conveys to the child our inner uncertainty. When we're unsure of our position, we can hardly expect his enthusiastic cooperation. If we doubt our judgment, the child may also come to question it. Thus, without being aware of it, we may be encouraging self-centeredness in our children.

Parents who think they must put their child first *at all times* are harming both themselves and their children. We all have limited reserves, and an exhausted parent can't be an effective parent.

Guilt feelings may push parents into doing things for their children when they're not really up to it. For example, a child may ask us to read him a story when we feel the need to relax. If we tell ourselves, "Come on, be nice — read him the story," and force ourselves to do it, he'll probably sense that we're not really happy about it. He won't derive any real pleasure from our self-sacrifice. There's nothing wrong, in this case, with giving preference to our own needs and telling the child pleasantly, "Sorry, honey, no story right now. I'm not really up to it."

Besides, constantly giving our children top priority may easily lead to our resenting them. This is bound to manifest itself eventually in excessive criticism or other aggressive behavior toward the child.

When parents feel guilty about burdening a child by requesting his help in the home, they should keep in mind that providing him with opportunities to be helpful benefits him, too. As parents feel less guilty about such demands and more confident that they constitute good training for the child, it will become much easier to act firmly.

Am I Expecting Too Much?

Lack of firmness sometimes results from uncertainly about what our expectations should be. For instance, a small child refuses to pick up his toys. The parent then hesitates, thinking, "Maybe I'm expecting too much. He's so young; maybe I shouldn't be so strict." It's important to decide what we expect and to stick to our decision.

Here is one mother's story, with a surprise ending:

> I have an 11-year-old son who frequently asks to go for long periods of time at the gym, which is fine if his studying and homework are done. But this is rarely so. So begins the pattern of my saying no, and his begging and pleading, totally ignoring my "nos." His pleas are of needing an outlet, being under a lot of pressure in yeshiva, a difficult, harsh teacher, and I begin to succumb — "Maybe he's right; maybe it will help."
>
> Then I started the workshop and wow! I nicely but firmly said "no" with a soft shake of my head and I continued this because my leader said that it's okay for children not to have everything they want — children don't always have to be happy! When his tears and pleas continued longer than three or four nos worth, I softly said, "The matter is closed, you can go outside and calm down if you'd like, and we'll go on to other topics."
>
> Finished? So I thought. I felt calm! Relieved! I went out to a shiur and came back to find a note:

>> Dear Mommy, From the heart of Yisrael Hillel to yours.
>> You may not really think I sound sorry but I am! And even if you still don't think so, then there's nothing I can do but ask you one thing. The sign for the month of Adar is fish. There is enough salt water in the ocean already for the fish and by my crying it certainly won't help the fish, so I'll stop but please think about this, "Can I go to gym next Wednesday?" This way we can both be happy.
>>   From Yisrael Hillel

He gave it to me with a calmness and a smile on his face.

As we reassess our children's capacities, we may decide to raise or lower our expectations. This must be done carefully and thoughtfully. It's counterproductive to change our expectations impulsively in the middle of an interchange with a child.

Don't be too concerned about your expectations. Expectations that are constantly much too high or much too low can be harmful, and so can inconsistency — but if your expectations are usually reasonable, occasionally expecting too much of a child does no real harm. You're bound to make mistakes. Forget about being perfect and just focus on trying to do your best.

FEAR OF DISAPPROVAL AND REJECTION

Another reason some parents don't act firmly toward their children is that they fear displeasing them. These parents make the basic mistake of linking their own worth to the approval of others — in this case, to the approval of their child. Thus they are overly sensitive to any suggestion of criticism from the child, incorrectly assuming that his disapproval must mean that they are not good parents.

It's unreasonable and highly unrealistic to expect that our children will always approve of our decisions. Yet some parents seem to think that if they try hard enough, care enough, and sacrifice enough, they'll win their children's constant approval. But some of our decisions are bound to disappoint our children. And they may express their unhappiness or disapproval. As long as we've acted with their best interest in mind, we shouldn't allow their temporary displeasure to disturb us.

If a child disapproves of us, that's unfortunate. Even if his feelings are warranted, he's at best wrongly confusing us with our actions. But the child may not be judging us at all; he may simply be unhappy. It's our own habit of judging ourselves negatively which seriously distorts our perceptions, and leads us to conclude that our child is judging us negatively, too.

Sometimes, parents fear that remaining firm and not giving in will make the child unhappy and spoil the relationship with him. They need to learn that this notion is false, as the following (actual) telephone conversation between a mother and her parenting workshop leader illustrates:

> MOTHER: *How can I set limits without offending my children?*
> LEADER: *What makes you think that by setting limits, you're offending your children?*
> MOTHER: *Because they make faces at me! I know they are unhappy and dissatisfied and I worry that it will spoil my relationship with them.*
> LEADER: *Why does that worry you so much?*
> MOTHER: *Well, I heard about a family where two children didn't turn out so well because their parents screamed at them so much. I got scared and stopped all my yelling. But just to be sure that my children should never be unhappy with me, I have been giving in to them on nearly everything. Now I see that with no limits, the situation has gotten out of hand. Isn't there some middle way?*
> LEADER: *Look, it's part of life that we can't always have what we want. Children need to get used to this idea from an early age. When you find it necessary to limit your child and he makes faces at you, you seem to fear that this will spoil your relationship with him. It won't. It happens that children are sometimes dissatisfied when they didn't get what they wanted. That's perfectly normal.*

Just then the mother's 5-year-old daughter tried to interrupt the conversation. The mother later told the leader that she'd put a finger to her lips to motion for quiet. True to form, the child had made a face, but the mother reminded herself, "That means she's unhappy. It happens. It won't harm our relationship. I don't need to worry about it." She later had a talk with her daughter in which she empathized with the child about her unhappiness. The girl seemed very satisfied afterwards. The relationship hadn't been adversely affected at all — to the contrary, it had improved.

Sometimes, our deepest fear about displeasing our children is that they'll stop loving us. Parents who are worried about losing their children's love may be afraid to deny them anything. The child, in turn, learns that everything will always go his way, and he becomes a small tyrant. Out of the motivation of "pleasing the child," they might very well end up with a not-so-pleasing child!

A small child who is angry at his mother will sometimes react with insults such as, "I don't like you!" "You're not my friend!" "Silly Mommy!" Instead of taking such remarks to heart, we should view them as a natural manifestation of the child's immaturity, and use our judgment to decide whether to ignore such statements or perhaps to answer softly, "I know you don't really mean that, but you're not allowed to say such things to Mommy."

Another way of handling this problem is described in the following account:

> My 3-year-old was in the habit of insulting me whenever my decisions did not suit her. She would say, "I don't like you," or tell me she was leaving the house to go live with a friend. I usually told her that it wasn't nice to say those things, but it had little effect. I decided to try another method. The next time she told me, "I don't like you," I said to her, "You really don't like me?" Amazingly, she burst into tears. Another time she said, "I'm going to live with Shanee." I said, "Do you really want to live with Shanee?" She said "Yes." I asked, "Do you want to try?" Somewhat sadly she answered, "No." I see I get much further with this way of handling it.

THE TRAP OF GIVING REASONS

Most parents are aware that children accept decisions more easily when they understand the reasons behind them. By giving children explanations in this way, parents also provide the child with a model of reasonableness.

Rabbi Hirsch writes that parents should give reasons for demands and restrictions so that the child not come to regard his parents as autocratic, but that children should obey because they submit to their parents' better judgment — not because their parents' reasons appeal to them.[8]

Sometimes, parents feel compelled to justify a request because they fear that otherwise their child might not cooperate. The child, sensing that logic has become the deciding factor, will eagerly begin arguing. After he rejects the first reason given, the parents fall into the trap of offering more reasons — only to have their child reject these, too, one after another. The result is much unpleasant arguing. The child may even reject all the explanations offered and refuse to accept the decision altogether.

Giving reasons no longer serves a useful purpose if a child has come to demand them and thinks his obedience is contingent on his approval of them. In such a case, asking "Why?" becomes a challenge rather than a legitimate request for a reason. Or it can be a complaint — "Why do I have to do it?" Asking "Why?" can even develop into a habit of arguing for argument's sake.

To discourage such habits it's best to give children one reason only. If it is rejected with an argument, remain firm. Have confidence in your ability to make your decisions stick. Offer no additional reasons; these only provide the child with new openings to counterargue. Be persistent. If you've asked your child to do something, insist pleasantly but firmly that he do as he was asked, and be prepared to continue to do so until he complies. Stay calm, pleasant, and nonjudgmental. When his arguments bring the child no satisfaction, he may soon learn to stop them.

Here's an illustration:

SIMCHA: I need $5 spending money for the class trip tomorrow.
FATHER: That's a little too much. We'll give you $3.
SIMCHA: But all the other kids get 5!
FATHER: (Notice he does not offer another reason, such as "We can't afford it") Sorry — three is all you can have.
SIMCHA: But I can hardly buy anything with $3!
FATHER: I'm sorry but it will have to do.
SIMCHA: Please, can't I have five?
FATHER: No, three is all you can have.
SIMCHA: It's not fair!
FATHER: I'm sorry but you can't have more.

If, the first few times you use this approach, your child continues to argue — be patient. The fact that you responded or yielded to his arguments in the past has probably reinforced his arguing habit. To start changing the situation now, you'll have to put up with some unpleasant arguing for a while.

Be especially careful not to let your child's arguing put you on the defensive. Suppose your daughter argues, "You always let the other kids stay up late when *they* ask." Don't respond defensively. Instead, redirect attention to the issue under discussion — "Let's not discuss that. Right now, we're talking about *your* asking to stay up late. And the answer to that is no." If your daughter continues to press her point, tell her, "I've told you my decision. Now let's end this discussion."

Do your best to control feelings of annoyance toward the child for her arguing. But there's nothing wrong with letting her know, on occasion, that you find it disagreeable — "You know, it's not pleasant when you argue."

Our expectations have a way of being realized, so we should try to develop an attitude which conveys to the child, in a friendly manner, "I expect you to accept my decisions even when you don't like my reasons."

One mother explained how she learned not to get sucked into endless arguments:

> There used to be a lot of arguing in our house. Looking back on it, I feel it was because I either didn't sound convincing enough, or else I lost my temper at the first no and immediately started yelling. Then I learned about avoiding arguments by giving one reason only, and continuing to be firm but calm even if that reason was rejected. After that, I felt emotionally ready for the next argument.
>
> The next day my 5-year-old Shulamith wanted to change her everyday dress for a Shabbos dress. I said no, as there was no time to wash it before Shabbos. She insisted. I firmly repeated myself, "Shulamith, you may not change your dress." I remained friendly but firm, as she continued to argue. Shulamith finally gave up and cheerfully went off to play — no tears, no recriminations. I guess she heard the confident determination in my voice!

Parents who are afraid that the child might not accept their real reason for a decision might be tempted to make up more palatable reasons. This bending of reality is good neither for parent nor child. Besides, if these reasons aren't completely honest, the child is likely to recognize them as mere excuses and try to argue them down. Therefore, it's best to stick to the real reason and completely ignore the child's reaction. For example, if a request for candy is being turned down, it's better for the parent to give his true reason — that it isn't good for the child to have too many sweets — than to offer the excuse, "It's too close to suppertime."

Rules ("Ice cream only on Shabbos"; "Rooms have to be tidied up before supper"; etc.) can be very helpful in eliminating the need for giving reasons, and can make it easier for children to accept limits. When the rule is established, the reason for it may be given. Thereafter, a friendly reminder is sufficient: "You know the rule about tidying up rooms."

In some situations it's not possible or even desirable to give a reason at all. If children have been taught to be obedient and accept their parents' better judgment, there should be no problem with enforcing a parental decision even when no reason is given. It should be sufficient to say, in a calm and pleasant manner, "I'm sorry, but I can't give you a reason now."

Chapter Four

PRAISE AND ENCOURAGEMENT

wo of the most powerful resources parents have for educating their children are praise and encouragement. The late Telzer Rosh Yeshiva, Rabbi Chaim Mordechai Katz, said that appreciative words help a person realize his own inherent worth and encourage him to utilize his attributes to the best of his ability.[1] Encouragement, praise, and appreciation bring out the best in a child, instilling a sense of security and confidence.

TEACHING THROUGH PRAISE AND ENCOURAGEMENT

Children have an innate need for affection and approval. They have a natural desire to please us, because this brings them, in return, expressions of love and praise. It is therefore important for us to let our children know what pleases us, by praising and encouraging their good behavior.

Children need to be told things like:

> "You fixed breakfast for all of us! That's grown-up behavior."
> "It was so nice to see you go to bed on time this evening."
> "I can really rely on you to take care of your little sister while I rest!"

Praise in front of another important person can be especially rewarding. For example, a mother can announce to her husband, in the child's presence, "Daddy, I want you to know that Benny got dressed like a *big* boy today!" She can enhance the effect of this praise, adding some delicious anticipation, if she tells Benny in the morning, "When Daddy comes home, I'll tell him how well you dressed yourself today."

There is a certain amount of effort involved in keeping an eye open for agreeable behavior. It's much easier to notice what children do that disturbs us. The children may be playing quietly in their room, and we take no notice of it. But if they begin to be noisy, we're likely to go in and ask for quiet. It's much harder to remember to go in to commend them for their quiet, good behavior *while* they're playing peaceably.

Try to be alert for improvements in a child's behavior and comment on them:

> "I hardly had to remind you this week to hang up your jacket."
> "I notice you're remembering more often to bring your dishes to the sink."
> "You've improved in your table manners."

Opportunities for praise can sometimes be created:

> Mother: (at the breakfast table) Aaron, let's see how carefully you can pour your milk this time so nothing spills.
> (Aaron pours carefully and succeeds)
> Mother: You were really careful. Nothing spilled at all!

Commend children for effort, too:

> "I notice you're making a real effort to get along better with your sister."

It takes practice. If a parent is not alert for opportunities to give praise, those chances will slip by unnoticed. But once the habit of expressing appreciation is established, it can bring about big changes in the children and in the atmosphere of the home.

HOW TO PRAISE

To be most effective, praise should be specific, appropriate, and objective.

Being Specific

When you praise, describe the behavior you liked. Avoid global praise such as "You're a wonderful boy," or "You're a very good girl." The intention of praise is to let the child know what specific aspects of his behavior are appreciated, so that he can continue them. That means focusing on what the child is doing.

If praise consists of general evaluations of the child, he may get the impression that his worth is measured by his actions and accomplishments, or that your love for him depends on his behavior. Restricting praise to specific behavior will prevent these misconceptions.

Avoiding Excessive or Inappropriate Praise

Although children benefit from frequent praise and appreciation, excessive or overfrequent praise is counterproductive. It may lead the child to depend on constant approval and recognition. The idea is to *teach a child to appreciate himself.*

Excessive or inappropriate praise may also be rejected by the child, who senses that he doesn't really deserve it. (For example, yesterday he hit his sister, so he knows he's not a shining example of perfection.)

Objectivity

It's important that our praise emphasize the value in the child's good behavior, and not merely our personal pleasure. For example, as you're helping your son put his toys away you might say, "The room looks nice when all the toys are put away," or "Isn't it nice when everything is in its place? Then we can find what we're looking for!"

The aim is to train children to be conscious of an objective good, rather than of simply having pleased others. The ultimate goal is for the child to become an adult who is motivated solely by the desire to do God's will. With this in mind, parents can begin to encourage more abstract values such as mitzvos and good character traits:

> "You did a real mitzvah when you helped that lady with her packages."
> "You washed the dishes even though you didn't feel well — that's showing *mesiras nefesh* (self-sacrifice)."
> "You showed real self-control by not hitting your brother back!"

This type of praise is incorporated in the custom of acknowledging good deeds with a blessing, "*yasher kochacha!*" (more strength to you).[2]

Self-esteem

The importance of self-esteem has been stressed to the point where it has become a major concern. Self-esteem (a healthy self-image is a more appropriate term) ought to be a given. All humans possess infinite worth, having been created in God's own image. Reminding themselves constantly of this will help parents to look for ways to build and reinforce this mindset in the child.

Parents frequently ask, "What can I do to insure that my child will have a healthy self-image? The answer is: Just avoid knocking it down! Doing so begins what may turn into a lifelong pattern whereby the child internalizes the parents' criticism, sees himself negatively ("Mommy yelled at me; she thinks I'm bad; I *am* bad!"), and ends up habitually picking on himself and putting himself down for perceived (or real) mistakes and failures.

More material on the problem of a low self-image may be found in Chapter 15. Although specifically dealing with its manifestation in teenagers, it is equally applicable to younger children.

ENCOURAGING ACHIEVEMENT

Encouragement helps build the self-confidence and enthusiasm needed to develop new skills. When we encourage our children, it's good to keep in mind that success at any particular task should not be our concern as much as instilling self-confidence in the child.

There are several aspects to encouraging achievement in children:

1. *Giving help.* When we introduce a new skill to our child, we must model how the task is done, explaining all the steps. But after the child understands the process, we need to withdraw a bit and allow him the opportunity to work things out by himself — at the same time, being prepared to offer our help when it's needed.

When a child runs into difficulty in some task, parents frequently encourage him with "Come on, you can do it," or "It's not so hard." This can be helpful, but it may often be more encouraging to the child when we first show some empathy: "I see this is difficult," or "I see you're having a hard time." The child can then be encouraged to keep trying. We might also remind him, *"Kol haschalos kashos"* (all things are difficult in the beginning).[3]

Often, a simple suggestion is all the child needs to help him over some difficulty. For example, "If you hold the sock the other way, it goes on more easily."

2. *Expressing confidence.* Encouragement can be as simple as a show of confidence in the child's judgment. Allow children to join family discussions and give them credit for the good ideas they contribute.

Also, try to avoid unnecessary cautions when children are working or playing: "Watch out, you'll fall!" "Be careful, that's going to break!" Even when it's necessary to caution a child, it can be done tactfully, such as, "Better not to make the cup so full."

3. *Constructive criticism.* When helping children improve their work, avoid merely pointing out what's wrong. Offer constructive suggestions and alternatives. For example, if a child has done a sloppy job on his arithmetic homework, say, "If you wrote those examples more clearly, they'd be easier to read," rather than, "It's impossible to read this!" You might also point to the most legibly written example, commenting, "This one is a pleasure to look at! Maybe you could write all the others just as neatly."

4. *Avoid comparisons and competition.* There are distinct individual differences among children. These must be taken into account. Allow each child to move at his particular pace without being compared to others.

5. *Encouraging through praise.* Make a point, from time to time, of finding some positive things to say about a child's work. For example:

> "Nice lettering on that sign."
> "What pretty colors in that painting!"
> "That's some job on those candlesticks — they really sparkle!"

PRIDE, AND FEAR OF FAILURE

Parents need to encourage and praise their children's accomplishments to help them develop self-confidence. But as children learn to value their own achievements, they need to be protected from two pitfalls: pride, and fear of failure.

Parents can protect children from pride by emphasizing how thankful we should be for any abilities and talents with which we've been blessed. Children should also be taught to be modest about their accomplishments. The Sages teach, "If you have learned much Torah, do not think highly of yourself for it, since for this you were created."[4] Parents can model modesty by reacting with gratitude, rather than pride, over their children's achievements, and by resisting the temptation to talk to others (especially in front of the children) about their children's cleverness and special attainments.

To protect children against both pride and fear of failure, parents need to teach them that their personal worth isn't measured by their accomplishments. While it's certainly rewarding to do well, it doesn't make us better people. Our Sages have taught that a person is required only to do his best. Whether he succeeds or not is not up to him.[5]

Parents should be careful not to pressure the child (or allow him to pressure himself) by insisting that everything he does must be perfect. They can also teach him that mistakes are the way we learn, rather than signs of personal failure or reasons to rebuke ourselves.

REWARDS AS A METHOD OF PRAISE AND ENCOURAGEMENT

Should rewards be used as incentives to encourage proper behavior in children? There are sharp differences of opinion on this question.

The view to be given here is that while it's certainly best to rely on praise and other verbal reinforcement to influence children to behave well, rewards do have their place. They do motivate children and encourage them. However, they should be used only to get children to conform to basic behavioral requirements, such as keeping a neat room or getting to bed on time. They shouldn't be used to induce children to do household chores, such as washing the dishes or taking the garbage out. (See "Reluctance to Help" in Chapter 8.)

Some people question the use of rewards or prizes to encourage good behavior because they think it's a form of bribery. This is a mistake. *A bribe, properly defined, is a prize or inducement offered someone in order to pervert his judgment or corrupt his conduct. But the intention of a reward is to reinforce good conduct.*

Another objection to rewards is that the child becomes accustomed to always expect rewards for good behavior. The assumption here — that the child will continue to perform good deeds for inferior motives — is a false one. The Gemara teaches, "A person should always fulfill Torah and mitzvos, even if he does so for ulterior motives — because he will eventually come to do them for their own sake."[6]

We should never lose sight of the ideal. As our Sages describe it, "Do not be like servants who serve their master for the sake of receiving a reward, but be rather like servants who serve their master without the intention of receiving a reward."[7] Ultimately, good behavior will bring its own rewards. But children, who haven't yet experienced that intrinsic satisfaction which good behavior brings, may need our help in getting such behavior started. Rewards are a way to *initiate* a child into better behavior.

Rewards need not necessarily be material rewards. A trip to a favorite spot can be a reward; so can the privilege to stay up late, or even to bake a cake. You can use as reinforcement whatever your child finds enjoyable. Being allowed to play with some special toy or game can work well. By observing what your child enjoys doing, you can pick reinforcers that will be effective for him.

Incentives tend to lose their effectiveness if parents keep reminding the child about them. For example, "If your bed's not made by the time you leave, you won't get your star." They will then be seen by the child as just another form of pressure to get him to behave as we want him to. Parents have to be careful to keep themselves emotionally detached from the situation.

The point system is popular with many parents. Tell your child which behavior he'll be rewarded for. In a conspicuous spot post a chart for accumulation of points. When he has accumulated a certain number of points, the child can trade them in for some prize — anything from a book or small toy to a mechanical pencil. Let your child choose which item he wants. You buy it and show it to him beforehand. Or a nonmaterial reward can be offered.

Star charts can be very reinforcing for young children. Glue on a star (let the child pick the color) every time your child makes his bed, for instance. No other reward is necessary.

As an example of an innovative reinforcement system, suppose you want to teach your children not to leave their belongings scattered all over their room. Give each child a small sum of money in the morning; but for every item found lying carelessly on the floor by evening (clothing, books, etc.), the child must give up a certain amount. Alternatively, to prevent argument, you might decide to give the money to the child in the evening, minus whatever has been forfeited during the day.

Drawbacks to Rewards

There are some serious drawbacks to using rewards. Though initially they may produce good results, they tend to lose their effectiveness with time. Also, sooner or later, rewards must be discontinued. There is then the danger that the child will fall back into his old behavior patterns.

To mitigate these shortcomings, rewards should be gradually discontinued when the new habits have been firmly established.

Instead of declaring the discontinuation of rewards, the mother might say something like, "You're doing so well. You make your bed so nicely almost every day! You know what? I'm going to give you a really nice surprise in your lunchbox sometimes."

From the beginning, rewards should be accompanied by appropriate words of praise; later, these words should be sufficiently rewarding to the child. Don't make the mistake of assuming that because you've regularly rewarded your children for good behavior, you have to continue doing so. The right kind of praise can be amazingly effective in weaning children from the need for rewards, as this mother discovered:

> It was evening and the children's room was a mess. I was in no mood to supervise cleaning it up. So I said to the children, "Oh, I'm so tired and now I still have the dishes to do, and then to come back and supervise the cleaning up of this room. How wonderful it would be if when I finished the dishes, the room would already be cleaned up!" Then I walked out to do the dishes. The children closed the door and cleaned up the room. In the past if they made a surprise of cleaning up unexpectedly, I would give them some small sweet, and if I didn't they would say something like — "Remember, last time we cleaned up, you gave us this — can we have it now too?" This time I wanted to get them away from that. When I opened the door to the room, I said, "Wow! What a beautiful job you did, what a nice surprise — you must feel so good! I was so tired and you've cleaned the room yourselves without my help at all, you must really feel good inside. I remember how good I felt when I made surprises like that for my mother!" None of them even mentioned a candy.

Rewards for Torah Study

Traditionally, rewards have always been given to children to encourage the study of Torah. The Talmud relates the story of an elementary-school teacher who merited that his prayers for the community were answered immediately. When queried by the great Sage, Rav, he answered as follows:

I teach young children....And I have a pool of fish, and whoever does not wish to learn, I coax him with fish, and I entice and appease him, until he comes to learn.[8]

Rambam suggests that teachers encourage the young child to learn with things he loves, such as nuts or figs or a bit of honey.[9] Rabbi Yoel Schwartz writes:

We may properly encourage better Torah learning through incentive rewards, for Torah studies are particularly difficult, and eventually, the child will feel the joy of learning without artificial inducements.[10]

In one home, the children were allowed to choose a colorful postage stamp from their father's collection every time they came to study Torah. The father also kept in his desk drawer several beautifully illustrated animal books, as well as scientific equipment such as a magnifying glass and a magnet, for the children's amusement after their lessons. These small enticements were all effective rewards for Torah study.

Chapter Five

DISCIPLINE WITH LOVE

There is a tendency to view discipline as a withholding of love. But according to the Jewish view, not only is discipline an expression of true love, but withholding it from the child is a sign of hatred! "For he whom the Lord loves, He admonishes."[1] "Who spares his rod, [it is as if] he hates his child."[2] (Here we interpret "the rod" in its broadest sense, to include all forms of discipline.)[3] The disciplined child is also a source of true gratification to his parents. "Discipline your child, and he will grant you repose; he will give delight to your soul."[4]

A newborn baby is compared to a little wild donkey;[5] he follows only his natural instincts and primitive desires. Discipline is necessary to instill in the child those basic controls which will enable him gradually to acquire a less self-centered orientation.

THE RIGHT HAND AND THE LEFT

In educating the child, the Sages advise, "Let the left hand push away while the right hand draws near."[6] We may see the right hand as symbolizing the direct expression of love — affection and understanding — and the left as representing the indirect expression of love, which appears as restriction and discipline. Rabbi Samson Raphael Hirsch explains that, though we combine love with strictness in our education, the "right hand drawing near" must predominate. "We will have difficulty succeeding in our education with excessive strictness, which only incites to rebelliousness." Only by expressing our constant love for the child can we succeed in educating him.[7]

Excessive severity is counterproductive and may lead to rebellion, but the withholding of discipline is no less harmful. Parents sometimes fail to discipline their child because of inappropriate feelings of compassion for him, or because they worry about interfering with his natural development. They're making a basic mistake. Perhaps the most tragic story in Scripture is that of Absalom's rebellion against his indulgent father, his violation of his father's wives, and his murderous drive to destroy his father. What could cause such perversion of human nature? The Midrash explains that the parent who deprives his child of discipline will cause him to follow evil ways and, eventually, to hate the parent. Because King David didn't chastise or discipline his beloved son, Absalom became depraved, and even wanted to kill his father.[8] An absence of firmness and a reluctance to discipline children can be basic causes for later rebellion against parents.

Note that the Sages refer to the withholding of discipline as *deprivation*. Discipline is necessary for the child; he has a right to it!

The strict left hand and the compassionate right hand may also be viewed as working together in another sense. When imposing discipline, we should do so in an obviously loving manner; this makes the child feel that we have his best interests at heart. Discipline which carries a message of love can never be interpreted by the child as rejection.

Modern psychology, too, recognizes the importance of discipline:

> Much has been written about the dangers of harsh, oppressive, unloving discipline; these warnings are valid and should be heeded. However, the consequences of excessive punish-

ment have been cited as justification for the elimination of discipline. That is foolish....[the child] wants to know where the boundaries lie and who's available to enforce them...[and the parents] need to know when to punish, how to set limits, and what behavior to inhibit. This disciplinary activity must occur within the framework of love and affection.9

ADMONISHMENT

The Torah commands us to admonish our fellow man when we see him behave improperly, as an expression of our love and concern for his welfare. This mitzvah applies to our children with even greater force, for they are totally dependent on us for the development of their character and values.[10]

The verse in Proverbs, "For he whom the Lord loves, He admonishes..." concludes with the words, "...like a father who delights in his son."[11] The *Gaon* of Vilna comments that the father-son relationship is unique. In other relationships, the rebuker may love the one whom he rebukes, but if the person won't listen, he eventually lets him go his way. But if a son doesn't heed his father's rebuke, the father doesn't desist; he continues to chastise him until the son improves his ways. He does this out of a love which is so great that it cannot bear to see wrongdoing, and desires only that the son behave righteously. The evidence that the father acts out of feelings of love is that when he's finished chastising his son, he speaks to him comfortingly and soothingly. When the admonishment is followed by words of consolation, it's unlikely to cause resentment, for the child will sense that it is really an expression of love.

Principles of Admonishment

Purpose: When admonishing their child, parents should clearly convey to him that they act out of concern for his welfare. As Rambam says: "Speak pleasantly and softly when you admonish someone. Explain to the person that you have only his benefit in mind, to bring him to eternal life in the World to Come."[12]

Timing: We should not hesitate to admonish our children, but there's a special obligation of "not saying that which won't be heeded."[13] This means that we may have to postpone the admonishment until the child is most receptive to being rebuked. (A child's wrongdoing must never be overlooked entirely; he may interpret our silence as approval.) Thus, with the exception of very young children, it is often better not to admonish a child on the spot, but rather to wait for an opportune moment. This may be an hour or so later, sometimes even a day or two. It's important that both the parent and the child be calm enough for a serious and friendly conversation about the behavior. It is said of Rabbi Eliyahu Lopian that before reprimanding any of his children or students, he would always allow enough time to elapse so that not a trace of anger remained. Once when one of his children did something extremely improper, he waited two full weeks until he censured him.[14]

In a large family where postponing admonishment might result in the parents' forgetting to deliver it altogether, it's a good idea to jot it down, perhaps in a special note pad. For example, one might write, "Talk to Shlomo — disrespect suppertime" or "Tzippy — complaining about my asking her to sweep floor."

Parents must also be careful not to admonish the child in front of others, lest they cause him embarrassment or shame.[15] (The prohibition against causing embarrassment or shame extends to private admonishments as well.)[16]

Avoiding anger: When admonishing a child, our goal is to influence him to regret his behavior and work to change it. This can't be accomplished with angry rebukes. A show of anger should be reserved for those rare occasions when we need to forcefully impress a child with the gravity of his wrongdoing. Even then, we only *act* as if we're angry; inwardly we remain calm.[17]

Positive expectations: When Aaron the *Kohen* met a wrongdoer, he would greet him in a friendly manner. When the transgressor was tempted the next day to do wrong again, he would think, "How will I face Aaron, who greeted me as if he considers me righteous? I feel ashamed to do wrong."[18]

When admonishing a child, one should convey that one expects the best of him. In the words of the Ran:

> Anyone wishing to correct a person who has done wrong should do this in two ways. First he must let him know that

he did wrong...second, let him know that he is capable of reaching a high level [of perfection] — that despite his wrongdoing he is beloved by his friend and remains in his good graces.[19]

The Shelah teaches us that if, when admonishing someone, we tell him that such conduct doesn't befit so intelligent and wise a person as he, he will feel complimented and more receptive to correction.[20]

If we are to influence our children, they must sense our belief in their ability to change. They must never receive the impression that we've given up on them.

When parents view their child's negative traits as fixed, they inevitably convey this by such statements as:

> "Batya can't do what I ask without giving me an argument."
> "Dinah makes a fuss about every little thing — she's such a complainer!"
> "Nothing remains in one piece after Benjamin is finished with it."
> "Pinchas can't make up his mind about anything."

The labels parents commonly give their children, such as "irresponsible," "lazy," or "stubborn," have the same effect. "Labeling is disabling," writes a noted child psychologist.[21] Rabbi Hirsch states: "If we give up hope concerning our children, and fail to muster the energy to guide them onto the proper path, they too will give up hope concerning themselves."[22]

We should be careful even in the case of very small children who, it is presumed, wouldn't comprehend what is said about them. Children often understand far more than we realize; it is best, therefore, to avoid all negative remarks about a child — regardless of his age — in his presence (and when not in his presence as well!).

Manner of Admonishment

People don't like to be told that they're wrong. Children are no exception, and should be admonished, writes the *Gaon* of Vilna, with "soft words and reprimands which will be willingly accepted."[23]

Our admonishment can consist of a few words delivered on the spot, or it can take the form of a serious discussion with the child. *What* we say is not as important as *how* we say it. If we are calm inside and feel loving concern for the child, then the words we choose will usually be the right ones.

Consider the following rebuke: "When I called you before, you ignored me and continued playing. Is that right? What are you supposed to do when I call you?" Imagine this being said in an accusatory tone of voice, and picture the effect on the child. Now think of the same words spoken gently, and imagine their very different effect.

We should be aware to what extent our tone of voice, even the expression on our face, can convey a put-down message, often far more effectively than our words. Watch yourself in a mirror as you say, "You shouldn't have done that," in three different ways: first angrily; then with mild annoyance; then lovingly. The child is no less aware of the contrast!

Keep in mind that a deep sigh, a look of disgust, folded arms, or even pursed lips can convey our negative thoughts about the child. Children are masters at studying our faces, stance, and body language in general for signals of disapproval, and we should do all we can to control such negative signals — and, ultimately, the negative thoughts behind them.

Admonishing a child with "Why did you...?" or "Why didn't you...?" is generally ineffective and should be avoided. These types of rebukes are really criticisms of the child and, unless said extremely gently, are unlikely to motivate him to improve his behavior.

Let's consider the following example: Your daughter has come home from school with her dress full of glue stains. You know that the stains won't come out and that the dress is ruined. You reprimand her: "Why weren't you more careful?" This supposed question really conveys, "You should have been more careful!" It implies a negative judgment of the child. She'll react either by defensively warding off your criticism, or by accepting it and feeling down about herself ("Mommy's right — I don't know why I'm so careless!"). In either case, she's unlikely to be thinking constructively about how she might avoid staining her clothing in the future. A better approach, more likely to succeed, would be to tell her, "Oh dear, those glue stains don't come out. What a shame, this dress can't be worn anymore. Please try to be more careful next time when you work with glue." (Of course, the way we say this makes all the difference.)

A mother writes:

> *Since starting the workshop two weeks ago, I've eliminated the word "Why?" from my vocabulary. It's terrific! The atmosphere at home has changed completely. I used to be constantly saying, "Why....Why didn't you do your home-work?...Why didn't you clean up?...Why didn't you do the dishes?" Now I try to avoid that.*
>
> *For instance, if one of my children gets up to play in the middle of doing his homework, instead of saying, "Why did you get up to play?" I say, "Please sit down and do your home-work." I am much more direct with the children. One of my children is terribly wild and destructive. I always used to ask him, "Why do you keep breaking things? ...Why...Why...Why?" though I knew it was harmful. Last week I saw that the shelf under the bathroom mirror had fallen. I was sure he did it — I didn't even have to ask! Before attending the workshop, I would have screamed at him, "Why did you knock down the shelf — why can't you be more careful?!" What did I do this time? I was aggravated, and then I calmed down. I went to him and quietly asked, "Who broke the bathroom shelf? Who knocked it down?" "Mommy, it was me," he said, "but not on purpose." "Okay, I said, "next time be more careful." This was a real breakthrough for me!*

Reprimanding the child with a description of his negative behav-ior is another pattern to avoid. A lively 5-year-old thinks it is delight-ful fun to use the sofa as a trampoline. Mother cries out, "You're ruining my furniture!" But these words don't convey her under-standable concern about the sofa. What they mainly convey is her annoyance over the child's behavior. Consequently, he feels put down and possibly even resentful. A better reaction would be, "Honey, please stop. The furniture gets ruined when you jump on it like that."

Another example: Eleven-year-old Betzalel is teasing his brother Noach, 19. "Be quiet!" Noach responds. "You're nothing but a little pipsqueak." A parent may unthinkingly scold, "Noach! That's no way to talk to your little brother. You make him feel like he's nothing!" Here again, this remark is likely to be seen as nothing more than a putdown. A better way of handling it would be to call Noach aside and say, "I know Betzalel's teasing bothers you. But calling him a pipsqueak belittles him and makes him feel bad. He'll just come back and tease you some more, to get back at you." From there the parent might go on to discuss with him ways of influencing Betzalel to stop his teasing.

Reprimands such as, "Look what you're doing!" or "You're not listening!" fall into the same category; make every effort to avoid them.

When correcting a child, remember to state your specific expectations clearly. It does little good to complain, "Why do you always run out in the middle and leave me with the rest of the cleaning up to do by myself?" Instead, say, "I'd like you to stay in the kitchen after supper to help me until everything is cleaned up."

It's good to sit down with the child during your talk with him. You might want to reassure him of your love by taking his hand in yours, or putting your hand on his shoulder. Try, whenever possible, to begin with something favorable:

> "I guess you probably forgot...."
> "Maybe you weren't aware...."
> "I know you were in a hurry before and that's why.... "
> "I realize it was hard for you to control yourself...."
> "I'm sure you didn't intend to...."

Don't corner the child. Give him a chance to explain things from his point of view. Don't knock his reasons down or label them excuses. You can show understanding at the same time that you point out what was wrong with his behavior. Often, a simple reminder such as, "Remember what we said about...?" is all that's needed. Try to end the session on an optimistic note, conveying confidence in your child's desire to improve his behavior.

Sometimes merely telling the child, "I'm disappointed in you," is enough. Or, "I guess I don't have to tell you that you acted wrongly before — you probably realize it yourself, don't you."

Even a look of disappointment — mingled with surprise — which lets your child know "I expect better of you," can at times suffice. You must let your child's nature guide you in deciding what forms of reprimand will work best. For some very sensitive children the mildest of rebukes is enough.

Here are the stories of several mothers who achieved excellent results with their children when they changed to a quiet manner of admonishing:

> *My two boys had had a fight. Eli, 7¹/₂, had torn a picture which his 5-year-old brother brought home from school. Normally I would have scolded him in a loud voice: "Eli, you shouldn't have done that — it wasn't very nice! How would you like it if someone did that to you?" His reaction would then have been defensive, something like, "He started it!" and so on, ending up in a very unpleasant argument.*
>
> *This time, I waited until evening. I called Eli in and told him quietly, "I want to speak to you." I had him sit down next to me and, taking hold of his hand, told him in a serious but quiet voice, "Eli, what you did this afternoon wasn't nice — it wasn't right — you shouldn't have done it...." At that point he burst into tears! I was so surprised. With a few quiet words, I got through to him so easily.*

> *It was suppertime. My son, aged 3, and my daughter, aged 7, were arguing over a favorite cup. My son moved a chair to the counter and climbed up to reach for it. While his back was turned, my daughter pushed the chair away. He slid down from the counter, missed the chair and fell, hurting himself. I told my daughter that her meal was over and sent her to her room. Later, after I cleaned up the kitchen and felt calm enough to talk to her without becoming angry, I went to her room. I said, "I know you realize that you made a mistake*

when you moved away the chair." She replied that she did. I continued and said, "I hope it won't happen again." My daughter replied, "It won't."

Previously, I would have screamed at her immediately, telling her it was "stupid" to move the chair and that she could have "killed" her brother. She would have yelled back defensively and cried.

I feel that by admonishing my child without accusations and in a calm fashion, I achieved the desired result without upsetting my daughter or myself unnecessarily.

"Well, it sure works!" I exclaimed, as I walked into my second workshop session. The day after my first session my 5-year-old daughter came into my room at 5 o'clock in the morning. Usually I'd screech, "Get out — I want to sleep!" Hearing that, she might not leave at all, or she might go out but come back five minutes later. This time I said instead, "Please, darling, — I'm very tired — I want to sleep. Please, go back to your room and rest some more, okay?" She went — no problem! And I got my sleep.

What we say to our children is important, but we shouldn't become overly cautious, worrying about every word we say. Although we should make reasonable efforts to avoid hurting the child, sharp words are sometimes necessary. Indeed, if parents are too careful to avoid all sharp words, the child may become overly sensitive to minor slights which others easily overlook.

There are parents who hesitate to admonish their children because they fear it might arouse guilt feelings in them. Often, the parent himself has that reaction to criticism, and therefore assumes the child will react in a similar way. We should understand that guilt feelings — the destructive type — result from *improper* admonishment, the kind that puts the child down. If we're careful to admonish children quietly, pointing out only what was wrong with their behavior, there is no reason to hesitate — we'll arouse appropriate and necessary regret alone. Maintaining a low tone of voice will go far to "help the medicine go down" with a minimum of discomfort.

When Repeated Admonishment Has Not Helped

It's no secret that staying calm is most difficult when repeated admonishment seems to have failed to have any effect on our child. At these times we're likely to think, "This is *it!* That was the last straw! I've talked to him about this nicely time and again, but it doesn't seem to make any difference! Now I'm going to let him have it!"

But parents should be aware that if they let themselves get angry at this point, their efforts to stay calm until now will have been largely wasted. Remember that one of the main reasons the child persists in his bad behavior is that he tells himself how bad he is for misbehaving, rather than making determined efforts to change. Our anger strongly reinforces his opinion of himself as "a bad boy," as well as the habit.

We must be careful, though, not to tell *ourselves* off for our inability to stay calm. That would be making the same mistake that our child is making! Recognizing our own difficulties in this area should help us to be more tolerant of our child's difficulties, so that we will show him more understanding.

It's when we feel we've come to the "end of our rope" that we must make special efforts to speak quietly. It's appropriate to ask questions which call for an explanation of his behavior, such as, "How is it that you're still doing this when I've talked to you about it so many times?" Said gently, this is bound to evoke in the child genuine feelings of regret. Sometimes we might add, "I know you're sorry. But that's not enough. You have to make up your mind to act differently next time." We might also gently rebuke the child, "It's not right for you to keep ignoring my requests like this."

Reactions to Admonishment

Often, children will remain completely quiet when we admonish them. This doesn't mean they're not listening. They could be taking in everything we say, without feeling like answering. Give them time to think things over and don't rush them.

Other children will defend themselves mightily even when they've been only mildly admonished. That's because admonishment triggers uncomfortable guilt feelings inside them, which they then try to ward off by a defensive reaction.

In dealing with these defensive reactions, avoid trying to prove the child wrong. If his defense is a flimsy one, he usually knows it; he doesn't need it pointed out to him! For instance, you ask your son why he neglected to put his toys back on the shelf. He answers with that best known of excuses, "I forgot." Don't argue, "How could you forget when the toys are right in front of you, all over the floor?!" It's best to take him at his word and answer, "Please try harder to remember next time."

Parents should realize that their manner of rebuking the child until now may have contributed to his guilt problem and subsequent defensiveness, and should be careful from now on to avoid triggering more guilt. If we keep our remarks objective and avoid put-downs, he'll get over his guilt feelings in time; then he'll no longer feel compelled to defend himself.

Ideally, our goal is to instill in the child the ability to admit his mistake and express regret over it. Consider the following exchange:

MOTHER: We've talked about not leaving your papers and books lying around the living room. This morning I found your things there again.

CHILD: But it was only a few papers!

MOTHER: (gently) Honey, you don't have to defend yourself. Just tell me, "I'm sorry, Mom, I'll try to remember for next time."

The child's guilt feelings can also trigger angry or hostile reactions. In this case he's blaming *us* for making him feel bad. Don't let such reactions put you on the defensive, and certainly don't let your child's angry outburst stop you from reproving him in the future. Tell him, "I see you're very upset. I'll talk to you later when you've calmed down."

Later, when the child has regained his composure, you can say, keeping your voice very low, "I realize you were feeling bad before and that's why you screamed at me. But you know that's wrong. If I say something which upsets you, you can tell me that you feel bad, but you're not allowed to yell." Try to get him to see that you correct him because you care about him, and don't want him to do things that are wrong. "I know you're very unhappy right now," you might say. "But please try to understand that when I correct you, it's because I care about you so much. I have only your best interests at heart."

Children, like adults, often feel very upset after being admonished. Your child may even be telling himself off for his poor behavior. You can ease his self-recrimination and guilt with the words, "I know you're sorry."

It also helps to reflect back some of his feelings, at the same time offering encouragement. For example, "I know — right now you're feeling miserable because of your poor self-control. You never *want* to yell at me, but then you lose control and do it anyway. But I know you can learn to control yourself better. It will take effort, but I think you can do it."

A child may act as if he isn't bothered at all by your rebuke. "I don't care," he says with a shrug. Respond by putting your hand on his shoulder and telling him, very lovingly, "I know you don't really mean that."

PUNISHMENT

In general, parents should rely on admonishment to correct their children's behavior. But when repeated reprimands haven't worked, we may sometimes need to punish the child. Punishment should not be seen as a last resort, but as an occasionally necessary disciplinary tool. Like admonishment, it is a Torah obligation.[24]

Some parents hesitate to punish their children because they are reluctant to cause them suffering. It may help these parents to overcome their qualms if they can regard punishment as a kind of bitter-tasting medicine which is sometimes the only cure for misbehavior. Would you hesitate to give your child a teaspoon of bitter medicine if he needed it?

Other parents hesitate to punish because they've been influenced by some modern ideas about punishment which claim that it is an unfair use of power that leads to feelings of hatred and revenge in the child. This may be so when parents punish vengefully or in anger — but that's clearly not the Jewish way. As Rabbi Shlomo Wolbe writes:

> [Sometimes] when the child does not immediately obey, the father feels personally offended. He then "punishes" the child. In truth, this is not *punishment* but *revenge*, and revenge is forbidden by Torah law toward a child too![25]

> The sensitive heart of the young child is strongly affected by every expression of pain on the part of his parents. And if we deprive him of part of his usual portion of sweets, this is already significant punishment; certainly so if he is deprived of all of it![26]

We learn from the Talmud that we should punish children only after they have been forewarned and know what to expect if they continue to misbehave.[27] Punishments should never be announced and then deferred, since in anticipation of a punishment a child may be frightened to the point of harming himself.[28] Either punish immediately, or overlook the misdeed. Parents are also cautioned to be extremely sparing in punishing older children.[29]

Always explain to your children why they're being punished. At the time of punishment, your manner should convey how badly you feel about having to administer it.

Physical Punishment

We'll discuss physical punishment first — not because it's the best method, but because it's used so often.

Usually, it is forbidden to strike others.[30] Nevertheless, it is permitted to hit a child, as punishment — but only to the extent necessary for educating him.[31] However, it is poor practice to rely on hitting as an educational tool.[32] The Talmudic Sage, Rav, advises: "When you hit a child, do not hit him with anything but a shoestrap (shoelace),"[33] to which Rashi comments, "In other words, a light stroke which can do no harm."

The *Gaon* of Vilna writes that a parent should not strike his child cruelly and out of anger for what he has done. Rather, the parent's intention should be to prevent future bad behavior. And he should not hit the child more than a few times.[34]

Jewish law forbids administering physical punishment to a grown child.[35] This prohibition is based on the Biblical injunction "You shall not place a stumbling block before the blind."[36] That is, by striking a grown child, one may incite him to hit back — thereby violating a serious Biblical injunction, against striking a parent. Even too frequently hitting a small child is wrong, and parents are liable to court sanctions for it.[37]

Modern psychologists have pointed out the harm done by hitting children (some even advocate the elimination of *all* forms of punishment!), and many parents have become extremely reluctant to do so. Yet the various objections raised regarding hitting children — that it is harmful and cruel; that it causes children to hate their parents; that it teaches them aggression and cruelty — should not concern us if we adhere to the above-mentioned limitations. When parents act only out of concern for their children's welfare, occasional mild hitting is neither harmful nor cruel — but beneficial. The child is unlikely to hate his parents for hitting him; nor is there any danger that he will learn aggression and cruelty from the parents' example.

The child should be impressed and pained not so much by the slap as by the fact that it was *necessary* for the parent to hit him. Remember that children are often very upset after being hit, and in need of reassurance that we still love them. Therefore, it's a good idea to show them some affection not too long after the spanking.

The following incident reported by one mother illustrates how effective a gentle slap on the hand can be:

> Our 4-year-old was in the habit of calling everyone, including me, "meshuga" (crazy). I reprimanded her several times in a quiet tone of voice: "Yaeli, I can't allow you to call me that." But she persisted in using the word. I tried ignoring her for a while, but this didn't seem to help either. I explained to her what the word means and how it hurts people's feelings to be called such a name, but this seemed to have little effect, since she continued her behavior.
>
> In order to help myself control my anger and annoyance at my daughter, I reminded myself that the child was not bad,

but rather that she had a bad habit, and that it was my job to help her break it. These thoughts enabled me to remain calm and to attempt to deal effectively with the problem.

One day when the older children were out of the house, my daughter asked me for something that I was unable to give her at the moment. Her reaction was to call me "meshuga." I walked over to her, took her hand and said quietly to her, "Yaeli, I have asked you to stop calling me meshuga, but I see that you forget. I have to hit you now, to help you remind yourself." Then I hit her gently on her hand. She ran out of the room crying. She cried for a long time. Since then, she has not mentioned the word.

Slapping children routinely for all kinds of minor misbehavior is poor disciplinary practice. Keeping children in line by constantly warning them, "You're going to get slapped if you do that!" is similarly ill advised. For hitting to be effective, it must be used very sparingly.

Other Kinds of Punishment

Sending a child to his room: This is an appropriate punishment for many kinds of minor misbehavior. For instance, the child may be wild and unruly. Warn him: "Either you settle down or I'll have to send you to your room." If he ignores this, say very calmly, "Please go to your room now for a while. You can come out when you're ready to control yourself." If necessary, take him by the hand and lead him to his room (or some other room). If he emerges soon afterwards and resumes his wild behavior, tell him, "I see you're not yet ready to control yourself. Please go back to your room." Or the child can be asked to stay in the room for a specified amount of time. To prevent him from popping out every few minutes to ask, "Can I come out now?" you can put a timer in the room, explaining that he can't come out until it rings.

When a child refuses to go to his room or to stay in it, we may need to forewarn him of other punishment to follow if he doesn't obey us. In the above situation, for example, you might say very quietly, "You decide — you can go to your room or miss your dessert tonight." But we have to make our punishments stick. Even if the child acts as if he doesn't care, he'll be sorry he didn't listen when he misses his dessert.

Another way of handling it: Firmly grasp the child's hand and lead him into his room. Tell him that he has to stay there and that you'll be holding on to the doorknob from the outside, ready to release it when he decides to remain in the room.

A child must not be forcibly kept in isolation when this obviously agitates him to the point of hysteria.[38]

How long should the child be kept in his room? It depends. Suppose you sent him to his room for continuing to climb onto the window sill in the living room, when you'd told him repeatedly not to do that. After 15 minutes you let him out, whereupon he promptly goes back to climbing onto the window sill. Obviously, the 15 minutes weren't enough. Perhaps half an hour will be more effective, or maybe even 45 minutes.

Another aspect to consider is: What does the child do in his room? If he's having a wonderful time playing with his toys, your punishment will have little effect. Maybe you'll have to put him in a different room, possibly your own bedroom; or, you can quietly remove the toys from his room before putting him into it.

Sometimes when they're sent to their room, children will begin to kick, bang, or throw things. Taking their shoes off will minimize damage to some extent, and may also teach them not to kick — because it hurts! If there's danger of any damage, this behavior must be stopped immediately, either by physically restraining the child or by sending him out of the house. (Naturally, we have to exercise good judgment as to whether sending him out may be risky if the child is too upset.)

Or try this method: Tell your child beforehand that he may come out of the room only when he's been completely quiet for a specified period of time (five minutes, or so). Also, that for every object he kicks or throws he must stay in the room for an additional period (a minute or two). This means you'll have to be at the door to hear what's going on inside. When things finally quiet down, tell him, "I have to add (so and so many) minutes for (kicking the door/throwing around toys, etc.)."

Timeout Chair: This works best with very young children. Place a special chair in a corner or the center of the room. Then tell the child (assuming you've already forewarned him of the consequences the next time he would misbehave), "This is your punishment. You have to sit in this chair." If he bounces up, we put him back — holding on to him if necessary so that he can't get up.

Depriving a child of treats: Be careful, when using this punishment, that it doesn't produce strong resentment. After your warnings of what will happen are ignored, reduce the child's usual portion of treats. Thus, give him his crackers at snacktime, but without the usual peanut butter; or give him only half a bag of potato chips or half a piece of cake for dessert.

Deprivation of privileges: You can also punish your child by depriving him of some privilege — perhaps, not allowing him to ride his bicycle for a day. For instance, if your child dawdles about getting to bed at night (and after your warnings about the punishment go unheeded), you might deprive him of a day's bike riding for each 15 minutes late to bed. If he's come in late several times, or if he misbehaves while outside, an especially fitting punishment is that he be kept in the house. True, this can be hard on you, but it may be worth your while to go through one difficult day if this will produce a change for the better in your child's behavior.

Punishment for disrespect: As discussed in Chapter 2, showing respect to parents is one of a child's basic obligations. Occasional disrespect is best dealt with by gentle rebukes. But when a child has been unusually disrespectful, sometimes punishment may be called for. One effective and suitable punishment is to refrain from speaking to him for, say, three hours. Since your purpose is to impress the child with the seriousness of his transgression, it is important to explain to him quietly beforehand that he is being punished. You might say, for example: "For the next three hours I am not talking to you. You shouted at me — you're not allowed to do that. This is your punishment." For a younger child, half an hour is usually sufficient.

Make it clear that this punishment is not a form of retaliation, but rather a measure deemed necessary for the child's welfare. Feeling no anger, calmly ignore the child for the specified time. Pay no attention to any complaining or carrying on about the punishment. Ignore it as you'd ignore his resistance to swallowing a bitter-tasting medicine. Nothing need be said when the punishment is over; resumption of normal relations can begin immediately. Don't make remarks such as, "I hope you learned your lesson." Like any other disciplinary action, however, this one loses its effectiveness if used too frequently.

Reactions to Punishment

Parents should not let a child's reactions to punishment affect them. To "get back at" their parents, children will sometimes sulk to show them how angry they are at being punished. If the parents ignore this, the child will see that he's only punishing himself and will stop. If children project an "I don't care" attitude, this should also be ignored.

On the other hand, violent protest — whether directed against objects or against the parents themselves — should not be overlooked. For suggestions on how to cope with such behavior, see "Abusive Behavior" in Chapter 3.

NATURAL AND LOGICAL CONSEQUENCES*

A very effective method of discipline is simply to refrain from interfering in the natural order of events, thus allowing children to experience the direct unpleasant results — that is, the natural consequences — of their misbehavior. For example, clothes which aren't put into the hamper don't get washed. A child who doesn't get up on time is inevitably late for school and must face the teacher's displeasure. Children who come in late for supper end up with a cold meal, or miss the meal altogether.

Logical consequences, by contrast, are the *arranging* of events so that unpleasant consequences follow. For instance, objects left lying around the house end up in a box kept in some out-of-the-way spot. A child who neglects to brush his teeth can't have dried fruit or other sweets because sticky foods, if not removed by brushing, can damage teeth. A child who misbehaves when the family is out visiting stays home the next time. Children should always be informed beforehand of negative consequences, so that they have a

---

* These concepts were first formulated by Rudolf Dreikurs in *The Challenge of Parenthood* (New York: Duell, Sloan & Pearce, 1948).

choice in the matter. Thus, the child who misbehaves on a visit is quietly told, "Either you behave nicely or we'll have to leave you home with a baby-sitter the next time we go visiting."

Always state consequences in a matter-of-fact tone of voice. If you use an intimidating tone, you're making a threat, rather than a simple factual statement of consequences. This usually makes disciplinary action less effective, because threats tend to provoke children into being resistant.

Chapter Six

DEVELOPING AN UNDERSTANDING RELATIONSHIP

*I*n elaborating on the mitzvah, "Love your fellow as yourself,"[1] Rambam writes: "All the things you want others to do for you, do them to your brother in Torah and mitzvos."[2] This principle has special implications for the way we nurture our children.

On the most basic level, of course, is the physical care we give them: our provision of a home, food, medical care, etc. But we also give of ourselves emotionally — with smiles and friendly words,[3] or, in a deeper way, by extending empathy. Empathy means putting yourself in the other person's position, imagining what things are like from his point of view, and letting him know that you understand. It is valuable to all people, and certainly to growing children, who are dependent on others for support and guidance. It is among the most lofty forms of *chesed* (lovingkindness), one of the cornerstones of Torah life.[4] (See Chapter 8.)

In addition to empathy and understanding, children want to have their ideas and opinions respected. They can usually tolerate disagreement, as long as they feel that their ideas are granted some legitimacy.

Children flourish best when we extend them this empathy, understanding, and respect.

LEARNING TO BE MORE EMPATHIC

When our children come to us with their problems, we often quickly jump in at once with our advice. We tend to discount their feelings or we tell them how they should feel. Instead, we should stop and ask ourselves, "How would I want someone to respond to me if I were in this child's position?"

One good way to become more empathic is to keep in mind how dissatisfying an unempathic response can be when we ourselves want some understanding from another person. For example, imagine that you're a housewife with four little children. It's two weeks before Pesach and you've been working hard all day. When your husband comes home you greet him with a wan smile as you tell him, "I'm completely worn out." He replies, "I keep telling you you're doing too much. Half the work you do is totally unnecessary." How do you feel? Not understood, and perhaps even upset. No doubt you'd have liked to hear something like, "I can see you're completely exhausted! You must really have worked hard. Why don't you go rest a bit while I put the kids to bed?" At another time, you might be willing to listen to the well-intentioned advice of doing less unnecessary work, but not at this moment when it's empathy you're seeking.

Becoming more empathic toward our children takes practice. Before we give advice, it's important to let the child feel that we understand his position. We have to learn to curb that initial impulse to tell him what he should do or how he should feel; instead, first take the time to really listen to him. This may require some effort, but the results are well worth it, as these stories illustrate:

> We had an ongoing problem with our 11-year-old son, who didn't want to go to his Pirchei group on Shabbas afternoon.

Then he would complain endlessly, "I have nothing to do." A 15-minute argument would then ensue — "Jonathan, go to Pirchei."

"Why should I go? We don't do anything there anyway."

"Just go — you'll have a good time."

"No, I don't want to."

"Jonathan!" (with the pitch of my voice raised an octave).

Finally he would go out the door, with both of us feeling bad.

This time when he came to me saying, "I don't want to go today," I turned to him and said, "Jonathan, I know you don't like to go to Pirchei, but it's so much better for you to go than to stay here and be bored."

He got up and walked out of the room. I was sure he was just going to read in his room, but in a minute I heard the front door open — he walked out and went to Pirchei!

Although ordinarily a gentle, well-behaved child, my 9-year-old Efraim has an occasional stubborn streak which I have never been able to get around. Whenever he set his mind to something that was contrary to what I wanted, I would find myself angrily forcing the issue. The results would always be an unhappy, sulking boy and a frustrated mommy.

On this particular morning, Efraim was feeling out-of-sorts because of fever blisters on his tongue — enough to make a child miserable but not enough of a reason to stay home from school. When I went in to wake him, Efraim grumbled. Three-quarters of an hour later I realized, amid my activity with the other children, that Efraim was still in bed!

Formerly, I would have stormed into Efraim's room to demand that he get dressed immediately, resulting in resentful compliance. This time, I was armed with our previous evening's parenting workshop discussion on empathy. Rehearsing mentally, I entered his room. Efraim was still beneath his quilts. "Efraim," I said gently, "I know you're not *feeling well this morning...but get dressed anyway." Having said that, I bit my tongue to keep from saying anything more and left the room.*

Three minutes later, I curiously peeked into the room. To my utter amazement, Efraim was up and entirely dressed — down to his shoes! And all this without even a frown!

I couldn't help reviewing and reviewing the scene excitedly all day in my mind, trying to figure out what had happened!

It takes practice. We can be on the alert for ordinary incidents, giving thought to how we might respond with greater empathy. For instance, parents will advise, "Don't scratch that mosquito bite — it'll bleed!" But the child continues scratching away. Now the parent says, "If you hadn't scratched, it wouldn't bleed." It's so much nicer, for us and the child, to feel with him and let him know that we understand what he's going through. We all know how very hard it is to resist scratching insect bites. Better to say, "It itches *so* much, and it's *so* hard to resist scratching! Come, let's put something on it to help stop the itching."

CREATING AN ATMOSPHERE OF UNDERSTANDING

In creating an atmosphere of understanding, parents must be patient, empathic, and good listeners. But there are several things to watch out for:

1. *Avoid contradicting or discounting your child's perceptions*: Try to give legitimacy to his opinions. For example, if he says, "Yuch! This milk tastes sour!" don't tell him, "Why, you can hardly taste the sourness." When he tells you that his drawing "didn't come out well," don't answer, "Well, I think it's nice."

We tend to respond this way because we're trying to influence the child. In the first example, we're trying to persuade the child to drink the milk. But the predictable outcome will be an argument, with each side maintaining his position. Far better to respond, reflecting the child's opinion, "The milk tastes sour to you?" The issue here is not whether the child must drink the milk or not, but one of showing respect for a legitimate opinion. You can suggest flavoring the milk to cover up the slightly sour taste. (If the child then still doesn't want to drink the milk, he should certainly not be forced to do so.)

In the second example, we want to encourage the child to continue drawing. But here, too, he'll most likely keep insisting that his drawing isn't good. An empathic, understanding response, one which confirms the child's point of view, might be, "You're not satisfied with the way your drawing turned out." Surprisingly, this is often more encouraging to the child.

Parents shouldn't try to get a child over any unhappiness or despondency by telling him, for instance, "Never mind. You'll get over it," or "Come on, it's not so bad. Snap out of it." Children (adults as well!) don't like being talked out of their feelings. It's better to acknowledge the child's feelings with, for example, "How disappointing! You were looking forward to that trip so much, and now it was canceled because of the weather," or "I'm so sorry you didn't get the window seat." Our empathy and understanding are usually enough to help children get over their unhappy feelings.

A further illustration: Your teenage son has torn his pants while crawling under a fence. He's unhappy because he realizes that his carelessness means you'll have to pay for a new pair of pants. Don't console him with, "Never mind — we'll buy you new pants." He'll feel better if you reflect his feelings. "You're unhappy because you're blaming yourself for your carelessness and you're thinking about how much money we'll have to spend for new pants."

In reflecting your child's feelings, exercise certain cautions. For example, complaints about another person's behavior usually constitute forbidden derogatory speech, and you should gently point this out. If your child tells you he's angry at his friend, it would be wrong to answer, "Boy, you really felt like punching him in the nose, didn't you!" Anger is a bad character trait. We don't condemn a child for his anger, but we must not encourage it.

Understanding your child's feelings doesn't mean you have to agree with them. Often it's a mistake to do this. For instance, in the previous example of the canceled picnic, it would be foolish to say, "You're right. It really is terrible that the picnic was called off."

Sometimes, children are totally unreceptive to empathy, preferring to be left alone. You can find out if the child wants to talk or would rather be left alone by asking, "I see you're upset. Do you want to talk about it?"

At times, children actually want to be talked out of their feelings of discouragement. One mother, whose 15-year-old was worried about the possibility of his ankle injury becoming permanent, described the boy's reaction when she empathized with him by reflecting his feelings. "I don't want to hear that," he told her, "I want you to assure me that it's nothing serious." We need to sense what's appropriate in each situation.

2. *Avoid challenging the child*: Questions such as, "Do you mean to tell me...?" or "Are you sure?" or "How do you know that?" put the child on the defensive. They convey a lack of trust in his judgment. (Parents should refrain, in general, from "cross-examining" children and asking too many probing questions.)

3. *Avoid imposing your opinions on the child*: Don't get into arguments about who is right or whose ideas are better; this only results in polarization of positions. Try, whenever possible, to find something in the child's statements with which you can agree. Even when you don't agree with what a child says, you can still comment, "That's interesting," "I hadn't thought about it that way before," "That could be." Remarks such as "That's ridiculous," or "How could you say something so silly?" or "You don't know what you're talking about" show disregard both for the child's opinion and his feelings.

When we do express disagreement, it can be done pleasantly — "I don't quite agree with you," "I don't see it that way," "I have a different opinion." When children suggest a way of doing something which we must reject, we can say, "I'm sorry, but I can't accept that idea."

4. *Give advice sparingly.* As well meaning as our advice may be, children want and need a chance to learn from their own experience. Too much interference in their affairs can lead ultimately to resentment and a general resistance to all advice. If we wisely reserve our advice for when it's asked for or really needed, it's far more likely to be accepted.

If your advice is rejected, don't argue. For example, a teenage girl studies every evening late into the night. "I think it might be a good idea to study a little less and go to bed earlier," the parent advises, "I'm worried that you're not getting enough sleep." "Don't worry," she says, "I can manage. I'm not tired." Further efforts to induce her to go to bed earlier are unlikely to succeed. It's best to end the discussion at once, conveying confidence in her ability to make sensible decisions.

A good way to offer advice, when it wasn't specifically requested, is to ask in a straightforward way, "Would you like some advice on this?" or "Would you like to hear what I would do in your situation?" This spares children from having to ward off unsolicited advice, and spares us the unpleasantness of having our suggestions turned down.

Do your best to avoid getting into "yes, but" discussions, where you keep offering suggestions which your child turns down with a "yes, but" reply. If he rejects your suggestions, respect his right to do so. Don't warn him of the dire consequences. Don't show resentment or make deprecating remarks. Also, don't tell him in disgust, "Okay. Do whatever you want."

Keep in mind that your child wants your approval of his ideas, and will try hard to win it by presenting reasons to support them. To influence him to accept your point of view, first show that you understand his position, only then presenting your suggestions in a friendly way. Say, for instance, "I understand what you're saying but I'm wondering if..." If he remains uninfluenced, you can always end the discussion with, "All right — why don't you think about it a little?" Children do often reconsider and even accept our advice later (though they may not announce it), after they've had time to think things over and feel less threatened by loss of honor because of capitulation.

Often, children learn "the hard way" that they would have been better off following their parents' advice. At such times, refrain from moralizing. For instance, your family is about to leave on a long bus trip and you remind the children to go to the bathroom. One child insists that he doesn't have to go. An hour later, when you're on the bus, he suddenly tells you he does need the bathroom. Don't say, "Why didn't you go when I told you?" or "You see what happens when you don't listen to me?" Limit your words to, "I'm really sorry, but you'll have to wait until we're off the bus." On future trips, he's likely to follow your advice.

When children come to discuss their problems, we shouldn't assume that they always want help. Advice may even sound to them like criticism because it implies that they aren't handling the situation well. Usually, all the children really want is a sympathetic ear, a sounding board, a chance to "get things off their chest" or to clarify their own thinking. If we listen and respond with an occasional "Hmm" or "I see" or "I know what you mean," they may well solve their problems all by themselves. Sometimes, by simply reflecting their state of mind, we greatly facilitate the "unloading" process for them. For example:

> "You're having a hard time deciding whether you want to take piano or guitar lessons."
> "You're feeling discouraged about Gemara."
> "With so much homework you're thinking you won't have any time to play."

Even when our children ask for our advice, we don't always have to give it immediately. We can try sometimes to help them arrive at solutions on their own by asking, for example, "What do you think you could do?" If the child replies, "I don't know," we can suggest, "Have you thought of...?"

But there are times when we need to intervene to prevent our child from making a major decision which could be unwise. For example, an older daughter wants to enroll in a school which you think isn't suitable for her. You can tell her, "This is a very serious decision. Have you thought it through? Let's sit down and discuss the pros and cons." If you've decided to permit the girl to make her own decision, let her know from the beginning that the final choice will be hers.

Parents should tell their child when they think he's making a rather serious mistake. For example, if a teenager decides to spend a large sum of his own money on an item which you feel isn't worth it, you can let him know how you feel. Children are often thankful to their parents later for their advice.

Being only human, parents will occasionally err in their judgment. When this happens they shouldn't hesitate to say, "I'm sorry, I made a mistake." Don't worry that appearing fallible will undermine your authority or your child's confidence in you; on the contrary, it builds up confidence. Children feel more inclined to rely on parents who admit when they're wrong.

What about truly major decisions, such as marriage? When the issue is one of a serious character flaw in the prospective spouse, parents should stand their ground, caringly and as calmly as possible. If until now you've built a relationship of trust and confidence, this storm, too, should be successfully weathered.

EMPATHY AS A MODEL FOR OUR CHILDREN

When we show our children empathy, it also serves as a model for them to emulate in their relationships with others. The following incident was reported by a mother, who observed that her children were becoming far more empathic in their relationships with each other and with their friends as a result of her showing more empathy toward them.

> I usually lie down for an hour after coming home from my morning teaching job. One day while resting, I heard tremendous crying and screaming from outside. I then heard my eldest son, age seven, go out the door. When he came back, I called him to my room. He told me, "Mommy, I went outside to see what happened — maybe someone hurt himself. I saw that Moshe was crying. He and his brother Joshua only have one bike and they were fighting over it. Joshua wasn't being fair — he wasn't giving Moshe a turn. I had a solution. I told Moshe, 'Don't cry. I'm not using my bike now 'cause I'm doing my homework. You can use mine in the meantime. Put it back when you're finished.'"
>
> I was so proud. I hugged my son and said, "What a chesed you did! And I know how important your bike is to you." He said, "You're right, but I felt bad for him. And, Mommy — I also didn't want you to wake up from all the yelling."

HELPING CHILDREN TO UNDERSTAND THEIR EMOTIONS

Children greatly appreciate it when we show them that we understand their feelings. But we can go beyond this and actually teach them cognitive principles that will increase their own self-mastery. When children are calm and in a receptive mood, we can show them how they largely bring on their own unhappiness by their particular way of viewing events in their lives. We can explain that we all have the choice to make ourselves either happy or unhappy, depending on what we think or tell ourselves about the things which happen to us. The following metaphor is readily understood even by a first-grader:

> Life is like a big store. There are two counters in this store, one on the right and one on the left. The counter on the right has a big sign over it which says HAPPINESS. That's where we buy thoughts which make us feel good. Over the counter on the left side is a sign which says UNHAPPINESS. That's where we buy thoughts which make us feel bad. We have a choice. We can decide which counter we will buy at. We can decide what we will think and how we will feel.

After relating this metaphor, you can ask your child what kinds of thoughts are bought at the unhappiness counter. Then go on to help him identify his own upsetting thoughts. If he has difficulty, you might suggest some likely possibilities — "Were you by any chance, telling yourself...?" (For cognitive methods that can be readily adapted for use with children, see Chapter 1.)

Don't try to teach cognitive principles while a child is upset. A subtle way to bring home these ideas is to ask, after an unhappy child has calmed down, "Which counter were you buying at before?"

HELPING CHILDREN TO OVERCOME ANGER

Helping children to overcome anger toward siblings or friends is discussed in Chapter 12. Here we will discuss the problem of the child who gets angry quickly when confronted with minor difficulties and frustrations, such as a stuck drawer or a missing toy. A mother told about her son: Six-year-old Ariel quickly lost his temper when frustrated, venting his anger by yelling, throwing things, and the like. For instance, when his younger sister, Meira, tore the page on which he was writing, Ariel screamed, "I can't take this!" and turned over all the kitchen chairs.

That same evening at the supper table, when told that orange juice was reserved for Shabbos, Ariel reacted violently, throwing things and again overturning chairs. When Ariel's mother didn't give in, he eventually quieted down and came back to the table. Then he noticed that Meira had sipped from his cup — and promptly there was another outburst!

Ariel's mother was very concerned about the situation. Her child truly believed that he was unable to tolerate unpleasantness. Also, she was in a constant state of anxiety about the next outburst and how she would handle it. Since her main goal was to avoid confrontations, she usually gave in to Ariel's demands — while at the same time realizing guiltily that surely that was no way to teach him to tolerate frustration.

Ariel's mother was advised not to let him damage objects or furniture. When he'd begin to kick or to throw things, she was instructed to hold him firmly and say, "I can't let you damage things in the house."

It was suggested that she choose a moment when Ariel was calm, and conduct a conversation with him along cognitive lines.

The next week Ariel's mother reported:

> *Friday evening after supper I sat with my son and, placing my hand on his shoulder, said to him, "I'd like to talk to you about what happened yesterday with the orange juice. Do you like to get angry?*

ARIEL: *No, I don't like to get angry.*

MOTHER: *So why do you get angry if you don't like to?*

ARIEL: *Because people annoy me and do all kinds of things I don't like.*

MOTHER: *And that's terrible that they do this? You can't stand it?*

ARIEL: *Right. I can't stand it.*

MOTHER: *But you don't like getting angry. Would you like me to help you so you won't get angry?*

ARIEL: *Yes.*

MOTHER: *Okay, let's talk about it. How would it be if the next time, instead of thinking "this is awful", you'll think, "it's not so awful". Tell me, when I didn't give you the orange juice yesterday, was that awful?*

ARIEL:	No, that wasn't awful.
MOTHER:	It was ...
ARIEL:	Not so awful!
MOTHER:	If you think that way when others do things to you which you don't like, do you think that will help you to not get angry?
ARIEL:	Yes, that will help.
MOTHER:	Let's talk about really awful things. When someone gets killed in a car accident, is that awful?
ARIEL:	Yes, it's awful.
MOTHER:	If you build something with your blocks and someone breaks it — is that awful?"
ARIEL:	(laughing) No!
MOTHER:	I think this will help you to overcome your anger.

Shortly after this discussion Ariel was building with his Lego blocks, when Meira unintentionally knocked over the building, scattering the pieces. Seeing that he was about to get angry I quickly asked, "Is this awful?"

ARIEL:	No.
MOTHER:	It's...
ARIEL:	Not so awful!
MOTHER:	Let's think about something that's really awful. If someone would break his head or leg, that would be awful.

The next morning at the Shabbos table, my husband was giving out slices of challah. By mistake, he gave a slice to Meira before Ariel. Ariel got up and began yelling but I quickly asked him, "Is this awful?" He laughed.

MOTHER:	So what is it? It's just...
ARIEL:	(immediately) Not so awful!

Again, I told him to imagine something really terrible. "If we didn't have anything to eat and were starving, would that be awful?"

ARIEL:	Yes.
MOTHER:	But if your younger sister gets her challah before you, that's not terrible. That's just not so pleasant.

That afternoon, I asked him, "Which do you like — being happy or being sad?"

ARIEL: *I like to be happy.*

MOTHER: *When you're angry, are you happy or sad?*

ARIEL: *I'm sad.*

MOTHER: *With Hashem's help, you're going to be happy now almost all the time. Because you'll overcome your anger. (Ariel's eyes lit up when I told him this.)*

After Havdalah, I pointed out, "Just now we said, 'The Jews had light and joy...' That means they were happy. 'So shall we be.' B'ezras Hashem (with God's help), this week will be a much happier one than last week. Do you know why?"

ARIEL: *Why?*

MOTHER: *Because, b'ezras Hashem, you're learning to overcome anger. Now I'm going to make a sign that will help you whenever you feel anger coming on. I'm going to write on this piece of oaktag "it's not awful, it's just not pleasant". We'll hang it on the kitchen wall. Tomorrow, I'm going to buy you a little note pad. And every time you manage to control your anger I'm going to write it down in the pad — each time on a separate page. When the pad is full we'll buy you the watch that you've been wanting!*

Later that night, my husband said he was going to Har Nof. Ariel began whining that he wanted to go along, that he'd never been to Har Nof.

MOTHER: *Oh, it's terrible that you can't go to Har Nof, right?*

ARIEL: *(laughing) No, it isn't terrible!*

Several weeks have passed since then. Ariel's mother reports that the frequency of his outbursts has decreased from twice a day to twice a week. What's more, while she'd previously focused almost exclusively on the problem of his temper, to the exclusion of his many good qualities, now she is able to pay more attention to, and reinforce, his positive attributes. As a result a great change has taken place in her relationship with her son; they've become good friends.

(Ariel's little "game" may be "played" by quick-tempered grownups, too — with equally good results!)

Chapter Seven

EDUCATION FOR
TORAH LIVING

As Jewish parents, we are obligated to prepare our children to be Torah Jews, living Torah lives. This means teaching children Torah so that they will know their responsibilities as Jews, and *mussar*, general moral education, so that their character be God fearing and upright.[1] We must also train them in the practical observance of the various mitzvos. Finally, sons must be taught a trade or profession to enable them to earn a living and not to be dependent on others.[2]

There are several places in our prayer book where we refer to our children; these are opportunities to beseech God's help for success in these endeavors.[3]

The responsibility for educating the children in Torah-living rests primarily with the father, but mothers, too, are obligated.[4] This is supported by the fact that, according to our Sages, the Torah was given to the women first, "in order that they should guide their children."[5] One authority comments, "Their sons, too, will hear [Torah] first from their mothers.[6]

TORAH STUDY

Fathers are obligated to teach their sons Torah, as it is written, "And you shall teach them to your sons."[7] A father who cannot teach his son must hire someone else to teach him.[8]

A woman's share in the reward for Torah study is earned largely through her efforts to encourage her husband and sons in their study of Torah.[9] While women and girls have no duty to study Torah, if they do so, they are rewarded for it.[10] Girls must be taught the laws pertaining to those mitzvos which they are required to observe. According to recent authorities, they should be taught much more, especially studies which cultivate a Torah worldview, such as the tractate of *Avos* and *Menoras Ha'Maor*, a classical, annotated Talmudic anthology.[11] Rambam states that as soon as a child begins to speak, we should teach him: "*Torah tzivah lanu Moshe...,*" "*Shema Yisrael....*" and then other Torah verses one by one, until he reaches age 6 or 7 when he begins to go to school. *Aleph-Beis* is taught to the child in his fourth year.[12]

Thus from the very start, the child receives a strong sense of the centrality of Torah: "For it is our very life."[13] Throughout his life, he will always give Torah study its rightful priority; it will mold him, shape his outlook, and become the point of reference in all his dealings.

TRAINING IN MITZVAH OBSERVANCE

Rabbi Yehoshua Neuwirth's *Shemiras Shabbos Kehilchasah*[14] includes an extensive compilation of mitzvos to teach children. Since it covers the topic so well, we present some excerpts here:

> The commandment of *chinuch* (educating children) requires us to accustom children to keeping the mitzvos while still young, so that they will fulfill them when they are grown. Once a child has reached bar or bas mitzvah — 13 for a boy and 12 for a girl — he/she is considered a Jewish adult with all adult obligations. *Chinuch* applies to both sons and daughters, though one need not accustom daughters to observe the various time-related mitzvos from which women are exempt.

Children should be taught mitzvos according to their age and level of comprehension....Accordingly when they seem ready, we teach them the blessings recited before performing mitzvos and before eating. Adults are allowed to pronounce the holy Names in order to teach the child to recite the blessings, even though the child is saying a blessing in vain. One does not answer "Amen" to the blessing of a child below his fifth birthday, even if he says it appropriately before actually partaking of food or performing a mitzvah. We teach the child to say *Birkas Ha'Mazon* (Grace after Meals) a little at a time, until he knows it completely....

As soon as the child can chew solid food we give him the required minimal portion — about two tablespoons of matzah and *maror* (bitter herbs — usually romaine lettuce) — during the Passover Seder. He is also given the Four Cups of wine [or grape juice], each the required minimal amount — about one-third of a cup. However, he need not drink more than a mouthful each time....

When a boy is ready to don a *talis katan* (four-cornered garment, with fringes called *tzitzis*) — i.e. to keep two *tzitzis* in front and two in the back and to hold two of the *tzitzios* in his hand when saying the *Shema* — we are obliged to buy him one. It is customary for boys to wear a *talis katan* from the age of 3 years....

When a boy is 5 years old the father should train him in the mitzvah of *sukkah*...and should not permit him to eat a meal outside the *sukkah* [snacks may be eaten outside of the *sukkah*]....

The commandment of *chinuch* applies to Rabbinical regulations as well as Torah law....Thus a father should have his child recite the blessings over the *lulav* (Four Species) not only on the first day, but also on the latter six days of *Sukkos*; to hear the reading of *Megilas Esther* on Purim; to recite the various prayers which were all Rabbinically instituted; to kindle Chanukah lights, etc....

Concerning restraining a child from transgressing a prohibition, there are three age groups to be considered:

1. Regarding a child who has no understanding, i.e. until

age 2 or 3, it is not necessary to restrain him from any transgression. However, one may not cause him to transgress or feed him forbidden food.

2. Regarding a child of 2 or 3 who is capable of understanding when told that something is not allowed, the parents must restrain him from both Torah and Rabbinical prohibitions. However, others taking care of the child are not obliged to do so.

3. Regarding a child of 6 or 7, all are required to restrain him from Torah transgression, though not from Rabbinic transgressions.

When a sick child needs to eat forbidden food, a Rabbinic authority should be consulted....

It is permitted to give a child something to eat before he has said his prayers or before hearing the Kiddush on Shabbos....

A child who needs it for his health may be given milk one hour after eating meat, even in homes where the custom is to wait six hours, [provided it is not given at the same meal]....

Children should be trained from the age of 9 to fast part of the time on Yom Kippur by delaying breakfast, and waiting more time than usual between meals. In the case of a frail child, we begin this training only after age 10....

Until age 6 or 7, a child may wear leather shoes on Yom Kippur [and Tishah b'Av]. Beyond this age we should accustom him not to wear them.

INSTILLING LOVE FOR GOD'S COMMANDMENTS

In one of his responsa on children's education, Rav Moshe Feinstein writes:

Teaching the child to have faith in God and His Torah is the main aspect of his education. Parents should make him aware that everything that they give him is a gift from God. Thus they will instill in the child a love for Him, and for the parents whom Heaven has delegated to provide his needs.[15]

Rabbi Feinstein points out that love of mitzvos is also inculcated by explaining to the child, according to his level of comprehension, the reasons for each mitzvah, at the time of its performance.

Thus for example, before teaching the child to say the *berachah* (blessing) for bread, the parent should briefly describe how bread is "brought forth from the earth," emphasizing that by saying this blessing we acknowledge that the bread we eat, as all our other food, comes from God. Parents should show pleasure and praise their children for saying *berachos* while they are in this learning stage.

Countless opportunities arise in daily life to instill a love of *chesed* (lovingkindness). For example, on the bus, a child who is able to stand should be encouraged to rise for an elderly person. Say pleasantly, "Look! There's a woman who needs a seat. You can do a big mitzvah by getting up for her!" Gentle pressure may be exerted to have him do so. Of course, he should be praised after relinquishing his seat.

RESISTANCE TO TRAINING

Sometimes children resist our efforts to train them in mitzvos. Parents are often unsure about how to react in such a situation. When your little girl refuses to recite a blessing though she knows how, should you insist? When your second-grader is home for the day, should you make him recite all the lengthy prayers he normally says at school, even if he doesn't want to do so?

Keep in mind that children aren't obligated to recite blessings or prayers until they reach the age of bar or bas mitzvah. Remember, you want your children to come to love to do mitzvos and not to regard them as a burden.

To your little girl who doesn't want to recite a blessing you can suggest, "I'll say the *berachah* and you just say the last word." If she doesn't want to cooperate even to this extent, don't make an issue over it. Never shame a child by saying things like, "What? You don't want to thank Hashem for the nice apple?" This strongly implies that he is a bad person for not wanting to recite the blessing and accomplishes nothing.

It's also better not to make an issue over the morning prayers. If your second-grader complains that the prayers are too much for him, you can tell him, "Praying *is* hard work." (The Hebrew word for prayer, *avodah*, means "work.") "I'll tell you what — you're not bar mitzvah yet, so you don't have to say everything. Say as much as you can, all right?"

Even after children are completely familiar with a mitzvah, they may still need some prompting now and then. A pleasant way to do this is to say, for instance, "Let me hear how nicely you say the *berachah*." Occasional praise afterwards, when the child has made the effort to say the blessing properly, is very effective. For younger children, keep the morning and evening prayers brief, as well as *Birkas HaMazon*, and lead them through the words.

If we notice that one of our older children has forgotten to recite a blessing or has neglected some other duty, we should quietly remind him of it. We need to be careful, however. Out of genuine concern for the child's moral development, it's all too easy to fall into the habit of constantly reminding and checking up: "Don't forget to say a *berachah*." "Did you remember to wash your hands?" Besides being unpleasant, such prompting is apt to give the child the feeling that we don't trust him to remember to do these things by himself.

Rather than worrying what will become of our children, we should have optimistic expectations of them. We should express confidence in their ultimate willingness to fulfill their religious obligations, when these will become incumbent upon them. Indeed, children will often surprise us by their readiness to take on all obligations, once they know that it's halachically required of them.

Parents sometimes become angry over their child's neglectfulness because they interpret it as a sign of not caring about the mitzvos. They need to examine themselves to understand the source of their anger. Does it stem from a genuine zeal for God's honor which the child treats lightly? If so, they're making a serious mistake, for children below the age of 20 are not liable to Divine judgment; they aren't sufficiently mature.

More commonly, the anger stems from an intolerance of their perceived failure as parents for having thus far been unsuccessful in mitzvah training. This then turns into anger toward the child. After all, it's *his* neglect which has made them into failures! Demands for perfection might also underlie the anger. Or, the parents may be unwilling to contend with the trouble their child is causing them.

The sad truth is that anger is no way to instill love for mitzvos. It makes the children think that they have to keep mitzvos for *our* sake, as if *we* benefit in some way from their observance. If we want our children to care more about their obligations, we have to make it clear that we train them in mitzvos out of concern for *their* welfare. By focusing on concern for the child rather than on our personal displeasure, we'll eliminate anger, allowing training to proceed in a caring and patient manner.

Lastly, parents should refrain from negative self-evaluation for any lack of success on their part. Whatever mistakes may have been made, lessons can be learned from these. As in all problem situations, effort should be concentrated on positive action — this cannot be done in an atmosphere of self-criticism.

LOVE AND REVERENCE FOR GOD

From their earliest years, children should be raised to love and revere God. Even at a very tender age, they should be exposed to holy influences. We learn this from the fact that when the people of Israel were assembled to hear the reading of the Torah, even children not yet capable of understanding were to be present.[16]

Rabbi Yehoshua ben Chanina, one of the great scholars of the Talmud, was praised by his teacher: "Happy is she who bore him." This is because his mother would bring his cradle to the *Beis Midrash* so that he absorb the sounds of Torah learning.[17]

It is good to bring children to the synagogue, to expose them to its holy environment and familiarize them with the public *davening* (prayer services). But there are certain restrictions to be observed:

> The father [presumably, the mother as well] must accustom his children to proper awe and reverence in the synagogue. It is better not to bring young children to the synagogue than to have them running around, distracting the worshipers.
>
> When bringing his young child, the father should make sure there is no trace of excrement on him or on his clothing, since it is forbidden to pray in the presence of anything disgusting.

The father must properly supervise his young children and see to it that they sit quietly next to him. The child should be taught when to answer "Amen"; according to the Sages, this makes him merit the World to Come. It is good to have him kiss the Torah scroll when it is carried around, to encourage him in performance of mitzvos.18

Don't insist that your child stay in the synagogue for longer than is appropriate to his level of maturity. Encourage him to follow the service, but only to the extent that he's ready for this.

What if an older boy, not yet bar mitzvah, altogether refuses to accompany his father to synagogue? A somewhat lenient policy is best here, yet the problem shouldn't be ignored. The father can discuss with his son the purpose of prayer in connection with our duties in life as Jews, and reach an understanding about an appropriate amount of time to stay in the synagogue. Though the child has no doubt heard this from his teachers, it carries special weight when it comes from his parents.

The boy should not be criticized or made to feel bad for not wanting to go to synagogue. Keep in mind that below the age of bar mitzvah, he is not obligated to attend services. To motivate him the father can try using a point system, whereby the boy earns points towards some prize for going to synagogue. This is in line with the Talmudic dictum: "A person should always fulfill Torah and mitzvos even if he does so for ulterior motives, because eventually this will bring him to do them for their own sake."19

MORAL TRAINING

To succeed in raising a child with high moral standards and conduct, parents must provide a good model of moral behavior. As Rabbi S.R. Hirsch writes, "In the life of his parents, the child sees the picture of what will one day be his own life, and he copies it eagerly and quickly."20 Thus, parents have the responsibility to examine their own conduct and correct any weaknesses in their character:

> Before attempting to rid our children of the hideous faults and bad habits we consider unacceptable in them, should we not

first seek to eliminate these same vices completely from our own perceptions and attitudes, from our own words and actions...?

Our children can learn to walk and to talk only by seeing us walk and talk. How else, then, should they be able to learn from us patience, equanimity, gentleness, sincerity, honesty, moderation, humility, justice, and lovingkindness if not through our example? How else should they learn to control themselves, to put up with unpleasantness, to forgo willingly what seems to be pleasant and gladly perform their duties in level-headed cheerfulness, except by having us personally demonstrate to them...?[21]

We are obligated to restrain our children also from *lashon hara* (derogatory speech), lying, cursing, fighting, and the like. In this respect it is essential that we keep our priorities in order, as Rabbi Hirsch points out:

It is not our major trespasses against moral law but our attitude toward the petty offenses of daily life that pose the greatest threat to our children's moral development. If a cup clumsily dropped and broken...or a torn dress provoke us to more anger than a favor denied one's little sister, or a slap administered to a little brother in revenge...or a word that circumvents or distorts the truth, then we unconsciously indicate to our students in the art of morality that we cannot be too concerned about timeless moral values since, after all, we seem to be far more upset about the loss of an object of merely transient value.[22]

Parents have the responsibility to protect their children, as far as this is possible, from corrupting influences. This is especially important today, when the streets and the media are steeped in violence and immorality. We must exercise the greatest care in selecting to which influences we allow our children to be exposed.

On the other hand, excessive shielding of children from harmful influences can be bad for them too. We need to find the right balance between overprotection and no protection at all. Rabbi Yoel Schwartz writes:

A Torah home which is too insulated, however, could have an adverse effect when the child grows up and goes into the outside world, for whatever legitimate reason, such as livelihood. The sights and sounds of the nonreligious world could appear exciting if the child's home has been too austere. So within the Torah home, there should be room for a permissible range of modest and prudent entertainment. Both overstrictness and over-reacting can actually cause children to break away from the Torah fold.[23]

Rambam describes the importance of living in a good environment:

> It is the nature of man to be influenced in his ideas and actions by his friends and acquaintances, and to live in keeping with the accepted norm of his town. Accordingly, one should befriend the righteous and be always in the company of wise men in order to learn from their deeds....Furthermore, if he lived in a town where...people are not honest in their ways, he should move to a neighborhood where the people are righteous and conduct themselves properly.[24]

Children love to listen to stories. We can utilize this love to inculcate in them ethical and moral values with Bible stories and Talmudic legends. The leisurely Shabbos meals are an ideal time for this.

Literature for children should be carefully selected. "What a pity," writes Rabbi Hirsch, "to quench the child's natural thirst for stories with fairy tales devoid of educational value or Jewish spiritual content....Far better to tell him stories based on reality, with moral and educational content."[25]

Today, fortunately, there is available a wealth of children's books, with material which inspires while it entertains. There are stories depicting episodes from the lives of great Torah personalities, tales drawn from Midrashim, and life experiences of characters both young and old, to absorb the child's interest and teach Torah values as well.

Chapter Eight

HELPFULNESS AND CONSIDERATION

*I*n Judaism, the commandment to practice *chesed* (lovingkindness) is a major precept governing interpersonal relationships.[1] The very survival of the world is seen as dependent on *chesed*.[2] *Chesed* is not just a commendable quality but an obligation.[3] As the prophet states: "What does God require of you but to act justly, to love *chesed*, and to walk humbly with your God."[4] A person should desire to practice *chesed* whenever possible, and rejoice at the opportunity.[5]

Chesed has an "active" and a "passive" aspect. The former is *helpfulness* — extending ourselves to improve the happiness and well-being of others (this includes empathy, discussed in Chapter 6). The latter is consideration — refraining, as the Torah enjoins us, from causing injury to someone else's feelings or property.[6] Indeed, the Talmud views this passive aspect as central to Judaism.[7] Helpfulness and consideration together constitute *chesed* — the very foundation of society, as is written in Psalms: "The world is built on *chesed*."[8]

These traits, basic to Judaism, are not acquired automatically; parents have the responsibility to foster them in their children. This can be accomplished in two ways. First, parents must serve as an example of helpful and considerate behavior toward each other, toward their children, and toward others. But this role-modeling, although essential, is not enough. We must also provide opportunities for our children to practice such behavior; the home is an obvious and ideal place for such practice. By encouraging our children to help with household tasks and teaching them to avoid causing inconvenience or harm to others, we provide early and invaluable experience in being helpful and considerate.

In addition, children should be taught that *chesed* is a mitzvah — that God wants us to feel empathy for others and to help them whenever possible, and that helping their parents is a special form of this mitzvah, a special kind of *chesed*. This teaching, reinforced with stories of our forefathers and Sages, will help to develop a strong foundation for *chesed* in the child's personality.

HELPFULNESS

Benefits of Helpfulness

When they request help from their children, parents shouldn't feel that they're acting selfishly or imposing a burden. While our children's helpfulness may make things easier for us, at the same time we're giving them an opportunity to fulfill the mitzvah of honoring their parents. Also, we allow them to show gratitude for all we do for them. Finally, love flourishes best when it expresses itself in action; and children who are taught to do things for their parents are being given an opportunity to develop love for them. This point is discussed extensively in Rabbi Eliyahu Dessler's writings.[9]

Parents are obligated to help their children convert their self-centered orientation into an altruistic one — that is, to learn to love their fellow as themselves. Personality is shaped by actions;[10] the best way to develop altruism in children, therefore, is to have them do things for others. The first step in this learning process is acquired naturally in the family, when parents accustom their children to doing things for them and for each other.

Practicing helpfulness at home also benefits children because it promotes a sense of self-assurance and accomplishment, as the psychologist Rudolf Dreikurs notes:

> Children should be drawn at an early age into active participation in domestic life. This promotes their social interest and the capacity for cooperation. Moreover, it strengthens their self-assurance and starts them on the way toward useful accomplishment.[11]

It should be explained to children that the members of a household are a team; each does his share, for the benefit of all. A mother's job, especially when there are small children in the family, is often too heavy a load for one individual. To function effectively, she needs help with many of the household chores. Thus, it's important for children to share in the responsibilities of the household.

A 40-year Harvard University study has turned up some startling truths about the many benefits children receive from being given opportunities to help around the house. The study followed the lives of 456 teenage boys from inner-city Boston, many from impoverished homes. Those boys whose parents had them do household chores became far more successful adults than their less industrious childhood playmates. They earned more money and had more job satisfaction. They had better marriages and closer relationships with their children. They were healthier and lived longer, and they were far happier.[12]

Encouraging Helpfulness in Young Children

Young children are normally eager to assist their parents. They feel "big" and grown up when allowed to help. But, naturally, they are somewhat slow and clumsy and sometimes their help can be more of a hindrance than a benefit. Young children are also not concerned about getting things done in the same way that adults usually are. Because they regard work as play, children aren't in as much of a hurry to finish a given task. Parents who let themselves become impatient with young children who are trying to be helpful are apt to squelch the children's natural enthusiasm for helping altogether. Many parents don't let their young children help at all because, as one mother expressed it, "They take forever! I'd rather get it done quickly, myself." A child who wants to help may be told, "No, you can't do it. You'll make a mess." Such treatment is a pity, for the child is denied the many benefits that helpfulness brings. It may also make it more difficult to accustom him to helping when he's older and more capable. Parents should learn to tolerate some inconvenience and disruption of their routine, so that, in the long run, everyone will benefit.

Even a very young child can be allowed to help, for instance, with bringing dishes to the sink or wiping off the table. By the time they are 5 or 6, most children are quite capable of washing dishes and will be eager to do this as well. A stepstool will be needed, or the child can kneel on a chair. It's worth it for parents to spend time on this kind of training, which is relatively easy to accomplish while the child is still young. Later, these habits are much more difficult to establish.

One young mother was asked why her children so greatly enjoyed helping with the cooking. She answered, "My children always saw my work in the kitchen as play. At a very young age I allowed them to be with me in the kitchen to join in 'Mommy's playing.' I gave them all kinds of things to do — whatever they could — even slicing tomatoes (with a nonblunt saw-edged knife!). To this day they love cooking."

As mentioned before, children naturally love to help with chores; but they can come to regard them as a burden — often under the negative influence of the adults around them. In the Torah view, work is of central importance;[13] it is seen as our completion of God's creation.[14] Shemayah, mentor of the renowned Sage, Hillel, teaches that one should love work.[15] This obligates us to nurture such love in our children by letting our own happy and cheerful attitude toward work be an example to them. Parents sometimes refrain from asking for much help from their children, telling themselves, "Let them enjoy life while they're young; they'll have enough responsibilities when they get older" (as if responsibilities are incompatible with enjoyment!). This attitude isn't conducive to developing the love for working and doing which is the Torah ideal.

A change in attitude here can lead to astonishing results:

I have always wanted my children to have a relaxed, pleasant childhood with a strict minimum of helping; make their beds, put their clothes away, and nothing more. But lately I'd been exhausted from overwork. When my 6-year-old daughter Zehava came home from school I was lying down and simply didn't have the strength to move. Just then my next-door neighbor called to invite my daughter for the afternoon. Normally I would have agreed, thinking again, "Let her enjoy her childhood...."

But this time, after hearing in the workshop that we should not hesitate to ask our children to help, I just said point blank, "Zehava, I'd like you to make supper for tonight."

Zehava, looking amazed, asked, "What should I make?"

"Green peppers stuffed with cottage cheese, rice crackers, tuna fish and chocolate yogurt."

"What should I do with the green peppers?"

"Cut them in half, put cottage cheese inside, put two popcorns from your birthday party and an olive in the middle."

Her eyes brightened. "And the chocolate yogurt? How should I make that?"

"You take plain yogurt and put two big spoons of chocolate Shake and mix it very well."

Zehava ran to the kitchen. She came back a few times to ask which way she should cut the peppers, etc. But I sensed her great feeling of importance and self-worth. She did a great job!

When I got up an hour and a half later, I felt so rested and happy. All I did was pop some potatoes in the microwave. And when my husband came home, Zehava was thrilled to let him know that she actually made supper!

Manner of Requesting Help

The way we request our children's help critically affects their eventual attitude toward helping in general. Avoid prefacing your request with, "I want you to..." This places your wishes too much at the center. A friendly, matter-of-fact, but not effusive, manner of requesting is best: "Please take this garbage down," rather than "Be a darling and take this garbage down for me, please." Requests such as, "Would you mind cracking these eggs for me?" or "If it isn't too much trouble, could you diaper the baby?" should be strongly avoided; these convey a sense of uncertainty, both about your child's willingness to help and about your right to ask. Similarly, "Come help me with the dishes" is better than "Do you want to help me with the dishes?" If your child answers, "No," you're in trouble. In fact, it isn't always necessary to ask directly for help. For instance, you can say, "Ruthy, you can set the table for supper." or "Come, Yonah — you can help me slice the cucumbers." At times you can suggest, "It would be helpful if you would...."

Never plead with a child. Also, don't tell him how tired you are; this sounds apologetic. Simply say, "I need your help." Parents shouldn't feel they have to give a reason for requesting help.

This take-it-for-granted attitude toward helping was neatly summed up by one mother of eight:

> When the children were little, there was just no question about their helping — I couldn't manage otherwise. It was understood. Each child had his job and it was taken for granted that everyone had to do his share. The kids seem to have absorbed this attitude — that I expected it of them. After all, I couldn't do everything!

Our attitude toward requesting help can be crucial in gaining our children's cooperation. As these mothers discovered:

> In the past, when I had asked my children for help, they frequently reacted negatively. As a result, I often didn't ask for help when I needed it. Finally I became convinced that I had every right to ask for help, that not only was it for my benefit but even more so, for the children's, and that I didn't have to be perfectly fair in whom I chose. My attitude then completely changed. The next time I asked for help I did it

very matter-of-factly, with a lot of self-confidence. Amazingly, every child went to his task without a word of protest!

I came home one day to face a houseful of work and not enough energy to do it all. My first job was to straighten up two bedrooms, in preparation for the carpet cleaners who were coming soon. I took two large boxes and asked my 4-year-old to fill them with items from the desk top, bed, floor, etc. It was a fairly large job and I expected some resistance. Armed with my newly acquired "tools," I said, "Estee, I need your help. Please pick up all the toys, books, and clothes from the floor, desk, and bed, and put the things in these boxes." Ten minutes later the job was done — perfectly! The interesting thing is that in the past I would have explained how tired I was and how I wasn't feeling well, so could she please help me. With that approach I always got resistance or no help at all. This time, I not only got the help I asked for, but my daugher even surprised me later on by scrubbing the kitchen table of her own accord — without even being asked.

Even when parents are tired or rushed, they should make the effort to ask for the child's assistance in a calm and pleasant way. Parents should be careful, when asking for help, that their tone of voice doesn't convey resentment, annoyance, or anxiety. A sharp "Come in here and clear this table!" for example, could reveal resentment that the child doesn't help enough. The hidden criticism in the parent's request is picked up by the child, who might feel offended and thus be unwilling to help. On the other hand, a hesitant manner of requesting, as mentioned above, reveals the parent's anxiety that the child might not want to help; often enough, the outcome is the very thing the parent fears. It's worthwhile for parents to learn to control these harmful emotions by identifying and changing the attitudes which trigger them.

Showing Appreciation

Parents should express appreciation when their children have been helpful. They thereby demonstrate the proper and desirable response when one person has helped another, effectively modeling *hakaras hatov* (gratitude). Effusive displays of gratitude, however (as opposed to the take-it-for-granted attitude mentioned above), are inappropriate and may make children suspicious that their help wasn't really expected. Also, they may come to depend on such praise and believe that any contribution they make deserves high commendation. They could even develop a need for constant approval of all their actions, not only from their parents but from others as well. A simple "thanks" should suffice for a small task.

Be careful, in expressing appreciation, not to link your child's helpfulness to his character. Like exaggerated praise, expressions such as, "Shoshana, you're a good girl for helping me," may lead to her helping in order to be liked and to gain approval. Objective praise such as, "You worked hard and did a nice job," or "You were very helpful today," or "You did it gladly — you felt happy to do the mitzvah!" helps her perceive the intrinsic value of her behavior.

Keep praise realistic. Children feel uncomfortable with praise which is neither true nor deserved. In fact, it may even trigger misbehavior — the child realizes he's not the "wonderful boy" you claimed he is, and hastens to prove that he can't live up to this uncomfortable image.

Assignment of Chores

Some parents manage well by asking for help whenever it's needed. But others find that it works better to assign routine jobs regularly in advance. In this way, each child knows what's expected of him, and the need to ask for help is greatly reduced. For example, the serving of courses at the Shabbos table can be assigned to various children ahead of time. Charts listing each child's chores for the week are very useful; they prevent much unnecessary arguing over whose turn it is to do a chore next. Children should be allowed to participate in drawing up these charts, as in other decisions concerning delegation of tasks. They are more likely to accept their obligations cheerfully when they're given a choice in the matter. Begin by gathering all the children together and telling them, for instance, "There are many different jobs that have to be done in the house. It's a little too much for Mommy to do by herself, and she needs your help. Let's make a list of what you children can do."

Mothers can usually rely on their common sense to help them decide what can be expected of children at various ages. If they're unsure, they can discuss it with a more experienced mother. Those who are skeptical about the abilities of very young children may want to read about the amazing accomplishments in Montessori schools, where from age 3 children learn to sweep, serve hot soup, and polish silver — all part of their training in the "exercises of practical life."

Since children generally dislike doing the same job every day, most families adopt a rotation system, with different jobs for each child for every day of the week. Still, a weekly rotation system is often preferred because it involves less frequent changes. Charts are drawn up listing each child's job. (See samples.)

JOB	SUN.	MON.	TUES.	WED.	THURS.
PEEL VEGETABLES SET TABLE	Tamar	Elly	Rachel	Naomi	Chaim
CLEAR AND CLEAN TABLE SWEEP FLOOR	Chaim	Tamar	Elly	Rachel	Naomi
WASH DISHES*	Naomi	Chaim	Tamar	Elly	Rachel
DRY DISHES EMPTY GARBAGE	Rachel	Naomi	Chaim	Tamar	Elly
PREPARE LUNCH BOXES	Elly	Rachel	Naomi	Chaim	Tamar

* If there is a dishwasher, loading and emptying it could be one job.

Or make a workwheel, that can be turned each week to assign different sets of duties to different children. Make separate charts for *Erev* and *Motza'ei Shabbos* (Shabbos eve and the night following Shabbos). Draw pictures for younger children who haven't yet learned to read. In some families it works out well for an older child to be given the job of supervisor; this relieves the mother from having to check to see whether chores are done properly. Older children can take over drawing up the charts as well, dividing chores as they see fit. A self-monitoring system is a good idea; each child puts a checkmark next to his name after he's completed all his chores. If the chart is made up with a marker and the checks put in with a pencil, there's no problem with erasing them at the end of each week. Or the chart can be laminated with a transparent plastic covering; checkmarks are then drawn with a water-soluble marker and wiped off at the end of the week.

JOB	WEEK 1	WEEK 2	WEEK 3	WEEK 4
BASEMENT TOYS HELPING WITH BABY	Ruthy	Shuly	Debby	Yitzy
KITCHEN HELPING	Shuly	Debby	Yitzy	Ruthy
LAUNDRY	Debby	Shuly	Ruthy	Shuly
ERRANDS	Yitzy	Ruthy	Shuly	Debby

If you prefer to have certain jobs done by the same child every day, make up individual lists for each child. Another method is to tack the children's names to a bulletin board and post underneath them each day a slip of paper listing jobs for that day. Or use a board with a wipe-off surface.

Charts are a big help with regular chores, but you'll still need to request help with less routine jobs. One mother of a large family relates:

> I need only to call out, "There are vegetables to peel. Anyone have time?" There is always someone ready to do it. Similarly, when we need bread I announce, "We're out of bread. Who can go to the store?" Every morning I prepare a list of items to be bought at the grocer's; the first one ready does the shopping.

This mother finds that this system works well for her; others prefer to turn to one child in particular and assign him the task.

Children who think they are given more than their share of tasks sometimes complain, "It's not fair! Why do you always ask *me*?" Rather than responding defensively to such accusations, proceed as if the child's perception is valid. Don't try to prove the child wrong, but simply reply, "You seem to feel that I ask you more often than the others. We'll talk about it later, but for now, please do what I asked anyway." Later, at an opportune time, you could start a discussion — remembering not to argue with the child or to respond defensively. Some empathy, with assurances that you always try to be fair, will put him at ease. You might also use this opportunity to discuss with the child any disrespect which he may have shown earlier. However, if the child's complaint is justified, resolve to distribute chores more carefully in the future. But don't be too concerned. Overzealous attempts to be fair invariably help bring about the very jealousy they're intended to prevent.

There's an understandable tendency for parents to request help more often from children with a positive attitude than from those who show reluctance. But, in addition to reinforcing the attitude of the reluctant child, this can lead to resentment and a negative attitude on the part of the child who wants to help but now sees the situation as unfair. It's worth making the effort not to take the easy way out. Unpleasant as it may be, parents should see to it that the reluctant child does his fair share of work as well.

There's always bound to be some unevenness in distribution of chores. Obviously, younger children are given less to do than older ones. A child of high-school age preparing for final examinations or a child approaching bar mitzvah might temporarily be allowed to devote all of his spare time to studying. Since boys have a special obligation to study Torah, we'll want to encourage them in this. If we need help while the boy is occupied in Torah study, we will, whenever possible, ask a daughter to help instead. If you notice resentment in a child who's required to do more because of such extenuating circumstances, explain the situation and do your best to help your child accept it.

Reluctance to Help

Reluctance to help is quite normal in children, but many parents are troubled by a show of displeasure. They want their child to be happy, and dislike forcing him to help when he clearly doesn't want to. Often, unpleasant memories of being forced to help when they themselves were children are what underlies such parental reluctance. Or, they may fear that the child will come to resent them. Thus, when a request for help is met with reluctant compliance, these parents are apt to say something like, "You don't have to do it if you don't really want to" — which, unfortunately, does nothing to encourage further cooperation. Other parents so dread the fuss that might ensue that they refrain from asking for help for that reason alone, preferring to do things themselves, much to the detriment of all concerned.

More commonly, parents react with annoyance to the child's reluctance to help. For example, they may scold, "Why do you make a face — don't you want to help?" or "Aren't you ashamed that you want to leave me with all the dishes!" — or, with obvious bitterness, "Never mind — I'll do it myself." But this only makes the child feel resentful and even less inclined to help. Such complaining and criticizing most often results in the child's internalizing our negative view of him, and in establishing as a fact that he doesn't want to help. It's as if the parents have pinned on the child a label which says: "I don't want to help. I'm bad."

Many parents, fully aware that their scolding and criticizing do no good, berate themselves relentlessly for their nonconstructive conduct. Instead, they should remind themselves that people — including children, and especially older ones — don't readily change long-established behavior patterns. Even if parents stop criticizing their child and adopt more effective methods of requesting his help, this does not guarantee that the child will promptly change his attitude. If he doesn't, it can be very hard for parents to avoid falling back into their old habits of disapproving and complaining. They may then begin to evaluate the child poorly, or to see themselves as having failed as parents.

Therefore, rather than paying any attention to displays of displeasure at having to help, ignore these completely. When a child, for example, offers obvious excuses such as "I'm too tired" or "I have too much homework" (watch your own similar statements — the child may be copying them!) you can show understanding but still, in a friendly way, insist that the job be done. For instance, you might respond, "I know you're tired, but peel the potatoes anyway" or, "I'm also tired sometimes, sweetheart, but I still do my work." A loving stroke on the cheek as you say this can work wonders.

Even when a child actually refuses to do a job, saying, "I don't want to" or "I don't feel like it," your response should still be as before — or you can say, "But I asked you." Strictly avoid giving answers such as, "What do you mean you don't want to do it? I said so and that's that!" Later, explain to the child, very quietly, that he's not allowed to refuse his parents' requests. Another way of handling such refusals is to ask, "Shall I do it?" But you have to ask this very softly or it can have the wrong effect, and you have to judge whether this approach will work with this particular child.

Here's a story illustrating how one mother handled this problem:

> I was feeling helpless about the situation with Shuli, my 8-year-old, who wouldn't cooperate in doing household chores. I would ask her nicely to do something, like washing the dishes. After

several refusals I would get angry and yell, "Do the dishes already — it's your job!" or, "Everyone has their job and you have to do something too!" When she still refused I felt extremely frustrated, like a total failure. Then I would scream at her even more. I felt awful doing this. If Shuli did do the dishes, she would make a sour face which angered me even more.

I tried identifying my thoughts — what was causing my anger? I was thinking, "How terrible to be so helpless and not know what to do!" and I was judging my daughter: "How self-centered of her not to do anything!" I worked on moderating these thoughts: "It's not the end of the world that she doesn't want to help — I can tolerate it. Besides, who says she has to be happy doing dishes?" This helped me tremendously to calm down and change my attitude.

The next evening I asked my daughter, as usual, "Please Shuli, do the dishes." She refused, giving a variety of reasons: "I have no strength," "I'm tired," "Why me?" But I stood my ground as I repeated my request, "The dishes are waiting for you. Please do them." I ignored her for a few minutes and then said again, "Please get started on the dishes," in a quiet but determined voice. Nothing helped. She decided she was tired and wasn't going to wash the dishes. She put on her nightgown and got into bed looking very angry.

I did the dishes myself. Then, feeling quite calm, I went into her room and said quietly and gently, "This evening you didn't do the dishes. It was your job. I hope that tomorrow you'll do them." Shuli was touched by my gentle tone (she'd expected the usual tongue-lashing) and softly stammered, "I'm sorry!"

The next evening she washed the dishes, but with a sour face, muttering, "Only I have to work so hard — only I have the hardest job!" I gave her a sad but understanding look, remembering how I'd disliked washing dishes when I was a girl. Then I said, "I saw that you didn't want to do the dishes, but you made yourself do them anyway," and I hugged her very warmly. The next day Shuli asked me, "When I finish the dishes tonight, you'll hug me strongly just like you did yesterday, okay?" I agreed and since then she does the dishes happily, she gets her hug, and the situation has improved unbelievably.

Another mother reported good results with the following method: When one of her youngsters doesn't want to do some chore, such as sweeping the floor, she says, "I expect the floor to get done," and then walks away, leaving the child alone. The job invariably gets done.

We would certainly prefer it if children did their tasks gladly, but we should learn to be satisfied for the time being with the job getting done at all. However, don't say to a grumbling child, "I don't expect you to love washing the dishes, all I expect is that you do it," or "I don't care if you don't like emptying the garbage, you have to do it anyway." This reinforces his negative attitude. If you consistently ignore all signs of displeasure and maintain a pleasant but firm manner, your child's attitude is likely to improve eventually. Though he may never learn to enjoy doing dishes, he'll come to see it as an opportunity to fulfill the mitzvah of honoring his parents. He'll also feel the satisfaction which comes from participating and doing his share, and the knowledge that he's able to do something for his parents in return for all they do for him.

An interesting story was related by one grandmother:

> I was washing dishes on Motza'ei Shabbos, while visiting my son and his family. Ten-year-old Yisrael was watching me. Suddenly he asked, "Grandma, do you enjoy doing this?" I answered, "You know, darling, I'm not especially fond of washing dishes. But when I think of how it takes a load off your mother and makes life easier for her, I feel really happy inside, and that makes the dishes an enjoyable job." He walked away, a thoughtful expression on his face.

Having a serious talk with the child can be very helpful too. You might say to him: "You know, doing what Mommy and Daddy ask is a big mitzvah. Part of the mitzvah is the happiness you give us when we see that you're glad to do it. But when you show us you don't feel like helping, it makes us unhappy. Then, even though you do it in the end, your mitzvah is much smaller." A mother related how touched she was by her 8-year-old daughter's response to being told, "I feel bad when you tell me that you don't want to do what I've asked." At first the child replied, rather thoughtfully, "I didn't know that." Later she came and asked, "Why didn't you tell me before that you feel bad?"

When a child shows reluctance to help, never say to him: "Okay, don't come asking me to do anything for you!" When he asks for a favor from you, don't counter with: "You don't want to do things for me, so I don't want to do anything for you either." This is not only vengeful, but nonconstructive as well. Also, avoid mulling over the child's supposed ingratitude: "After all I do for him, he doesn't even want to do a little bit for me in return!" This will only build up resentment toward him. Instead, try to view his reluctance to help as a sign of poor inner discipline.

Sometimes, there are situations in which it works out well when the reluctant child is left alone. One mother with an unusually helpful older daughter and a much less cooperative younger daughter decided against insisting that the second daughter do her share. She reasoned, "When the older girl leaves the house and the younger one sees that I need her help, she'll pitch in gladly." Several years later when her older sister got married, the younger daughter indeed changed dramatically for the better, gladly helping out with all the household chores and with caring for the younger children. This is a case of the power of optimistic expectations: The daughter realized that her mother expected that she wouldn't let her down when her help was really needed.

There are times when a little encouragement is all that's necessary to get a child over his reluctance to help. For instance, you've asked your daughter to go to the grocer's, but she complains that she's tired and has no strength to do anything. You can say, "Please try your best to get over your tiredness and see if you can do it anyway." If she then succeeds, praise her liberally: "How wonderful that even though you had so little strength, you forced yourself and went anyway!"

On occasion, refraining from insisting that the child do his chore, but letting him know at the same time that his behavior is wrong, can have a dramatic effect on his attitude:

My 8-year-old son Hillel was carrying on about having to polish his father's shoes. I told him, "Look, Hillel, I'm not going to make you do it. But you should know that it's wrong of

*you to act this way. Think about it." He didn't say anything
— but five minutes later I saw him take out the shoeshine
box and begin to polish the shoes!*

Parents sometimes pay or reward their children to motivate
them to do their chores. As mentioned in Chapter 4, rewards can be
useful for instilling basic good behavior patterns; but they have serious drawbacks when used to bring about compliance with doing
chores, which children should learn to see as an expected contribution to the household. Rewards for chores can develop in children an
attitude of "What do I get for this?" — to the point, sometimes, that
they may refuse to do tasks without a reward. Moreover, rewarding
or paying children for doing chores sets the parent-child relationship
in distorted perspective. Children receive everything they need from
their parents; let them do what they can to show their appreciation.
Regarding this concept, Rabbi Yoel Schwartz writes:

> [The child] must know that going to the grocery store or tak-
> ing out the garbage is his obligation both because he must
> honor his parents and because he should contribute his part
> to the family enterprise. If we promise him candy or money,
> we block his developing this sense of obligation.[16]

What if your child complains that other children get paid for
doing chores while he does not? A nice way to respond to such complaints was presented by this mother:

> *Occasionally my 9-year-old son Joel complains: "How come
> my friend gets paid $5 for shoveling the snow, $2 for taking
> out the garbage, and $3 for tidying up the basement?" My
> answer is: "We are a family. We are a team and we help each
> other. If I would pay you, it would be insulting to you, as if
> you were a stranger who was hired to do a chore. Every
> member of our family is very important."*
>
> *Recently I was making a birthday party for my 7-year-old
> daughter, Julie. I was feeling panicky — there would be 26
> children coming! I thought of calling my teenage baby sitter
> and pay her to help me. Then I said: "Wait a minute! What*

about Joel? When I have such a big boy, such a helper, why should I ask an outsider?" Joel, a difficult child who is extremely jealous and was previously resentful of the birthday party, felt so important and helped me tremendously throughout the party.

Novel ways can often be found to motivate children to do the jobs they dislike:

My children always liked hanging and taking down laundry, but no one wanted to fold it. So I said to them one day, "Come, let's play 'Personalities' while we fold the laundry." Everyone had a good time and gradually they learned to enjoy doing it.

Negligence in Taking Care of Chores

Some children raise no protest when asked to help, but avoid doing their chores by procrastinating or "forgetting." Discovering that a chore has been left undone can be annoying to parents. But again, outbursts such as, "Why do I have to be constantly after you to do everything?!" are counterproductive. Instead, learn to view your child's procrastinating behavior not as a sign of bad character, but as a bad habit. You can proceed to teach him to change his behavior.

For instance, you can explain to him, maintaining a very low voice, "You know, when Daddy or I ask you to do something, you should take care of it right away and not make us remind you. Doing what we ask is your mitzvah. If you're in the middle of something, you can always ask, 'Can I finish this first?' and I'll usually say okay. But otherwise, jobs have to be done right away."

Mild reprimands, such as the following, can also be helpful. "You know, I had to ask you several times to clear the table before you did it. That's not right. Next time, please do what I ask right away."

Procrastination is a tenacious habit, and your "forgetful" child will not change it in a day. Be patient; refrain from telling your child, "Please don't make me remind you so often to do what I asked" — this is frequently received as a complaint. Even the word "please," when given a certain emphasis, can convey great annoyance: "Will you *please* go in and do those dishes?!" Avoid letting your child's negligence make you feel powerless; he'll usually sense this and it strongly affects the way he responds to you. Instead, keep your cool and give quiet, consistent reminders.

With the occasionally negligent child, cuing is often a helpful technique. For instance, a child who was supposed to sweep a room can be quietly handed the broom. Sometimes a word or two will suffice — "Amos, the dishes." Use notes, too, as reminders; they can be "delivered" via a brother or sister. Charts also offer good opportunities for cuing; when a child has forgotten to fold the laundry you can tell him, "Take a look at the chart and see what job you were supposed to do."

What about the consistently negligent child, who ends up doing very little work — often much to the resentment of his siblings? Remind him in a friendly way that your family is a team with everyone doing his share. Stress to him, gently but firmly, the importance of cooperation and of everyone pitching in.

In general we should exercise patience. But on occasion when it's too inconvenient to wait, we might decide to do the work ourselves. Don't make the child feel guilty about this. If he says, "I was going to do it," simply answer, "I'm sorry but I couldn't wait."

Sometimes a procrastinating child will "progress" from not doing chores at all to doing them poorly. Don't hesitate to check up on his work and ask him to repeat a poorly done chore. Stick to objective evaluations and descriptions, telling him directly and simply what you want him to do — "This floor wasn't swept well. Please do it again." Whenever possible, first find something good to say about the work — "Hmm — let me see this pot. Nice job! But this cover is still dirty. Please go over it once more." Don't expect perfection; if you say anything critical, make it constructive — "I think you can do a better job than this."

At the same time, avoid hovering over your children to make sure they're doing everything properly. Children need to sense that we have confidence in them and expect them to do a good job. For instance, when children help with cooking, they may not always notice bits of food or peels which drop to the floor while they work. It's disagreeable for us and for the child if we badger him to pick them up. Here a simple "There are some eggshells on the floor," or "A few apple peels dropped over there" will do very well.

Flexibility

Although it's generally best to accustom children to doing what we ask of them right away, there is room for flexibility. We can teach a child to ask, when he wants to postpone a particular job, "Can this wait a few minutes?" or "Can I first do (such and such)?" But when our answer is no, we should stick to it and permit no arguments.

A child may sometimes have a legitimate reason for finding it difficult to help. Nevertheless, since it's wrong for him to refuse to do what his parents request, he should be taught, in such situations, to express himself appropriately. For instance, if he's truly overburdened with schoolwork, a proper way to express this would be, "I'm just loaded down with homework. Is it okay if I don't go to the store?" Parents can safely assume that the child's reason is legitimate, especially if he's normally happy to help and does so without complaint.

A readiness to compromise once in a while is important. Thus we might offer to do some of the dishes if the job seems like too much for the child. If a particular task doesn't have to be taken care of right away, we can let the child decide when to do it. Empathy is important too:

> I asked my son to set the table and fill the peppers with cheese. He cried, "It's too hard — I can't do it!" Formerly I would have responded, "It's easy — I'm sure you can do it" or "This is what I asked you to do and you have to do it." An argument would then ensue and often I would end up doing it myself rather than make a fuss. This time I remembered to be empathic. I said to him, "You think it's too hard for you to do that. I'll tell you what — go ahead and start and see how you do. If you have trouble I'll help you." He calmed down immediately and began to fill the peppers.

Parents frequently give in to a child's protestations about a job being too hard because of their uncertainty about whether it is indeed too much for him. Usually, there's no basis for such doubt; rather, the parents' uncertainty is rooted in self-critical attitudes. Parents can avoid such quandaries by making certain in their own minds, before making their request, that the child is capable of doing the task. In any case, as mentioned in Chapter 3, they shouldn't worry too much about this but should simply try to do their best.

Regard for the child's needs: Another important aspect of flexibility is to show consideration toward the child and his needs. For instance, if you must interrupt a child who is engrossed in some activity, express your regret at having to do so. To a child who's preparing for a test you might say, "I'm sorry to have to interrupt you while you're studying, but I need your help." It's always a good idea to give children advance warning — "When you're finished with this game, I'll need your help with vacuuming the rug."

How far should the parents' consideration toward their child extend? Should parents, for example, release a scholastically ambitious child from his obligations to help at home and let him devote his time to his studies exclusively? Should they forgo an older daughter's help and allow her to spend many hours with her friends, preparing an elaborate and impressive graduation exhibit at school? In answering these questions, we should weigh the relative importance of the alternatives involved. Which is more important — the five or so extra points on the examination, or taking some of the workload off an overburdened mother? Extracurricular activities may be a source of much genuine pleasure to the child, but they shouldn't take precedence over parents who need help. Even when the activities serve a charitable purpose, it should not be forgotten that "charity begins at home." In the words of the prophet, "Do not hide yourself from your own flesh."[17]

CONSIDERATION

In his summation of the entire Torah as "What is hateful to you, do not do to your fellow," the Sage Hillel teaches the fundamental role that consideration plays in Judaism.[18] Consideration means regard for others' emotional well-being as well as for their belongings; it is an attitude that should govern our entire manner of relating to people. When our Sages portray the ideal person who, by his example, attracts others to Torah, they mention only two traits — both of which suggest a person marked by consideration for others: "His dealings are faithful and his conversation with people is gentle."[19]

Lessons in consideration, as in all character traits, begin at home — with teaching children how to behave considerately and parental modeling of consideration in their behavior. If, for instance, a child is studying with the light on in the room when her sister wants to sleep, the parent shouldn't complain unthinkingly, "Why do you keep the light on? Can't you see your sister wants to sleep!" but should say softly, "Your sister needs to sleep. How about studying in another room?" Inconsiderate behavior outside the home should be handled with equal calm. A child who pushes ahead in a bus line, for example, can be quietly told, "Let's let these people get on first — they were here before us."

Teaching Consideration

Returning objects. Children often neglect to return objects to their proper place. This may greatly inconvenience the parents, but their main focus should be on the child's welfare and the need to inculcate in him, for his own good, a more responsible attitude. They'll handle the situation better if they can manage to control their annoyance. For example, a father discovers that his pliers are missing from the tool chest. Rather than calling out angrily, "Who took my pliers? Can't you kids put things back where they belong?!" he could quietly ask each child, "Have you seen my pliers?" When the child who borrowed the pliers produces them, the father might say to him, "I guess you forgot to put them back. Next time, please try to remember."

Later at some opportune time, the father could discuss with the child the importance of returning whatever is borrowed, explaining that failure to do so inconveniences others, wasting their time with needless searching. He can also, if appropriate, remind the child that he must ask permission before borrowing anything. By thus refraining from showing any personal annoyance, the father can successfully focus the child's attention on an important educational lesson: the harm we cause others through our neglect.

Handling the situation is easier if we know who took the missing object, as, for example, when we find it on a particular child's desk. Then we can simply say to the child, "You took my (stapler, Scotch tape) and you didn't put it back."

Helpfulness and Consideration □ 169

When children persist in failing to return borrowed objects to their place, they can be refused permission to use them. For example, if the child has neglected for the third time to return the screwdriver to the tool cabinet, he can be told: "I'm really sorry but I can't let you use the screwdriver for the time being. This is the third time you forgot to return it." If he then takes it anyway, some appropriate punishment is in order.

One mother, whose kitchen scissors were forever disappearing from the drawer, despite the fact that each child had his own scissors, tried tying a note to the scissors: "PLEASE RETURN THESE TO THE DRAWER AFTER USING." When this didn't help, she changed the note to: "THESE ARE NOT TO BE TAKEN OUT OF THE KITCHEN." After that the shears remained in their place.

Cleaning up messes: Another way children can cause considerable inconvenience is by leaving messes for someone else (usually their mother) to clean up. Rather than thinking with irritation, "They shouldn't leave me their messes like this!" parents should concentrate on how to remedy the situation. For instance, if your daughter has left spilled milk on the counter, calmly hand her a rag and ask her to clean it up. If she wants first to finish the sandwich she prepared for herself, tell her very pleasantly, "Please do it now. I can't work at the counter this way."

A mother reports her experience:

> My Uri sat down with a bag of peanuts at a freshly cleaned-up Erev Shabbos table. In the past, I would have become upset and scolded him for the innocent action of messing up the table. Instead, implementing the knowledge gained in the workshop, I calmly went over and showed him how to clean up the peanut shells by sweeping them with his hand onto a paper plate and throwing it all into the garbage. He did a pretty good job and I saved myself needless annoyance.

Children should be taught to clean up their own messes. Often, parents will yell at a child who has made some mess, "Look what you did!" — but then clean up for him! Usually, the parent is afraid that the child, if permitted to clean up the mess himself, won't do a good job. Parents who tend to react this way should work on changing their attitude. The child should be encouraged to do the best he can, with some assistance if necessary; the parent can always go over it later (preferably, not in the child's presence). If the parent decides to clean up the child's mess for him, this should be done quietly and without recriminations. Keep a box of old rags handy in the kitchen, and teach children to use these for quick cleanups. On the other hand, parents should avoid being excessively fussy; they should be able to overlook a bit of a mess here and there.

Older children who come in at odd hours and don't always eat with the family should be expected to clean up after themselves. If they forget, it's best to call them over and tell them quietly, "You forgot to clean up."

For a detailed discussion of order and cleanliness, see Chapter 9.

Understanding parents' needs. Children can be taught that parents' needs go beyond wanting a neat and orderly house. When a mother requires some quiet, or a chance to get her work done without the children underfoot, there's nothing wrong with explaining this quietly and pleasantly to her children. For example: "Kids, I need some time to take care of this pile of laundry and to prepare supper — please play in your room now"; "I have to get this work done now — later when I'm finished I'll come to you."

When mother and father want some quiet time with each other, they can explain to the children: "This is Mommy and Daddy's time to be alone." A timer can be set so the children will know for how long they are not to disturb their parents.

If you have a headache, or you're exhausted after a long night up with the baby, don't wait to talk to the children until your nerves are so totally frayed that you'll find it difficult to remain calm. A simple explanation such as, "Children, I have a bad headache; you'll have to leave me alone for a while now," will suffice.

It's particularly important to deal calmly with children when under pressure, such as on *Erev Shabbos* or before Pesach. If the children continually come into the kitchen for drinks or snacks while things are hectic, have a "no snacking" rule for such times and maintain it pleasantly but firmly. Or, so that children won't need to come into the kitchen, they can be given a bowl of apples and something to drink in their room. Older children should be in the kitchen to help, with the exception of the one who occupies the little ones or takes them out for a walk. If you finish with the cooking well before candle-lighting time on *Erev Shabbos* and you want your children to remember to stay out so that the kitchen will stay clean, you can post a sign on the door: "KITCHEN CLOSED UNTIL SHABBOS."

Visits and phone conversations: To what extent can a mother expect her child to let her chat uninterrupted with other adults? Many mothers experience inner conflict over this, fearing that they may be harming their child by ignoring his demands for attention at such times. Children, in turn, have an uncanny way of sensing this conflict, and can make their mother miserable with unceasing demands on her attention.

It's not necessary, however, to suffer inner conflict. Children don't need constant attention, and will manage very well without it for a surprisingly long time — provided we expect it of them. If we stop talking in order to give them attention every time they inter-rupt, we reinforce this behavior. Stopping repeatedly to tell the child "You're interrupting" has a similar effect.

Children can be taught to let us talk with other adults. When meet-ing an acquaintance while out with your child, say, very pleasantly, "Let me talk to my friend for a few minutes." When a guest arrives, explain that you'll be busy for a while with the visitor. If the child comes to tell you something, you can say, "Sweetheart, I'm talking right now to (so and so)" or, "Is this very important, or can it wait?"

Of course, you can show the child small tokens of attention to assure him that you haven't forgotten him. If he comes over to tell you something you can stroke his cheek, stop a moment to smile or nod — just enough to satisfy him — and take notice of him in small ways here and there.

If your child's disruptive behavior whenever there are visitors has persisted for a long time, you'll have to put him through an ini-tial training period. He'll keep trying hard to get your attention as you converse; but you must continue to give him only token signs of attention. If he cries and seems very unhappy, you might take him in your arms to soothe him, but still go on calmly with your conversation.

Comments such as "He never leaves me any peace!" should be strictly avoided; as should asking the child, "Can't you leave us alone for awhile?" These tend to strongly reinforce the negative behavior. To handle things differently, we need to identify the thoughts underlying our irritation: "I *shouldn't* have this annoyance! He shouldn't interrupt me and bother me like this!" We should moderate these thoughts, substituting for them a preference: "I'd *prefer* not being interrupted, but things don't *have* to be the way I want. It's not so bad."

The telephone can also pose a problem. Unlike seeing you talking to a visitor, when you speak on the phone your child doesn't see the person on the other side of the line and is therefore less aware of it when he interrupts. Stop the conversation for a moment and tell the child, "Please wait a few minutes — I'm on the phone" or simply, "I'm on the phone now." Don't protest loudly at him.

Children can be told that they should interrupt phone conversations only for something important. However, it's unrealistic to expect a child to wait too long. There's nothing wrong with saying, "I have to close our conversation now — my children need me." Some mothers disconnect their telephone every day for an hour or so to devote some exclusive time to their children.

Manners

Manners and politeness are an aspect of consideration. The Talmudic Sages considered them so important that they devoted two minor tractates (*Derech Eretz Rabbah* and *Zuta*) to the subject. Though some people disdain manners as automatic or superficial rituals, and etiquette can be taken too far — still, without manners our lives would lack that extra friendliness and warmth which are so important in human relationships.

We teach pleasant manners to our young children mostly by our good example, and also by occasional friendly prompting. For example, if the child says "I'm hungry, — I want a cracker," we can quietly ask him to say instead, "May I have a cracker please?" or we can prompt, "How can you say that nicely?" Children should be taught that thanking others is not only good manners but is meritorious as it shows *hakaras hatov* (gratitude). We should also explain to the child that we're obliged both to greet people and to respond to the greetings of people we know when we encounter them.[20] Teaching children to speak pleasantly to others is another aspect of good manners which should not be overlooked.

A child's lack of manners can be a sensitive spot for parents. Many parents are highly conscious of what others think of them. When a child publicly displays poor manners, they fear that he'll make a bad impression and thereby reflect poorly on themselves. If, for instance, the child doesn't take a proffered hand, they'll rush to make excuses. As effective educators, however, we must learn not to overly concern ourselves with others' opinions of us. Learning manners takes time, and our child's lack of them doesn't necessarily imply failure on our part.

The parents' concern over their child's lack of manners may express itself in continual prompting of the child to be polite. Although this may be effective at the moment, a child who is regularly reminded to "Say 'please'" or, "Tell the lady 'thank you' for the raisins" is unlikely to internalize politeness. Indeed, with a child who requests impolitely, relying on "Ask nicely and I'll give it to you" simply teaches him to respond to your cues, so that he remembers his manners only after being prompted.

A more constructive approach is to explain to the child, when you're alone with him, why courtesy is desirable. You might say, for instance, "There are lots of ways to ask for things. How does it sound when I say 'Pass the butter!' or 'Bring me a glass of water!'? It sounds like I'm giving you orders, doesn't it? But how about if I say it this way: 'Please, pass the butter' or 'Would you please bring me a glass of water?' That sounds much nicer, doesn't it?" This kind of modeling is particularly effective.

A good way to avoid frequent prompting was presented by one mother. When one of her children forgets to be polite, she turns her ear to the child, pulling at it slightly, as she smiles at him; the child invariably gets the message.

Many parents are especially embarrassed when a child asks for food in someone else's house. Again, don't respond on the spot, but let the child get the requested food (or drink); discuss the matter only afterwards, on the way home or at home. Explain to the child that he must wait for food until it's offered; if he's thirsty, however, he may ask for water.

Role playing is another useful teaching method. For example, anticipating a visit from Grandma, who's certain to bring a gift for her grandchild, you might rehearse with the child as follows:

MOTHER: Grandma will be here soon for a visit — she'll probably bring you a present. Let's practice how you'll thank her. You be Grandma — go out and ring the bell — I'll make believe I'm you. (Child goes out and rings bell; mother opens the door, prompts the child to say "Hello")

CHILD: Hello.

MOTHER (acting as child): Hi, Grandma! (again prompts child)

GRANDMA: I brought you a present.

MOTHER: Thank you, Grandma!

The roles are then reversed, with the mother acting as the grandmother and the child as himself. When the role play is over, the mother can say to the child, "That was very nice. Grandma will be pleased when you thank her so politely." If the child behaves as practiced, the commendation should be repeated after the visit: "It was nice the way you thanked Grandma for the present before."

Interrupting: Our Sages disapprove of those who interrupt others, even referring to one who does so as a "clod."[21] Children interrupt impulsively, and must be taught to allow others to finish speaking before they themselves speak. In addition to being worthwhile in itself, this provides good practice in learning self-control. Be patient. Don't rebuke your child with, "You're not letting me finish!"; it is better to pleasantly say, "Please let me finish." Be prepared to keep asserting yourself gently but firmly until your child learns not to interrupt.

Likewise, when several children are standing around us, each interrupting the other and all wanting to be heard at the same time, we can say, good-naturedly, "Kids, I'd like to hear what all of you have to tell me but I can listen to only one person at a time. Suppose we take turns. We'll start with...."

Table manners: Teaching table manners requires persistence with most young children. They need to be taught that it's forbidden to behave in a way that disgusts others.[22] They should be shown how to use a spoon and fork as soon as possible, and encouraged to do so. But don't be too fussy or demanding; strictly avoid comments like "Look how you're eating!" or, "You're eating like a pig!" A gentle word here and there is enough. When a child tries hard to eat correctly he should be complimented; this will encourage him and may also motivate the other children to emulate him.

A nice way to remind a child who uses his fingers instead of his knife and fork is to simply point to the cutlery or quietly hand it to him. Sometimes, it helps to set aside a few minutes at mealtime for paying special attention to manners.

Thoughtfulness

We can require and teach children to be considerate of others' needs for order, cleanliness, and quiet. More difficult to instill is thoughtfulness, the positive counterpart of consideration. It is the ability to sense what will give others pleasure and satisfaction, and to act on it. Thoughtfulness is so difficult to teach because it must be self-motivated. Modeling is necessary, but parents can also encourage thoughtful deeds which the child initiates. For instance, when an older child offers to watch the baby so that his mother can rest, she can accept with a pleased, "That's very thoughtful of you." Parents can also sometimes suggest small acts of thoughtfulness. A mother could, for example, hint to her son, "Your brother is late for school this morning. How about making his bed for him?" A subsequent commendation of the child's thoughtfulness reinforces his behavior.

Giving appropriate compliments is a form of thoughtfulness too. Try to make your children aware of situations where compliments are appreciated. Modeling is particularly effective here. For example, while the family is seated at the Shabbos table the father can make a point of praising his wife's cooking. Then, while the mother is in the kitchen, he can ask the children, "Isn't the soup delicious? Let's tell Mommy; that will make her feel good!"

A mild reproof at times for a child's failure to show thoughtfulness may be beneficial, but outbursts such as "Why can't you do something, for once, *without* being asked?!" will only arouse the child's ill will. Most children, if trained to be helpful and considerate, will eventually begin to behave thoughtfully as well.

Chapter Nine

ORDERLINESS AND CLEANLINESS

isorder causes much waste of time, as well as inconvenience. Habits of orderliness not only enable us to function productively; they help us develop an organized and efficient mind — "for a person is shaped by his actions."[1] In the list of outstanding characteristics of our greatest sages, Rabbi Akiva is praised for his beautifully ordered mind.[2] (Perhaps it was this trait that qualified him to lay the foundation for the entire Talmud.)[3] The story is told of a rabbi who traveled many miles to his son's yeshiva to see how the boy's learning was progressing. When he arrived he went first to his son's room. After merely noting that the room was organized and tidy, the father went home, certain that the boy was learning well.[4]

Parents should foster an attitude of "It's our house; we work together to keep it orderly and clean." Some mothers regard their children as more or less a hindrance to their efforts. This attitude leads to reproaches such as, "Look what you're doing to my clean kitchen floor!" This is not the way to develop a spirit of cooperation and teamwork.

EARLY TRAINING

One of the first ways to teach a child order is to show him how to put his toys away. Suggest to him that each toy has its place: "Let's put the train set here; the puzzles can go over here...." A low shelf is advisable; it is more conducive to organization than a toy chest into which all toys are tossed. Keep toys with many parts in sturdy boxes or plastic containers, such as are used in kindergartens. Large plastic gallon-size bleach bottles with their tops cut off (and washed out well) also make good containers. Since your small children will frequently wish to play near you, it's helpful to have a cart with select toys that can be wheeled in and out of their room. Or give your child a plastic laundry basket which he can pull from room to room for playing and quick pickups.

Young children will enjoy putting their toys away if we teach them to regard it as a sort of game. A little song (you can possibly record it) can engender real enthusiasm. Try the following, sung to the tune of "The Farmer in the Dell": It's time to clean up now (2), heigh-o the derry-o, it's time to clean up now. First come the blocks (2), etc. Next come the dolls (2), etc."

Children generally get much satisfaction from creating order in their environment, but we should give them time and not demand perfection. If there is no older brother or sister to help the child, the mother should work together with him at first, gradually doing less and less until he can do the whole job by himself. Comments such as, "How nice the room looks now!" heighten the child's feeling of pleasure and help to develop a love of order. Our cheerful manner as we help him instills a positive attitude, too. By the time they are 4, most children no longer need help with cleaning up; but we should still be willing to lend a hand at times.

It is unreasonable to expect that a child's room always be in order. Establish a regular time at which rooms must be tidied; before supper is usually best. That way you won't constantly have to remind your children to straighten up their room — which can bring them to view neatness as a burden. To give them enough time, remind your children well in advance. A timer set for about 15 minutes gives them an idea of how much time they have left and discourages dawdling. When they're finished, they should call you to inspect. Comments such as "Nice job!" or "I'll tell Daddy this evening what a good job you did" are encouraging. If the room's appearance is not as it should be, you can point out what still needs to be done. Serve supper only when everything is in order.

Even though a special time is set aside for cleanup, a child should still be taught to preserve some semblance of order in his room while playing. For instance, there can be a rule that no more than two toys be taken out to play with at one time. Toys with many small parts can be kept in boxes on an upper shelf so that children can't get at them without asking for help.

All of this may not be so easy when there are several children, some of whom are inclined to be neat and others less so. A tidy child is apt to become annoyed with his less orderly brother or sister. If he complains about the state of his room, take him aside and understandingly tell him, for example, "I know it bothers you when your sister leaves her toys all over the room, but it doesn't help to get annoyed. Why don't you just remind her quietly to put a few things away?"

Don't become involved in discussions about who took out which toy. Rather, tidying the room should be considered a joint effort. But when two children share a room, the older one can be made responsible for cleaning it up. Try to encourage a spirit of friendly cooperation among the children. If one child protests, for example: "I didn't take the blocks out! — why should I put them away?" answer with a smile, "I know, but put them back anyway." When your child has friends over to play, you can remind him to ask the other children to help with cleanup before they go home.

Children should also be taught to keep their clothing in order. Even a young child can learn to bring dirty clothes to the hamper; older children can fold or hang up clothing they've worn as well. Here again, the mother should assist the child when first teaching him, and can encourage him with comments such as, "It's good when the room is in order; then we can find everything easily."

As soon as they are capable, children should be required to make their beds. When they're still too young, older children can be asked to do it for them. Show the child how to make the bed, and perhaps help him the first few times. Even if it means he'll be late for school a few times, rules about making beds should be upheld. (Of course, the situation is more complicated if he goes to school by bus or other transportation; see "When the Child Relies on Special Transportation," in Chapter 10.) If, nevertheless, a child runs off without making his bed, leave the bed as it is. When he comes home tell him — without lectures or scolding — "You left your bed unmade this morning. Take care of it now please."

COPING WITH DISORDERLINESS

Teaching habits of orderliness is, perhaps, the area where parents experience the greatest frustration. How is it that parents who themselves provide a model of neatness encounter such difficulty instilling this trait in their children? We can best understand this problem by tracing its roots.

In teaching the child to be orderly, our aim should be that he develop a love of orderliness that will motivate him to be neat on his own. Such an attitude can best develop if the parents proceed calmly and with patience, and without exaggerated expectations. Parents who lack such tolerance are apt to nag and scold the child, who then becomes resentful and ill disposed to value tidiness. Thus the attempt degenerates into a futile and never-ending struggle.

Many parents find it particularly hard to moderate their expectations, especially if they've believed for years that they can't stand disorder. They may tell themselves again and again, "I shouldn't make such a fuss — I shouldn't get so angry when the kids leave their things all over — but I just can't stand the mess!!" As long as parents demand inwardly that things always be neat, they'll continue to have trouble maintaining the self-control necessary to train their children in neatness. Mothers who drive themselves to keep their houses constantly in order can expect only frayed nerves and unhappy children.

The parents' anger is often intensified because they view their children's disorder as evidence of their own failure — "What kind of mother am I that I can't get my kids to keep their room in order?" Parents who know they have this problem can tell themselves, "It's true that I haven't yet succeeded in teaching my children orderliness, but that doesn't make *me* a failure." When parents realize that they don't have to think in terms of "failure" or lack of self-worth, they'll find it much easier to cope with their anger.

Some parents also begin to worry about the children's character — "What will these kids grow up to be if they're so careless and disorderly now?" This, too, contributes nothing to solving the current problem.

It may help to consider the matter from the child's point of view. He hasn't developed the habit of putting things in their place. He knows he *should* but he hates to; he'd much rather read or play a game. So, he puts it off. In this way, more and more items accumulate — until his room is in such a state that the last thing he wants to do is clean it up.

The more we tell him what a slob he is, and how he doesn't care at all about the mess in his room, the more he comes to believe it. His reaction then is: "Okay, so I'm a slob — so I don't care what my room is like. That's the way I am." He may still be blaming himself for being this way, but he does nothing about it.

Caught in a cycle like this — often for years — parents sometimes become so weary of the entire ordeal that they finally give up, telling themselves, "All right, it's his room. Let him keep it as messy as he likes." This may relieve some of the tension, but it's obviously no solution. Besides, maintaining such an "I don't care" attitude is difficult; sooner or later, parents usually go back to getting angry at the disorder.

If they wish to succeed in changing their children's disorderly habits, parents must first learn to control their anger. This means refraining from sarcastic remarks such as, "It's no wonder you can't find your notebook in this mess!" It means that, instead of telling themselves, "Those miserable slobs! I can't stand their messes anymore! They don't care about *me* at all!" they must practice thinking, "I don't particularly like this mess but I *can* tolerate it. Besides, getting angry over it just makes me miserable and doesn't get me anywhere. They just have bad habits, and I'll have to patiently teach them better ones." (The problem of teenagers' disorderliness is discussed in Chapter 15.)

To make a fresh start, call a conference on the subject of orderliness. Discuss the importance and advantages of neatness — it gives us pleasure, it's easier to find things, it helps us function better (let the children contribute their ideas, too). Then say, "From now on we're going to set aside 15 minutes every day before supper for straightening up your room. I'll remind you, and I'll be around to give you a hand, too."

See this as a training period. Developing new habits takes time. You must start at (or return to) the beginning, showing the children how to straighten up their rooms and helping them with it. Little by little you can withdraw from the enterprise — leaving them to do the job by themselves.

As you help the children, be careful to refrain from any critical comments such as "Look at the way this room looks! Books all over, clothes lying around...and what's this junk doing on your desk?" A pleasant atmosphere should surround this activity. For example, if you come in at the appointed time and find your child busy with a book instead of cleaning up, very calmly take it from him, take him by the hand and say, in a friendly way, "Come, let's start cleaning up."

Don't start putting things away as the child watches, expecting him to join in. Instead, ask: "All right — what would you like me to help you with?" Surprisingly, when they see your willingness to help them, the children may very well say, "It's okay, Mom, we can do it by ourselves."

Teach your child that when he thinks he's finished, he should stand at the door and survey the room to make sure everything's in order. Prepare a checklist for him, including, for instance:

1. Books and games put away
2. Desk tidied
3. Floor cleaned up, etc.

Remember to praise his efforts.

Set aside a few minutes before bedtime, after your children are in pajamas, for having them bring dirty clothes to the hamper and for preparing fresh clothing for the next morning. Do all this together with them. You can sometimes solve the problem of dirty laundry by hanging a colorful pillowcase with a loop sewn onto it on the back of the closet or bedroom door.

If, for instance, the child persists in dropping his clothes all over the room and leaving them there, you might try applying some logical consequences. Since it's impossible to clean the room with so much clothing lying around, clothes get dumped on the bed and remain there (this may mean no clean shirt for Shabbos). By the time several days' clothing has piled up, the child may be so bothered by the mess that he decides it's better to put his things away. One mother who tried this with her 9-year-old son reported that one such experience was enough to rid the boy of his habit.

Carelessness

Practically all children occasionally leave items such as books and jackets lying around. Calmly tell the child, for example, "You left your briefcase in the hall." Or, you can call him in and say, "Take a look and see what has to be put away." If he left his things in the kitchen, tell him, "I can't work here with these things lying around." It helps to have a special "tchatchke" or junk drawer for each child where they can keep small odds and ends, items *you* may well see as worthless but which they deem too valuable to throw away.

Discussions can be helpful too. For example, "Kids, there's a problem with the books left lying around the living room after Shabbos. What shall we do?" A mother whose children had developed the habit of dumping their jackets and briefcases in the hall when they came home from school related her way of solving the problem. "I kiss them when they come home and then say, 'I won't talk to you until you hang up your coat and put away your books.'"

But what if children habitually leave their belongings strewn about, causing perpetual disorder in the house? Then, more drastic measures may be called for. You may have to gather the children together and tell them, "Kids, it's unpleasant to have to ask you to put your things away. On the other hand, I don't want to be putting them away for you either. So from now on, when I find your things, I'll be putting them in this bag." Show them where the bag (or box, if you prefer) will be kept — perhaps hung in the kitchen closet, or in some out-of-the-way place so that they'll experience the maximum of unpleasant consequences from their messiness. Or you can allot a shelf for quick clearance of items left lying around; even the top of the refrigerator can be used. But you must do all this quietly and pleasantly; the method loses much of its effectiveness if, for example, you start off by saying, "I'm going to teach you kids not to leave your stuff all over the house!"

Children frequently have a habit of leaving clothing and towels lying around the bathroom. Quietly call the child in and, with a slight gesture of the hand, tell him very simply, "Look." No more words are necessary; he'll get the hint and know what to do. A discussion about the situation may be appropriate, but at some other time.

Use humorous notes from time to time. To a pair of carelessly thrown pajamas pin the note: "HOW I LONG TO BE UNDER THE PILLOW!" To the uncapped toothpaste tube tape the note: "I LIKE TO BE IN THE CABINET WITH MY COVER ON." This can convey our message better than spoken words. Try to think up other amusing and novel ways of handling problems of disorderliness. For instance, if books are left lying around, you can hand a child a pile of them and say, "Here — you just became a librarian."

Don't help children who frequently mislay their things to find them. If a child complains, "I can't find my notebook," respond merely, "I'm awfully sorry," refraining from any lectures. In this way he may learn to put things away more carefully. To foster greater responsibility, you can require your children to pay for replacements of lost school equipment from their own savings or pocket money, if they have any. As for lost sweaters, jackets, boots, or briefcases, they should at least contribute toward the purchase of new items. Replacing a lost sweater or jacket with a worn-out hand-me-down can be a good punishing consequence. The fewer words said about this, the better. Usually the child is sufficiently self-critical about his carelessness and doesn't need any admonishment from us. It's a good idea to label all articles which could get lost.

CLEANLINESS AND APPEARANCE

When our Sages depict a ladder leading to perfection of character, they list cleanliness as the fourth rung.[5] Just as royal statues are washed daily, so must we, who are created in God's image, keep our bodies clean.[6] Cleanliness is even considered an aspect of holiness.[7]

In teaching cleanliness to their children, parents should try to be tolerant and relaxed. It's unreasonable to expect a child to be constantly clean, and a mother who insists on this is likely to wear out both herself and her child. What very often prompts the mother is concern over what others will think of her. Once she's aware of this motivation she can work on reducing her dependence on the approval of other people.

On the other hand, children needn't be sloppily dressed. To remind your child about his appearance, give cues such as, "Take a look and see what you need to do with your shirt." This is more effective than constant reminders to "tuck that shirt in."

For children who don't like washing their hands, a dab of hand cream every time they've done so can serve as an incentive. Try to keep washing routines cheerful; avoid statements such as, "How did you get yourself so dirty?" or "Get those filthy hands washed right away!" An older child can be told in a friendly and matter-of-fact way to wash his hands; a younger child can be led to the sink as you say, "Come, your hands need to be washed." It pays to be patient and not push the child to get himself clean in a hurry. We may get a little less done, but the reward, in terms of developing a positive attitude toward cleanliness, is well worth it.

Keep a sturdy stepstool next to the sink to encourage self-help. Likewise, a small mirror at child height helps develop good habits. Towel hooks should be low, and strong loops sewn to hand towels to keep them on their hooks.

A FINAL WORD

Because mothers are usually more directly involved with maintaining order and cleanliness, they are the ones to speak to the children most often about it. As a result, children sometimes get the idea that neatness and appearance aren't really so crucial since they seem to matter to only one parent. Therefore, it's important that fathers join mothers in stressing the need for maintaining a clean appearance, neat rooms, and an orderly house.

Chapter Ten

MORNING AND BEDTIME ROUTINES

MORNING ROUTINES

ornings are a time of tension in many homes. Many parents nervously rush their children through the morning routines: "Come on, get up!" "Stop dawdling and get dressed!" "Get going or you'll be late for school!" "Hurry up, eat your breakfast!" By the time the last child is safely out the door and on his way to school, parents often feel ready to collapse. What's to be done?

The main problem seems to be that we've taken over for the child. By rushing him, we make him think that his getting to school on time is *our* responsibility. So he starts to rely on us, becoming lax himself. If we want the child to take charge instead, we have to step back and allow some natural consequences to take their course.

This means, first of all, maintaining a pleasant, relaxed atmosphere in the house each morning. It's amazing, once we've stopped trying to run the show, how quickly children catch on and begin to assume responsibility themselves, as these mothers report:

> In the mornings I used to nag my Natanel constantly, in order to get him to school on time. Following a discussion in the parenting workshop, I decided that perhaps he was old enough and could be made responsible for going on time without my nagging.
>
> I didn't discuss this with him or do anything. Every 15 or 20 minutes I would nicely tell him the time (he can't read the clock as yet). After a few days he caught on that it was up to him to stop dawdling and get out on time. Still, this was not so easy for him and at first, he would often come to school five or ten minutes late. Now, a few weeks later, he's almost never late.

> My kids were very busy when they woke up in the morning, coloring, playing, talking — they absolutely never thought of getting dressed. I was always saying, "Get up! Get dressed! It's late!" I hated doing it — but always ended up doing it anyway.
>
> Finally I made up my mind — no more! It's their job to go to school and get there on time. I managed, with nearly 100 percent success, to stop nagging. But they, as usual, were coloring, talking, and playing — while I was relaxing, wondering what would happen. To my great surprise, at a certain point, they looked at their watches and when they realized how late it was, began to rush like mad. I still catch myself hoping they'll get to school late, to teach them not to dawdle — but it doesn't happen!

A little planning and organization will also help. If we take out time in the evening to lay out clothing for the next day, prepare lunches, and get briefcases ready for school, there's that much less to do in the morning when time is at a premium. (This is especially important when there's a baby to care for as well.) And needless to say, getting up early enough can make all the difference.

Of course, incentives can always be tried. This mother describes a rather novel system which proved to be highly motivating for her children:

> *Mornings were always very difficult, getting my 5-year-old and 6-year-old ready for school. I felt I constantly nagged them to get dressed and be ready for the car pool.*
>
> *I realized that both boys loved to give extra money for tzedakah (charity). The plan we developed was: On the days they were dressed before their father came home from shul, they would get two pennies for tzedakah. Later I expanded this: If they were dressed before I woke up (meaning that I wouldn't have to wake them or remind them that it's time to get dressed), they would get three pennies for tzedakah.*
>
> *It really worked! Now mornings are a pleasure in our house!*

Getting Children Out of Bed

If possible, give children their own alarm clock; that way you won't have to wake them up. If you're the one to wake them up in the morning, do it pleasantly. Pull up the shades and in a friendly manner announce, "Time to get up." Some children can rouse themselves quickly; others need a couple of minutes to get used to the idea. With a child who has particular difficulty, it helps if we commiserate — "I know — it's so hard to get up in the morning." There's nothing wrong with giving a reminder, but don't go into the room repeatedly to urge the child out of bed.

Making Beds

As discussed in Chapter 9, once they become capable, children should be required to make their own beds. A good rule is "BBB" — beds before breakfast. In other words, a child doesn't get breakfast until he's made his bed.

Dressing Young Children

Children of nursery-school age who are as yet unable to dress themselves will often resist us as we try to dress them. It sometimes helps to tell the child a story while dressing him. Another way of handling this is to leave the child alone and tell him that when he's ready to be dressed, he should call. If he doesn't seem to care, preferring to stay in pajamas, inform him that children who aren't dressed can't come to breakfast. This usually does the trick.

Teaching Children to Dress Themselves

The child's first efforts at self-dressing are rather clumsy. It seems to take him forever to get each piece of clothing on. He may also complain that it's "too hard." Sometimes, poor coordination may underlie his difficulties.

When children dawdle about dressing or complain that they can't do it, we may be tempted to jump in and quickly do the job for them. But if we can remain patient and encouraging during this period, letting the child do what he can and helping him with the rest, it pays in the long run. Empathy helps as well. For instance, "I know it's hard, but I'm here to help you."

The better the child gets at dressing himself, the more you should withdraw to let him handle it on his own. You can say, "Here are your clothes. Whenever you can't manage, call me and I'll help you." The child, however, may still want you to stay with him; in that case, you can divide things up. For example: "You put on your underpants and I'll do the shirt," "You do one shoe and I'll do the other."

The fact that a child has learned how to dress himself doesn't mean that he always wants to do it. He may tell you, "I can't get my shirt on," when he really can do it quite easily. It's best to answer, "I know you'd like me to help you but I think you can do it." Of course, all children like a bit of "babying" now and then and we should be willing to help them with dressing occasionally even when they don't really need it.

Choosing Clothing

In general, children should be allowed to decide for themselves what to wear, but it's probably better to put a younger child's clothes out for him. If the child wants to wear something else, you can respect any reasonable request.

Sometimes an older child will have trouble deciding what to wear in the morning. This is particularly so with daughters. They'll stand in front of their overflowing wardrobes, dramatically declaring, "I don't have a *thing* to wear!" or they'll wear you thin with "I can't decide. Should I wear the pink blouse or the purple one?" Often, they'll turn down all suggestions. Here an empathic response is best: "I know — it's so hard to decide"; then leave the child alone.

There's no need for arguments about putting on a sweater. Send the child out to check the weather, or the outdoor thermometer if you have one, and then let him decide. If he's uncomfortable for a day because of an inappropriate choice, he'll learn from that experience. If, however, you're worried that the child will catch cold, insist that he put on a sweater even if he doesn't want to. You can avoid arguments by not responding to his protests but answering simply, "I know, but please put the sweater on anyway."

Yet another alternative is to hand the child his sweater and say, "Here, put this in your briefcase so you'll have it in case you're cold."

Timers as Aids

A kitchen timer is useful for discouraging dawdling in young children who can't yet tell time. Set the timer for when they have to be finished dressing and teach them to check it now and then. You can make a game out of being dressed before the bell rings. The timer can also remind children how much time remains for eating breakfast or before they have to leave the house.

When the Child Is Late

If it looks like your child may be late for school, do nothing. Allow him to be late and experience the teacher's displeasure. Don't write him any excuse notes. (You can offer to write him a note such as: "Chayim is late this morning because he played instead of getting dressed." Most children decline such offers!) If the teacher is permissive about lateness, you might write a note asking that some consequences be applied.

This doesn't mean that you're unconcerned. Explain to your child that punctuality is a virtue and that it's important that he be in school on time. But it's *his* responsibility, not yours.

What about breakfast? You can save yourself much unnecessary annoyance by leaving it up to the child to decide how much breakfast he wants. If he decides to eat a skimpy breakfast or none at all because he's running late, don't be too concerned about it. True, food is important, and some mothers find it very difficult to send a child off to school hungry, seeing this as neglect of their duty. But what's really worse for the child: to go a little hungry, or to be subjected to an hour of nagging every morning? It becomes easier to deal with our feelings of compassion when we view the situation from this perspective.

When the Child Relies on Special Transportation

Don't nervously rush the child to make it on time for the school bus or car pool. Instead, try setting the timer and telling him that if he isn't finished dressing when it rings, we'll have to do the rest for him. If he isn't ready when the timer goes off, go in and stuff him rather unceremoniously (but not angrily) into the rest of his clothes. (If he's actually still in bed, pull him out at this point.) Try to make your dressing him sufficiently unpleasant so that he won't be eager to have you do it again. We can explain, as we stuff the child into his clothes, "I'm sorry but I have to do this quickly because we're in a big rush."

Another way of handling the problem is to offer the child some kind of incentive. Set the timer for a specified period — say, 15 minutes. Explain to him that if he has all his clothes on before the bell rings, he gets some small reward such as a special sandwich spread for lunch. If the bell rings and he hasn't made it, you'll still put his clothes on him — but he won't get the special treat.

If your child is likely to be distressed over missing school, you can try leaving him alone, allowing him to miss the bus or car pool. One day at home should be sufficiently punishing to motivate him to prevent a recurrence. To ensure maximum punishing consequences, don't be particularly attentive to the child. You can say, "I'm sorry you missed the bus, but I have a lot of work to do, and I don't have too much time for you." Or you might say, "Well, since you missed the bus, I guess you'll have to stay home. But you know, this is my time to do housework, and your time to be in school, so I think you'd better stay in your room — that way you won't disturb me in my work."

BEDTIME ROUTINES

Toward evening, most of us begin to look forward to that wonderful hour when our children are in bed and we can have a little time to ourselves. Much as we may want some peace and quiet, however, we need to avoid becoming anxious about it and telling ourselves, "I've got to get those kids into bed! I must have some rest or I'll surely collapse!" When we're nervous about getting our children to bed, we inevitably show it by our irritable way of talking to them; the children are then more likely to resist our efforts.

We need to view the situation more calmly. Even if the "worst" happened and the children were all still up hours after their bedtime, we'd still be able to cope somehow. Instead of anticipating possible difficulties as some sort of catastrophe, we can think to ourselves, "Even if I don't get the kids to bed on time, I'll still be okay. I'll survive." When we then proceed getting the children to bed without so much anxiety, we'll be more likely to gain their cooperation.

Getting Younger Children Ready for Bed

Allow plenty of time for the bedtime procedure, starting right after supper. Try to be relaxed, leading the children pleasantly through the various routines, so that it can be enjoyable for both you and them. You can remind children before putting them to bed to take drinks if they're thirsty, as there's to be no coming out of their rooms later to ask for them. Try to spend a moment or two with each child as you tuck him into bed and say the *Shema* with him; then give him a hug and kiss, turn out the lights and leave.

If a child now pops out of his bedroom and asks for some drink or snack, tell him very pleasantly that he can have these in the morning. Whatever reason he comes out for, don't make yourself angry by thinking, "Why can't he stay in bed?!" Instead, lead your child calmly yet firmly back to bed right away. As you do this, tell him, "No, you have to stay in your bed now," and be prepared to continue doing so, leading him quietly back to bed each time he comes out — the child is bound to get the message eventually. If a problem of this kind has gotten out of hand, a gate installed at the door can at least confine the child to his room.

If children call you to come, you can go in and quietly explain that now is their time to go to sleep. It reassures the child if you tell him where you'll be, and say you'll look in on him very soon. Tell children who no longer need toileting help that if they have to go to the bathroom, they should go quietly without calling you.

An especially pleasant way of saying good night to her children, and at the same time motivating them to be in bed on time, was devised by one mother:

> In our house we have "time together." The children who go to school get five minutes of private time with me at bedtime. If they're in bed on time I sit on their bed with them and talk to them for about five minutes. Sometimes they choose a story-book or short game instead. During this time no one else is permitted to interrupt or interfere with someone else's time together. Sometimes a child has something to tell me during the day and I don't have time to listen to it just then. I tell him, "Save it for time together." It satisfies him for that moment since he knows he'll get his chance to tell me later. They understand that this is a privilege and they are not supposed to complain on a night when they can't have it, such as if I have to go to a wedding, etc.

This mother, who still remembers the precious moments of "time together" with her own mother when she was growing up, added that she feels free to cut down the time spent with each child on days when she's sorely pressed for time.

Dawdling and Refusing to Stay in Bed

Some children habitually dawdle about getting ready for bed. Here, a small incentive can sometimes help tremendously. In one family, those who've put on pajamas, brushed their teeth, and are ready for bed on time can play in their rooms for an extra half-hour. It works like magic, reports the mother. You can also have children get into pajamas before supper; those who are ready on time get some small treat for dessert, such as an ice-cube "pop" (prepared from fruit-juice concentrate).

A star chart posted in a prominent place can be helpful too. Print the names of the children on the side; the days of the week can be initialed on top, with vertical lines separating them. Each day that the child is ready for bed on time, glue on (or draw) a star. You might decorate the chart with colorful bedtime motifs such as a toothbrush or pajamas.

More vexing is the problem of the youngster who has the unpleasant habit of persistently coming out of his room after being put to bed. The parents find themselves in what seems like an exhausting and never-ending struggle, night after night, to get him back into bed. What's to be done?

To begin with, make every effort to keep anger in check. Remind yourself that although your child's behavior is decidedly unpleasant and inconvenient, it's certainly *not* intolerable or unbearable.

Quietly explain to the child, at a time when both of you are relaxed, that you need your rest in the evening and that you can't allow him to be coming out of bed. Remind them that the rule is: Once in bed, there's to be no coming out. Toileting needs and drinks of water should all be taken care of beforehand. If the child now comes out to tell you that he isn't sleepy (or has some other gripe), tell him simply, "Sorry, you know the rule — once in bed, there's no coming out for anything." If the father comes home after the children have been put to bed but aren't yet asleep, he should go into their rooms to kiss them good night so that there's no excuse for them to come out.

If the child nevertheless persists in popping out of bed to join you, explain that you'll be forced to close his bedroom door unless he agrees to stay in bed. Merely shutting the door for a moment often results in the child quickly deciding that he really prefers to stay put in bed, with the door open. With a persistent youngster, you may need to hold the door shut for a while, ignoring tantrums, until he tires of screaming or of kicking the door and falls asleep on the floor, or in his bed.

One can go a little further, as these parents did:

> *Our 5-year-old came out of her room every night. Telling her to go back didn't work. So we attached a hook-and-eye type-lock high on the outside of her bedroom door — with a long enough hook to allow the door to open an inch or two so she could peek out. That way she wouldn't feel so locked in. Each evening we explained to her that if she came out, we would lock the door. We followed up on this. The first two nights she fell asleep crying next to the door. The third night she stayed in her bed. After two weeks she asked us to take the lock off. We did, and since then we've only had to warn her once about the lock.*

Or you might try the following reinforcement system. Fill a small plastic bag with a "nosh" food which the child likes (flavored popcorn is good for this). Show the child the bag, explaining that he will get it the next day. However, for each time he comes out of bed, you'll remove some of its contents. Keep the bag in the kitchen; if you then have to take anything out, do this in the child's presence.

You can't force children to sleep, but you can insist that they remain quietly in their beds. If a child has difficulty falling asleep, let him read a book or occupy himself with some other quiet activity.

Bedtime Routines for Older Children

As children get older, they'll no longer require your close supervision. Let them know when to start getting ready for bed, then check up on them from time to time, keeping reminders to a minimum. Use timers for signaling when to get out of the bathtub, or how much time is left for playing until the child has to be in bed. If the child ignores the bell, say, "The bell rang — you know what that means."

Instead of the usual nightly reminders — "Don't forget to brush your teeth" or "Did you brush your teeth?" — try hanging up this sign in the bathroom:

A pleasant way to remind a child about brushing his teeth is to ask, "Did you...?" as you gesture with your finger across your teeth.

Resistance

Don't argue with children about their bedtime. If a child says he doesn't want to go to sleep, or asks to stay up to finish reading a book or play some game, tell him, "I'm sorry, honey, but now is your bedtime."

With a child who regularly grumbles or makes a face when asked to get ready for bed, try a quiet talk. You might say to him, "I know how much you don't like going to bed at night. But you need your sleep — I can't let you stay up until all hours of the night. Try to be sensible about it, won't you?"

Sometimes a child will be more cooperative if you decide together with him on a bedtime which he then commits himself to stick to.

Chapter Eleven

JEALOUSY

A certain amount of jealousy among children is normal; we shouldn't be overly concerned about it, or invest too much effort trying to prevent it. Parents are often unaware that excessive concern about jealousy makes them act in ways that actually increase it. For instance, in cutting a cake, the mother will try hard to make each piece precisely the same size, hoping it will put an end to the children's eyeing each other's pieces to make sure no one got more. But the children now hover over the mother as she divides the cake, scrutinizing each piece even more carefully than before! The more we try to prevent apparent discrimination, the more vigilant children become.

The best thing we can do to prevent jealousy is not to worry about it. Most children experience some jealousy at one time or another; if no one pays much attention to it, they generally get over it on their own.

JEALOUSY OF A NEW BABY

Much has been written about the jealousy of the "dethroned" oldest child. At first, the explanation goes, he is an only child, enjoying the exclusive attention of his parents. Then suddenly he's ousted from this special position by a small intruder; as an inevitable result, he feels jealous. Of course, many older children do indeed experience such feelings toward a new baby; but we needn't assume that this is necessarily true for all children.

Signs of jealousy, if they do appear, are normal and are no cause for alarm. But it is a mistake to be constantly on the alert looking for them, and going to special lengths to appease the older child's jealousy — such as giving in to his demands while holding the baby, or hurriedly putting the baby down whenever the older child seeks attention; this strongly encourages further demands from the older child. Don't hesitate to freely show affection for your new baby, and don't feel you must give your older child a hug too every time you give the baby one. The important thing is to continue to show the older child liberal amounts of affection, just as you did before the baby's arrival. In addition, as you tend to your new infant, occasionally remind the older child that he too once received the same care. Children love to be told, "When you were a baby, I (fed, diapered) you just like this" — it lets them vicariously experience being a baby again.

Sometimes a little story can help the older child over his jealousy. One mother relates how this worked for her youngster:

> My 3-year-old Dovi was showing obvious signs of jealousy because of the special attention being given his new baby brother. Thinking over how I might help him better to understand why he no longer needed such attention, I decided that the best way would be with a story. I sat him down next to me on the bed and with my arm around him, began: "Once upon a time there was a little baby called Dovi." I went on to describe the trip to the hospital when he was born, and so on. Then I continued: "When he came home from the hospital with his mother, he couldn't do anything by himself! His mother had to do everything for him. She had to diaper him,

bathe him, feed him, dress him. And then Dovi started to grow. He learned to crawl, and now he could get to some things by himself. But his mother still needed to do everything for him. And then he learned to sit and he could eat by himself. Then he learned to walk, and he learned to talk, and he grew and grew until he could do almost everything by himself! He could dress himself, he could take a bath by himself, he could even open up the refrigerator and help himself to what he wanted."

At this point I stopped my story and said, "And now, Dovi, you are such a big boy and so independent that you can do more and more things by yourself. But this new baby that we have can't do anything by himself! He can't help himself to food from the refrigerator, he can't go outside and play by himself or draw pretty pictures. So I have to do everything for him. You see, he's not big like you, so in the meantime he needs lots of special attention. Maybe you could even help me sometimes — you could bring me his diaper, or put his pacifier in his mouth, or pat him on the back to get him to burp. Wouldn't that be nice?"

When I finished, Dovi seemed so pleased with himself. Now he often comes and tells me proudly about all the things he is able to do, and appears, on the whole, to be a lot less jealous.

There's a tendency for relatives and friends to shower all their attention on a new baby, leaving the older child out in the cold. Visitors who come to the house head straight toward the baby; in the street, friends and acquaintances peer into the carriage to admire the newcomer. If you notice that all the attention is causing jealousy, you might try, at times, to divert some of it to the older child. After the initial admiring of your new baby, you can call attention to something nice which your older child did. For example, you can say something like, "You know, Sari put her toys away all by herself today!" Or, you can focus attention on her in some other way.

You can help your older child develop a positive attitude toward the baby by giving him plenty of opportunities to help with his care, praising him liberally for any help. Children naturally sense a new baby's helplessness, and it makes them feel protective and anxious to do things for him. Your older child can fetch a bottle or a diaper, or even help with feeding or dressing the baby. When he asks to hold the baby, you can seat him on a carpeted floor to ensure safety.

Fortunately for everyone, new babies sleep much of the time in their early months and, except for purely physical care, don't require our attention. Thus we can give most of it to the older child, helping him gradually get used to sharing it with the baby.

On the other hand, there's bound to be less time for the next older child and any other siblings. Some mothers feel apologetic about this and, concerned about possible jealousy, try to compensate the older children, wearing themselves thin in the process. Far better to put such concerns out of your mind, try to be accepting of the situation and expect that the children will be accepting too.

If your older child is to be moved to a big bed to make room for the baby, do this several months in advance; otherwise your older child may come to resent the baby for pushing him out of his place. Also, if he is to go to nursery school, have him start a few months beforehand so he doesn't get the feeling that he's being sent from the house because of the baby.

To prevent the older child from disturbing you while you feed the baby, have some toys nearby to keep him busy. One mother of several young children reads to the older ones during this time. Before settling down with the baby she tells them, "Get your toys and books — we have our time together now." Of course, if you have older children who are around at the time, they can be asked to occupy the little ones; you can then enjoy the luxury of being all alone with your baby.

Often a child will react to a baby's arrival by wishing that he too could be a baby again. He'll ask for a bottle or a pacifier, or revert to other outgrown behavior. Such temporary regression is no cause for alarm. You can humor the child's desire to be a baby, to a certain extent, while at the same time emphasizing to him the advantages of being grown-up. If he wants to drink from a bottle for a while, let him; he's unlikely to want it for long. He'll discover that the milk's flow is disappointingly slow, and that the bottle isn't at all the great experience he thought it would be. As for a pacifier — since prolonged use can damage the teeth, it's better to let the child have one at bedtime only. You can remove it after the child has fallen asleep, explaining to him beforehand why you are doing this.

At times, the older child may show his jealousy with suspiciously strong hugs that make the baby cry. Don't suspect him of deliberately wanting to hurt the baby; assume rather, that it's a clumsy expression of affection. Thus, rather than calling out sharply, "You're hurting the baby!" tell him quietly, "Hug the baby gently." You can explain: "You're so big and strong; you don't realize when you hug the baby that it hurts — that's why he cries. Let me show you how to hug him (model on child). Now let's see how gently you can hug him."

Similarly, when you notice the older child playing too roughly with the baby, take his hand in yours and say, "The baby is delicate — we have to treat him gently. If we're too rough it hurts him." Then, with your other hand, gently stroke the child's face and hand as you say, "See — this feels nice. Now let's do it to the baby." With the child's hand, softly stroke the baby on his face and hands as you say, "See — the baby likes that. It feels nice. Now you do it." After letting him do it alone, praise him for it and hug him.

Physical attacks on the baby cannot, of course, be tolerated. Remove the child immediately as you tell him quietly but firmly, "I can't let you be with the baby if you hurt him." The child should be kept in another part of the house for awhile. It's important not to scold or shame him, as this may well heighten any existing feelings of hostility toward the baby, as this mother learned:

> My mischievous 3-year-old son was at it again. But this time when he hit his baby sister, I tried a different tactic. Instead of raising my voice and exclaiming, "Why did you hit her?!" I said gently, with empathy, "You're hurting her."
> He responded by kissing his sister! I couldn't believe it!

In extreme cases, it can sometimes help to let the jealous child know that you understand his feelings. For example, "I know it's hard for you now that I'm spending so much time with the baby."

JEALOUSY BETWEEN OLDER CHILDREN

Obviously, conspicuous playing of favorites by parents, especially between children close in age, can be harmful. The Talmud points out the dire outcome of Jacob's singling out Joseph for preferential treatment:

> One should never treat one child differently from the others, since for a weight of two *sela'im* of wool that Jacob gave to his son Joseph more than to his other sons, the brothers envied him — and as a result, our forefathers were forced to go down to Egypt.[1]

There's always bound to be some jealousy, but parents can keep it to a minimum by avoiding comparisons between siblings. Never say to a child, "Why can't you be like your brother (sister)?" Try not to praise one child or extol his achievements in front of the others when there's reason to believe that it could create jealousy. When a child is jealous of a more clever or gifted sibling, don't try to talk him out of his feelings by saying for example, "Never mind if you're not so smart — you're good at sports." Rather, show understanding — "I know — you wish you could get high marks like your sister." From here you might go on to remind the child of some special abilities *he* has. It's also well to look for opportunities to praise the jealous youngster for those things he excels in.

We can teach older children that jealousy is a bad character trait. It causes harm to others, but most of all to the jealous person himself. We can stress that though jealousy seems outer directed, it actually causes unhappiness, mainly for the jealous person himself — as he needlessly torments himself with longing for others' possessions or talents.

Frequently, a younger girl will be jealous of an older sister, who always gets the new clothes while she has to wear her hand-me-downs. The problem can sometimes be solved by taking *both* children shopping for new clothing (for the older one), and buying only those clothes which meet with the approval of both. This suggestion was submitted by a mother who got the idea when her younger daughter exclaimed in delight over her older sister's new dress, "Oh, how beautiful! You mean *I* get to wear that next?"

A younger child may envy an older one's privileges — such as a later bedtime. An empathic response such as, "I know, but your bedtime is now," usually avoids arguments and helps the child accept the situation.

At the same time, we must realize that it's neither feasible nor desirable to strive to treat all our children with complete equality. We should keep this in mind when a child accuses us of favoring a sibling. For example, 8-year-old Aderet gets a new knapsack because hers is worn out. Her older sister Miriam complains, "It's not fair! She doesn't take care of her knapsack and gets a new one, and I don't get one!" Resist the temptation of trying to reason with Miriam. Instead, show empathy. Rather than answering, "But look! Yours is in perfectly good condition — you don't need a new one!" you might commiserate with her: "I know, you'd like to have a new one too. But look, honey, you don't really need one." Surprisingly, such an answer is usually enough to help children get over their unhappiness and be accepting of the situation. Sometimes you might simply respond, with a friendly smile, "That's how it is." Certainly never tell a child, "You don't have to have everything he has!" This only makes him more unhappy and does nothing to reduce his jealousy. It's also best to avoid trying to balance things out — for instance, it wouldn't be a good idea to promise Miriam a new pencil case.

Remember, the child cries "unfair!" in the hope that it will weaken our stand, enabling him to get what he wants. Don't let him draw you into a defense of your position. Don't try to prove that you really are fair. And be sure not to let yourself become angry over the unfairness of *his* accusations!

All this isn't to say that a child's complaints are never justified. If, after thinking things over, you decide that they are, do your best to rectify the situation. But even then your response to the child must be without guilt or apology. Whether he's justified in his complaint or not, your answer need consist of no more than a gentle "We try our best to treat all of you fairly."

A child will sometimes accuse the parent of loving another child more. Criticism such as, "Why are you so jealous?" only reinforces the jealousy. Attempts to reassure the child by telling him, "You have no reason to be jealous — you know that we love all our children equally," generally aren't helpful either. An empathic response is best. Listen attentively, responding initially by reflecting his feelings: "You seem to feel that I love your brother (sister) more than you. Let me tell you something. I have a big heart with room for love for every one of you. I love each and every one of my children."

Just as we can't hope to treat all our children with complete equality, so is it virtually impossible, much as we might wish, to love them exactly the same at all times. It may be painful to recognize this, but we might as well face it — some children are just easier to love. We readily feel affection for the agreeably behaved child, or for the youngster with a friendly and outgoing nature. We shouldn't react with guilt if we find that we have trouble feeling affection for a particularly difficult child. Rather, we should see it as a challenge to truly love this child as well.

> My 3-year-old Aviva was born after our two boys. I guess my hopes were a bit too high — I pictured her spending quiet afternoons coloring and then helping me fold laundry.
>
> Aviva developed into a nag. I hoped the "terrible twos" would end on her third birthday, but things only got more difficult. I often told her to do something once, twice, and then resorted to either yelling, forcing or threatening. Obviously, this method was not working since she still refused to listen to me. I found myself responding differently to her than I did with my other children. It wasn't easy to love her, and I kept dwelling on that.
>
> My workshop counselor encouraged me to work on changing this inner convinction that I couldn't love my daughter. I should realize that I can be fond of her. It was important to avoid giving her negative responses (which is what she was getting pretty often). Instead, I should try to give Aviva a steady flow of love.
>
> I accepted the fact that I could love this child and reminded myself that she had good traits too. I tried to give her encouragement without being lavish. When she didn't do what she was told, I repeated my request over and over

again, but in a calm, quiet voice. It worked! But that wasn't the best part. My greatest reward was that by trying to become fond of Aviva, I really began to enjoy her!

Problems at Mealtime

Mealtimes are frequently the setting for a chorus of "It's not fair!" and "She got more than me!" Don't upset yourself by thinking how awful it is that your children display such bad character traits; try, instead, to see it all as a little funny. Refrain from responses such as, "Oh stop it, it doesn't matter!" Instead you might answer in a humorous vein, "So you don't want yours?"

Later, you can have a talk with the children. You might start by saying, "Suppose you're sitting alone at the table and you get a piece of cake. Would you be happy?" The children will no doubt answer yes. "Now suppose someone else is at the table and he also got cake, and you notice that his piece is bigger. Would you still be happy? No? Suddenly you're unhappy with the same piece of cake that you were so happy with before! Tell me, what would you have to do so you'd be happy again?" Someone is likely to give the logical answer; if not, you give it: "Just don't look at the other person's piece to see if it's bigger. You see, then you're happy."

In the future, when there's complaining again, you need only remind the children, "Remember what we said about not looking to see if someone else got more?"

Sometimes a simple response, such as the following, does the trick: "Would you like some more? Then ask! But not by telling me *he* got more."

Another method was presented by a mother who found that it put a quick end to her children's complaining. When they carried on about someone getting more, she simply told them, "Whoever complains, I'll take some away."

Here's a humorous adaptation of this method, as related by another mother:

I was cutting and giving out pieces of cake to the children, when one child began complaining that his piece was the smallest. I decided to show them, in a funny way, how trivial the whole thing was. I said, "Yes, I see the others all got more. I guess I'd better even up the portions." With that I began running madly around the table, cutting off small amounts here and there, repeatedly commenting "No, this piece is still bigger." In the end, I had one plate piled high with tiny bits of cake, while on the children's plates practically nothing was left of their original pieces. We all had a good laugh over it. Since then the kids think twice before voicing complaints about the size of a serving!

Another mother tried this:

My 9-year-old and my 6-year-old were forever comparing their pieces of cake, drinks, etc. Of course, since they never got exactly the same portions, the child with the "smaller" portion was always quick to point out that the other child got more. One day, I decided to show them just how trivial this was. I evened out the juice I had just served, pouring the extra drops into a third cup. When they were at last satisfied that their portions were equal, I very calmly said, "Look, kids, I want to show you what all this fighting was about." I held up this third cup containing the tiny amount of excess juice. Both children looked embarrassed. From time to time I have to remind them just how insignificant the difference is. That stops the comparing immediately.

If children are screaming all at once — "I want first!" "Give me first!" "It's not fair that he always gets first!" — simply ignore their carryings on and refuse to give out any food until there's quiet.

Chapter Twelve

FIGHTING

We don't like to see our children fighting with each other. As the Psalmist describes it: "How good and pleasant it is when siblings dwell together in harmony."[1] Yet, inevitably, children will fight; most commonly because of competition, jealousy, or disputes over the possession of some object or about who must do a particular chore.

The dynamics of a fight are fairly simple. One child does or says something which the other regards as objectionable. The second child then responds with verbal or physical abuse, the first child escalates the hostilities with further responses, and so on.

Parents differ in their reactions to fighting. Some try to settle their children's fights for them by playing judge. After a lengthy investigation, they decide who's right and who's wrong. Mr. Wrong then gets scolded or punished. What happens then? Mr. Right says to himself, "Hah hah! He got it! Mommy says he's wrong!" And Mr. Wrong ends up angry, both at his mother and at Mr. Right, thus setting the scene for the next battle! This approach also greatly encourages children to involve the parents in their fights, with each child trying to get the parent to side with him.

Some parents react by preaching to their children. "You're the older one — you should know better!" or "You children should love each other and not fight." However, such words are usually wasted. Children who fight are angry and in no mood for sermons.

Another way of handling fighting, generally not too effective, is to send back messages when one of the quarreling children comes to complain:

DANNY: Tzvi won't let me play with the fire truck!
MOTHER: Tell him he has to let you play with it.

RINA: Mommy, Shoshy hit me!
MOTHER: Tell her that's not nice.

Or, the parent may go in to personally reprimand the offending party. For instance, 7-year-old Shifra comes to tell Mother that 5-year-old Yoni won't let her write and keeps pulling away her pencil and paper. Mother goes in to take Yoni to task: "Stop bothering your sister — do you hear?" One problem with this approach is that while Yoni really may be bothering Shifra, you never know whether Shifra, the "victim," may not have first provoked the aggressive behavior she complains of, perhaps in order to attain the satisfaction of seeing Yoni "get it" while she glories in her innocence. Also children have old scores to settle; Yoni may well be getting back at Shifra for something she did to him the day before.

But victims aren't always treated with kid gloves either. They may be told, when they come to complain, "He wouldn't hit you for nothing. Come on — what did you do to him?" Unfortunately, the child thus accused feels bitter and is likely to go back to try to settle the score on his own.

Sometimes parents attempt arbitration. For example, they'll try to persuade one child that the other didn't intend to be mean or to hurt him. But the victim of abuse is usually left unconvinced and parents often end up in an unpleasant argument. Attempts to make peace *during* a fight are especially unlikely to work.

At times, when they feel they can't take it anymore — when it seems like they've heard nothing all day but "He hit me!" "No, she started it!" "He took my toy away!" "Mommy, she called me a pest!" — the parents' exasperation gives way to anger and screaming: "I can't stand another minute of this dreadful fighting! Stop it now — do you hear?!" Often they'll end up spanking both children, yelling, "I don't care who started — you're both getting it!" Such reactions of anger and violence may make the parents feel better for the moment, but they hardly encourage the peaceful resolution of conflict which the parents want their children to learn.

STAYING CALM

To handle this problem effectively, first resolve not to become aggravated over the fighting, nor to let it make you angry. As fervently as you want peace, you had better accept the fact that for the time being at least, there's going to be fighting: an unfortunate reality, certainly unpleasant, but not "horrible" or "unbearable."

Avoid blaming or judging your children ("Why is he so mean to her!" "Why can't she let her have the toy!"), even if it's only in your thoughts. Think in terms of how best to influence your children to get along better with each other. This calls for an objective and non-judgmental attitude.

Avoid also blaming yourself for your children's fighting ("What am *I* doing wrong that they fight so much?"). The assumption here seems to be that if you did everything right, your children would never fight. Realize that, even were you to do everything perfectly, your children would still probably fight. Squabbling and quarreling between children is so normal that there's practically no family that's free of it.

When you no longer see yourself as personally responsible for your children's fights, when you stop viewing each conflict as something you should have prevented, you'll find yourself much better able to stay calm enough to handle the problem.

While an unusual amount of fighting may be cause for concern, dwelling on thoughts such as, "When will they ever learn to get along?" and, "How will I be able to continue coping if this keeps up?" will only make you anxious; so try to put such thoughts out of your mind completely.

STAYING OUT OF FIGHTS

Next, difficult as this may be, learn to refrain as much as possible from interfering to settle your children's fights. True, it is your responsibility to teach your children not to fight; but this cannot be accomplished by intervening while any fighting is going on. Find another time for working out with your children ways and means of settling their difficulties peacefully.

But couldn't one child take unfair advantage of another child, when we remove ourselves in this way? Perhaps. But we haven't a hope of supervising matters to everyone's satisfaction so as to make everything always completely fair; we might as well give up such unrealistic efforts.

In the case of a bigger child actually persecuting a smaller child, we must interfere, for both their sakes, and teach our children that persecution of the weak won't be tolerated. But otherwise we should exercise self-control, and not interfere in normal sibling squabbles and tussles. We have to keep in mind that we can't always be around to protect our children from life's give and take. Sooner or later, they're bound to meet up with unfairness and unkindness; exposure to rough and tumble treatment may be necessary and valuable if they are to learn to tolerate life's difficulties.

If until now you've tried to settle your children's fights for them, explain that from now on you'll no longer interfere because you want them to learn to resolve their own conflicts. Now when you hear the usual agitated voices, resist the urge to run in to see what happened. Instead, calmly go about your business as usual. (How often we've dashed in frantically, only to discover that those ear-piercing screams were nothing more than acts which the child put on for our benefit — just to get us to come running, and, at the same time, powerfully impress us with how horribly he was being treated so as to get our protection as the victim!)

For instance, when one child comes to complain, "It's not fair — he's always starting up!" or when another runs in crying, "She called me stupid and said she'd tell her friends not to play with me!" tell him, "I'm really sorry that you're fighting. See if you can find a peaceful way to settle it by yourselves," or, "I have confidence that you can settle this quietly." The children must not conclude that you've suddenly become indifferent to their fighting. Convey to them that, quite the contrary, you care very much; but for the good of all you no longer mix in. Avoid responses such as, "I'm not getting into this — you kids have to settle it by yourselves," as these sound uncaring. If a child does complain that you don't seem to care, you can answer, "I do care, but right now it's better that you try to settle matters between yourselves. We'll talk about it some more later."

Children often come crying because they got "hurt" by a sibling, when you can see that nothing much really happened. Here too, it would be unfeeling to send the child away with, "See if you can settle this peacefully between yourselves." Though it's best not to intervene, you can nevertheless show some mild empathy. Avoid making light of the child's pain, telling him that he wasn't really hurt; this may be true, but the child will invariably interpret it as taking sides. This is especially important in cases of everyday minor skirmishes. For example, your daughter suddenly lets out a shriek because her brother accidentally bumped into her. Resist the temptation to say, "What are you screaming about — he didn't do anything." Instead you might say, exaggerating slightly, "Oh! — it looks like you got a bit banged up there. Do you want to show me where it hurts?" Your daughter is likely to get the hint and quiet down quickly.

Parents usually experience a great sense of relief when they no longer feel responsible for resolving their children's conflicts. Don't expect any sudden decrease in the incidence of fighting, but you may find that your children actually begin to settle these conflicts by themselves. Here are several examples:

I was a bit skeptical when our parenting group leader advised us not to mix in when the children fight. But the incident that followed proved to me that she was right. I was lying in my bed hearing my Rivka and Leah, ages 6 and 7, having a fight over a doll. Leah, the older one, was saying nasty words to Rivka. From my bed I listened and got upset, feeling that Leah was wrong and thinking: I have to teach them to be fair and talk nicely to each other. Their words grew louder and I grew angrier. The only thing that stopped me from yelling from my bed was the fact that the baby was sleeping right next to me. Then Leah hit Rivka, and Rivka started crying. I was ready to jump out of my bed but hesitated for a minute, reminding myself that it was better not to interfere. It turned out that my wait- ing was worthwhile. Hearing her younger sister crying, Leah felt guilty and changed her attitude. She said, "I'm sorry," to Rivka, gave her back the doll they were fighting over, and behaved just as I'd wanted to teach her to behave!

My 4-year-old was coloring with her markers. She warned her 3-year-old brother not to touch them, threatening that if he did, she would write on him. He ignored her, and as he reached for the markers, she wrote on his arm. My 3-year-old turned to me for help. When he saw that I wasn't getting involved, he got himself a stool and washed his arm off all on his own.

My teenage daughters Tova and Debby were supposed to be doing the laundry — but were quarreling instead. I decided to try the approach of not interfering. "Girls, can you manage to work this out between yourselves?" I asked. "But I'm doing all the work and Debby is just fooling around!" Tova, the younger one, countered. I turned to Debby and repeated myself, "Girls, do you think you can work this out on your own?" I then left. I was wondering what would happen. Would they stop arguing? Would they do the laundry? A few minutes later I couldn't believe what I heard. Both girls were singing as they worked together!

Fights tend also to resolve themselves more quickly when we stay out. One mother related her experience:

When I manage to keep myself from interfering in the chil- dren's fights, I find that, although there may not be fewer fights, still, the fights blow over more quickly. But most importantly, I have not become involved, upset, angry, and so on. I am not worn out as I tend to be when I do step in and then matters just go on and on.

Still another mother reported a definite decrease in fighting, once she'd learned to stop interfering:

I was constantly playing "judge" with my children, who fought a great deal of the time. Now I have learned to "bow out" of the fights, saying, "I'm really sorry you're having a problem — please try to settle it by yourselves." I find that the fighting has decreased a lot.

If you view your children's fighting as a never-ending affair, you might try to keep track for one day of the actual number and duration of fights. You may be surprised to find that total fighting time is far below what you'd supposed. One mother who'd complained about the "constant" squabbling between her two girls was amazed to find, when she kept a record, that there were only five brief incidents during the day, each lasting no longer than two minutes! Fighting certainly becomes easier to tolerate when we gain a truer picture of its extent.

Of course, if we have a longtime habit of settling our children's conflicts for them, we may not be able to give this up so quickly. Sometimes, exasperation gets the better of us; at other times we aren't strong enough to resist our children, who give us no peace until we settle some quarrel. Staying out of fights is no easy matter. Certainly we shouldn't be upset with ourselves if, in spite of a firm resolve not to intervene, we nevertheless find ourselves getting involved anyway.

WHEN TO INTERVENE

While it's strongly recommended that parents allow children to work out their differences by themselves, this doesn't have to become a hard-and-fast rule. For example, your 6-year-old son sits down on his younger brother's bed while he's trying to rest and starts kicking him. You might quietly take the older boy away as you say to him, "I don't think he likes being kicked that way." Or, two children are hurling insults at each other. You can tell them firmly,

"No name calling — we're not allowed to hurt other people's feelings." When a child comes to ask for help in settling some dispute, you can sometimes offer suggestions such as, "Have you tried saying it nicely?" or ask him, "What do you think you could do?"

Giving choices can sometimes be a good way to stop a fight, as the following little incident shows:

> My daughters Channa and Devora, ages 6 and 7½, were fighting over who would sit next to a friend who was their guest for the Shabbos meal. I said to them, "You can choose — either the two of you settle this between yourselves or you will have to leave the room." Just then my husband began to recite the Kiddush. I waited until he was finished. No sooner did the girls drink their wine than Devora, the older one, suddenly said, "Channa can have the place."

There are times, such as on *Erev Yom Tov*, when tension from being especially busy makes it particularly difficult to tolerate fighting. For example, one child begins to tease the other, quickly running away, and the other one then chases him all over the house trying to catch him. In this case it might be best to simply have the youngsters go into separate rooms for awhile.

Forcing children to share toys and possessions isn't a good idea, but at times we can help them work out a fair system. For example, when one child comes to complain about another who won't share a toy, we might ask, "How long does each of you want to have it?" and then suggest that the schedule be written down and posted somewhere in the room.

It's difficult to ignore squabbling when it goes on right under your nose. In this case, the best thing to do is to quickly leave the scene and busy yourself elsewhere. Alternatively, you can ask the quarreling children to leave the room. For example, say, "Kids, please settle this elsewhere." The children may first be given a choice: "Please, either stop the quarreling or leave the room."

Physical Aggression

You can decide to ignore children who are hitting or kicking in their room, intervening to separate them only when the fighting gets rough. In that case, say to them, "I can't let you hurt each other like this; I must separate you." Then put each child in a separate room for a cooling-off period. However, you shouldn't ignore any attacks that take place in your presence (not intervening is tantamount to conveying that this is acceptable behavior). Common sense also dictates that you intervene to protect babies from any onslaughts by an older child. A toddler or young child who attacks a baby shouldn't be scolded but rather removed from the scene as you tell him quietly, "I can't let you hurt the baby."

On the other hand, there are parents who feel that since it is wrong to hit, children must never be permitted to do so. Thus whenever there is any physical aggression — even if the parents didn't see it — the children are told, "You're not allowed to hit (kick, bite, scratch, pull hair)." If they still don't stop, they are separated. This doesn't mean, though, that you must intervene every time a child comes to tell you, "(So and so) hit me!" If you didn't see exactly what happened, it might be best to respond simply, "I'm sorry — I'll talk to him about it later."

Try to be empathic when talking to children about hitting. A statement such as, "I know it was hard for you to control yourself but you're not allowed to hit him (her)," shows understanding, and at the same time conveys that there are limits to acceptable behavior. A child who hits a lot because "the others make me angry" can be told, "The next time someone makes you angry, don't hit. Come and tell me about it instead."

As for biting, children will often sink their teeth into another child's arm without actually biting down. It doesn't hurt, but the other child comes to you to complain anyway. If you don't see tooth marks, you can be pretty sure that nothing much happened. The same goes for scratching. You can examine the child's arm as you say, "Hmm — it doesn't look too bad, but you can tell your brother (sister) that nails aren't for hurting people." However, if you see bad tooth marks or nail marks on anyone's arm, you should strongly reprimand the child who's responsible for them.

Don't try to teach a child not to bite, kick, or scratch by doing it to him to show him what it feels like. This sets a poor example for the child, and even if done for educational purposes, is likely only to cause resentment. A better approach is to tell the biting child, calmly, "The next time you bite, I'll have to tape your mouth closed." If he then bites again, cover his mouth with a piece of cloth tape one and a half inches wide. Don't leave it on too long — a minute or two will do. For a very young child, it's enough simply to hold his lips closed for a short time.

Scratching can be handled by cutting the child's nails very short, telling him matter-of-factly, "I'm cutting your nails very short so you won't be able to scratch." If he carries on, tell him, "I'm sorry if it hurts you, but I can't let you scratch."

Teach children not to kick by taking their shoes off whenever they do it.

Fighting in Public and With Friends

Fighting in public generally cannot be ignored. If your children begin to fight while on a bus, in a store, or in some other public place, warn them that if they don't stop they'll be punished later at home. (Since the punishment is conditional, this doesn't contradict the restriction against deferred punishment mentioned in Chapter 5.) Or you can use logical consequences. For example, anyone who fights while the family is visiting with relatives stays home on the next visit. Another example: If the children quarrel on the bus while you're taking them to buy new shoes, you give them a choice, "Either stop quarreling or we go back home without the new shoes." If they start to fight in a store take them out and tell them, "Kids, I can't let you disturb the other shoppers this way. Either you keep quiet in the store, or you'll have to stay outside." Of course, you must be prepared to follow through.

Before any trip it is a good idea to discuss with your children appropriate behavior. Concerning window seats or sitting next to Mommy or Daddy, you can suggest that they might switch places in the middle of the trip so that everyone gets a turn at these favorite seats.

Fighting during a car trip is easily handled: Pull the car over and refuse to continue until the fighting stops.

When children fight with friends, do your best to stay out of it. Avoid discussions about the fight with the other child's parents, and don't try to defend your child or blame the other child.

When small children have friends come to play, there's often considerable fighting over toys. It's best not to interfere; but you can go in to comfort any child who becomes upset. If the playing get too rough, send the visitor home.

In the park, let your toddler work out his problems with the other children by himself. If he grabs toys away from the other children and then gets hit, it may teach him not to grab toys. But you should definitely intervene if he's getting hurt, or if he's too rough with another child. A good way to stop an attack is simply to tell the aggressor, "Hey — that hurts him!"

If your child is constantly being hit by another youngster, it might be advisable to have a talk with the child's parents about the problem. Most parents will be apologetic for their child's behavior and try to cooperate, but there are those who always will take their child's side — to the point of indignation at the very idea that he ever does anything wrong. Sometimes it can help to teach your child to ward off attacks (see discussion on hitting in the next section); but often, the best solution is to have him leave the scene and come home when aggression begins.

Mothers often find their visits to friends' homes spoiled by constant fighting between their respective children. Try to ignore minor squabbles, but whenever the warfare seems to be getting out of hand you'll have to intervene, or cut your visit short.

Fighting at Mealtimes

Fighting during meals shouldn't be tolerated; it disturbs the peace of the entire family. The quarreling children should be told, "We can't enjoy our food when there's this disturbance at the table. You have a choice to behave pleasantly or to leave the table." If the children leave and then return to the table and behave well, remember to praise them: "How nice and pleasant it is at the table now!"

Fights Over Toys

With very young children, physical aggression is rarely a serious problem; the swatting, punching, and screeching that go on generally involve disputes over toys. But even very young children can be told that they're not allowed to hurt others, either physically or by saying things that make others feel bad. Three-year-olds can begin to be encouraged to share. Suggest, "It's nice to share our things with others," and praise the child when he does — "How nice the way you're sharing your new truck!" If a child is monopolizing a toy, don't try to make him share it but gently suggest, "Why don't you give him a turn? I'm sure he'd like one." When one child comes to complain about another's unwillingness to share, tell him, "I guess he wants to have it to himself for a while. Why don't you wait until he's ready to share?"

TORAH LAWS ABOUT FIGHTING

Even 5-year-olds understand enough so that you can begin to have individual talks with them about fighting — after tempers have cooled and the children are ready to listen. In addition to helping them work out more peaceful solutions to differences, remind your children about the Torah commandments and prohibitions which relate to fighting. Your words will carry more weight if you read the laws together with them from the original Hebrew. For those who prefer English, *Love Your Neighbor* by Rabbi Zelig Pliskin is a good source.

The following is a brief summary of these laws.

1. *Hitting*: Children should be taught that hitting others is not allowed. Even merely raising a hand to strike another person is forbidden.[2] But if someone raises his hand to strike us, or is actually hitting us, we may hit him to prevent him from hurting us. It's wrong to hit back in retribution.[3] Since most children find it very hard not to hit back, you might suggest that they can avoid the problem by following this advice: "When you see a hit coming, walk away."

If your child asks why *you're* allowed to hit *him*, explain that parents are allowed to hit their child to improve his behavior.[4]

2. *Causing pain with words or action*: Parents should teach their children that it is forbidden to do anything which causes another person to suffer.[5] Thus we must not insult others or call them by derogatory names;[6] this is forbidden even if the other person doesn't mind because he's gotten used to the name.[7] Neither may we speak to others in a harsh or critical manner, embarrass, tease, or

annoy them; this includes pestering behavior. Children should be taught the rule of Hillel the Sage: "What is hateful to you, do not do to your fellow."[8] Have them picture themselves in the other person's position — "Suppose you were Benny and someone said (did) that to you — how would you feel?" But remember always to say this gently.

3. *Lashon hara* (derogatory speech): Children often come to us complaining bitterly about the way a sibling or friend treated them. We have to point out that, difficult as it is to avoid, relating bad things about others constitutes *lashon hara* and is forbidden unless it serves some constructive purpose, such as in a situation where action must be taken.[9] It's best to tell the child, "I know you're very angry at (so and so) but you're not allowed to tell me any bad things about other people."

If a child complains about his sister because he wants you to admonish her, explain that he should first try to admonish her privately himself, and that only if that doesn't help, or if he's certain she won't listen, is he allowed to tell you.[10]

Since it's forbidden to accept as definitely true any derogatory report about another person,[11] tell the child, "Thank you for calling this to my attention. I'll talk to your sister about this some time." Later you can explain to him why you don't automatically accept what he says.

But what about the injunction of "not placing a stumbling block before the blind," according to which it is forbidden to encourage someone to speak *lashon hara?* Doesn't this pose a problem for parents? By listening to *lashon hara* related to us by our child, we're encouraging him to speak it. On the other hand, it's important to show our children understanding when they're upset — if we tell the child, "Be quiet — don't speak *lashon hara*," when he's angry at a sibling or friend, he'll feel that we're unsympathetic and uncaring. However, it is permitted to listen to *lashon hara* for the purpose of calming the speaker by giving him the opportunity to express his feelings.[12] Thus we may hear our child out, with the expectation that we'll be able to soothe his anger. Still, we can encourage our children, when they want to tell us about verbal or physical abuse by other children, to refrain from mentioning names — thus removing the derogatory information from the category of *lashon hara*.

A child who has learned that *lashon hara* is forbidden may wonder how we allow this. He may also have guilt feelings because he knows that what he's doing is wrong. Therefore, it's important to explain that if we listen, it's only in order to help him get over his anger.

4. *Holding a grudge or seeking revenge*: Children should be taught that no matter how badly someone has wronged or insulted us, we shouldn't take revenge or hold a grudge against him.[13] Just as God forgives us when we do wrong, so should we forgive others who have mistreated us.

The story of Joseph and his brothers can be cited as an outstanding illustration of true forgiveness.

5. *Judging charitably*: We should teach our children to fulfill the Torah obligation to judge others charitably, and to always try to see the good in others.[14] We can explain, "You know, we have to love everyone, and always judge their actions favorably no matter what they do. Sometimes it's hard — a person is mean to us and we think he's bad and get angry at him. But that's wrong. It helps us to judge another person charitably if we see him as someone who hasn't yet learned to behave better. Maybe it's hard for him to control himself, or maybe he just had a rough day." Even very young children can learn to think this way.

6. *The mitzvah of admonishment*: Children should be taught that we're not to feel hatred toward someone who has treated us badly. We have an obligation to tell him how we feel, but we must do it quietly and pleasantly.[15] If we yell at the other person, we offend him and are then ourselves guilty of wrongdoing. We must not judge another person for his wrong actions,[16] but should only point them out to him[17] — not while he's angry but when he's calmed down. We must then give him a chance to explain, and if he says he's sorry we must forgive him.

Also, because there's a special obligation of "not saying that which won't be heeded," there is no mitzvah to admonish if we're sure that the other person won't listen.[18]

7. *Asking for forgiveness*: Children should be taught that asking forgiveness of those we've hurt is part of doing *teshuvah*.[19] We can encourage this by suggesting to a child, when we see that a fight has left hard feelings, "He feels bad. Go tell him you're sorry."

SIBLING RIVALRY

Fights often start between siblings because one is trying to show that he's better than the other — by deriding his work, or denigrating his ability. Explain to the child that whatever talents and abilities a person has come from God. Rather than seeing ourselves as better people because of these endowments, we should be quietly thankful that we've been thus blessed.

Often an oldest child insists that because he's the oldest, all the others must do as he says. He bosses them around, sometimes harshly criticizing them, so that they become resentful and noncompliant. Gently explain to him that if he wants the others to listen to him, he must treat them with respect and speak to them in a way which doesn't hurt their feelings; then they will be much more disposed to respect and listen to him. As the Sages teach: "Who receives honor? He who honors others."[20] You can ask him to put himself in the others' position — how would *he* want an older brother or sister to speak to him? Then you might review an incident with the child, perhaps doing some role playing. For example, you can ask, "How could you have said that so he'd have really listened to you?"

HELPING CHILDREN DEVELOP GREATER TOLERANCE

The main reason for children's fights is their exaggerated negative evaluation of the other child's behavior. Try to help them see this. You might tell a child, "You see, when you think to yourself how *awful* what the other person did is, or when you tell yourself that it's *terrible* when he doesn't do what you want, what happens? You get angry and then there's a fight. So, what could you tell yourself so you wouldn't get so angry?" Try to elicit answers such as, "I could think that it's not so awful if he doesn't do what I want him to do" or, "I could tell myself that what he did to me wasn't really so bad." Sometimes, discussions with the child about "really terrible" experiences can help him develop a better perspective. You can also encourage greater tolerance by asking, "I know it's not easy, but do you think you can learn to tolerate it when he acts that way?"

Many fights develop because of the child's perception of something as unfair. Of course, what the child calls "unfair" is usually what *he* doesn't happen to like. Empathize with him at first, but then help him pinpoint the true reason for his distress — his demand that things always be fair. For example, if he comes to complain, "It's not fair! I had the ball and he just grabbed it from me!" first respond, "I'm so sorry." Then go on to point out, softly, "Honey, maybe if you didn't insist that everything has to be fair, you wouldn't feel so bad. You see, whenever we say, 'This isn't fair!' we get ourselves upset. It's much better for us if we can just learn to accept it." At another time, you might start a discussion about fairness: Can everything in life be the way we want it to be? And what trouble can it cause us if we insist on it anyway?

Older children sometimes display intolerance toward younger siblings who try to copy everything they do, or bother them with silly questions. Rather than telling the older child, "Don't you understand? He's just a little child — you shouldn't let it bother you," respond, "He looks up to you so much — he thinks you know everything! So he asks you whatever he wants to know. And he wants to be just like you — so he copies everything you do. It's really an honor for you. Try to see it that way."

Try at times to show your children how we spoil the present by continuing to mull over some unpleasant event in the past. Ask, gently, "How do you feel when you're upset? Not so good, right? Okay, something happened which got you upset. But it's over. If you keep on being upset over it, you're suffering twice as much. Okay — now let's find something else to do."

Helping Children Overcome Their Anger

Though most children express anger all too naturally, some "bottle up" their feelings, eventually exploding. If your child has this tendency, you need to be aware of it and help him to express his anger without damage to himself or others. At the same time, we can teach him the basic principles of cognitive psychology, along the lines described in this and other chapters. By applying these principles, he, too, can ultimately learn to cope effectively with his anger.

Because of the problem of *lashon hara*, we should encourage children whenever possible to get over any anger toward others by themselves. If this is difficult for them, then they should be urged to relate the derogatory information without revealing the other person's identity.

However, if you see that the child is very angry and complaining bitterly about the way another child treated him, it's probably better not to remind him of *lashon hara* but to hear him out, with the intention of helping him overcome his anger:

CHILD: I'm never gonna be friends with Michael again! He's a big cheater!

PARENT: I see you're really very upset. Come sit down and tell me everything that happened.

CHILD: Well, Michael had these trading cards and he told me they were very special. So I bought five cards. Then he tells me, "Ha ha, I tricked you. They're really plain cards — they're not even worth half of what you paid!" He's just a no-good cheater and I'm gonna beat him up!

PARENT: That was really very wrong of him to do, and he has to learn not to do things like that. But how can you teach him? By getting angry or hitting him? Is that going to make him stop?

CHILD: But he cheated me! He's disgusting!

PARENT: Wait a minute — he did a bad thing but that doesn't make him a bad person.

CHILD: He's a robber, that's what he is!

PARENT: Let's not call him names — let's stick to describing what he did. He took your money unfairly and that was wrong.

CHILD: I don't care — I'm gonna beat him up and tell him what I think of him!

PARENT: Then *you'll* be doing something wrong too, because we're not allowed to scream and yell at people and we're not allowed to hit.

CHILD: But I have to get back at him!

PARENT: If he deserves punishment, that's Hashem's business, not ours. But you can talk to him and tell him how you feel about what he did — not screaming or getting angry at him but just telling him — that's what we should do when people do things to us that aren't nice. Then you'll have done a mitzvah. You have to let them know that you're upset with them for what they did.

CHILD: But I'm so mad — I don't want to talk to him!

PARENT: You're mad because you're thinking what a bad person he is. Maybe if you just thought that he hasn't learned to behave better, you wouldn't feel so mad. Okay — so what could you say to him? (The child may not respond; if so, the parent can suggest some possibilities.) Well, you could say, "You really did a wrong thing and I'm upset with you about it."

Notice that no efforts were made to get the child to judge his friend favorably. An angry child is generally not receptive to such suggestions. Besides, it would have been difficult to find a favorable judgment in this situation. But we can help a child to look for mitigating circumstances which explain why another child behaved as he did; thus it was suggested to the child that he see his friend as someone who "hasn't learned to behave better."

Interestingly, modern research confirms that this is a very effective way to reduce a child's anger. In the past, it was thought beneficial to permit children to talk freely about their angry feelings, on the assumption that only in this way would they be able to get rid of the anger. Now there are experts who believe otherwise.

In one particular study with third-graders, children were frustrated and irritated by a little girl whom the experimenters had secretly enlisted in their cause:

The children were given one of three ways of "handling" their anger: Some were permitted to talk it out with the adult experimenters, some were allowed to play with toy guns for "cathartic release" or to "get even" with the frustrating child, and some were given a reasonable explanation from the adults for the child's annoying behavior. What reduced the children's anger? Not talking about it. Not playing with guns

— that made them more hostile, and aggressive as well. The most successful way of dispelling their anger was to understand why their classmate had behaved as she did (she was sleepy, upset, not feeling well).[21]

At times, a child may be so overwrought that we can't understand him. In that case it's best to say, "I'd like to hear what you're saying but I can't listen when you're talking like this."

WILLINGNESS TO FORGO

We can encourage children to be willing to forgo — that is, to let a sibling have what he wants or have his way — by pointing out that whenever they forgo in this way, they fulfill the mitzvah of doing *chesed*. Even though they may be giving something up, the good feeling that comes from doing the mitzvah of making someone else happy compensates for the sacrifice.

Even very small children are capable of experiencing such compensatory satisfaction, as we see from this account:

My 2-year-old son received a gift of two small books. His older sister of 5 wanted one and grabbed it from his hands. He began screeching. I told him the noise was hurting my ears and asked him to please talk to his sister instead of screeching. I also pleasantly reminded my daughter that it wasn't right for her to grab her brother's book from him.

My son now quieted down and with a very sad face asked his sister to give him back his book. Rather reluctantly, she handed it back. Now I turned to my son and said, "Your sister would really like to look at your book. You don't have to let her but if you do, then you will be doing a beautiful mitzvah. Do you know which one? It's the mitzvah of chesed! Hashem does chesed to us, and He wants us to do it toward each other."

His face brightening up, my son now relinquished the book and held it out to his sister. I had the impression that he felt genuinely pleased with himself, and not the least bit regretful or unhappy over his sacrifice.

Of course, children aren't always so receptive to our reminders that by forgoing, they're doing *chesed.* In such situations it's best to refrain from saying anything and quietly overlook it. Asking, "Don't you want to do the mitzvah?" is generally not helpful; it usually only causes the child to see himself as bad for not wanting to do a mitzvah.

Some parents like to use a point system to encourage forgoing. Every time the child forgoes, he tells the parent about it and gets a point. When a designated number of points have accumulated (at least five), the child is entitled to some special treat or a small prize.

You can also give points for specific acts of self-control which prevent fights. For instance, a child who starts fights by grabbing things away from others can be given a point whenever he controls himself and doesn't grab. The youngster who stirs up trouble by teasing gets points for controlling the urge to tease. Such incentives can sometimes provide the necessary motivation to make children work harder to prevent fights:

> *Suppertime was prime time for fighting among my five children, making this a difficult hour for me. Many of the fights revolved around my oldest son, Shimon, and although I had had several private conversations with him about the fighting, it hadn't helped.*
>
> *One evening as I paid particular attention to what was going on, I noticed that most of the fights occurred between Shimon and his younger sister Yael. For instance, he doesn't like very cold water but she loves it. So he takes the pitcher of cold water to the faucet and adds warmer water while she carries on. Yael, in turn, gets on his nerves with her constant teasing.*
>
> *I had an idea. That evening, after the younger children were in bed, I made the following proposal to my son: I would make a chart, and for each evening that he would do his best to avoid fights by, for example, ignoring his sister's teasing or forgetting about taking the chill out of the water, he would get a point. For each point, I would pay for development of one picture from the film in the new camera he had just received from his grandfather. The chart was to be a private matter between the two of us.*

Shimon liked the idea immediately and the next evening he earned one point. The following evening he forgot about the deal, but I reminded him later and also showed him a specific example of how he could have prevented a fight. The next evening he earned another point. By the time he had earned about 10 points, we began forgetting to keep track. But by then the fighting had substantially decreased, mostly because Yael saw that her teasing was not getting any results.

Several weeks later we received a letter from my father, asking when he could see some pictures from his grandson's new camera. That evening I told Shimon that he could take the last few pictures left on the film and that we would pay for development of the entire roll. I explained that although he had recorded only 10 points, he deserved it since he had really begun to make the effort to avoid fights, not only at suppertime but during the rest of the day too.

Sometimes one child always seems to be giving in to a more demanding sibling. If the youngster has an easy-going nature and doesn't appear to resent always being the one to give in, it's probably best not to intervene. True, the other child may be taking advantage of him, but you're unlikely to accomplish much by stepping in. The best you can do is to work to reduce the demanding child's need to have things his way, and to help him develop greater tolerance toward frustration.

But if the child who gives in resents it and comes complaining to you or, worse, finds ways to get back at the other youngster — then speak to him to help him with his problem. You can say, "It's a wonderful character trait to be willing to forgo. But not if you feel bad about it afterwards. It's nice to let others have their way, but you don't have to do it all the time. Make up your mind, before you give in, that you won't resent it afterwards, or else, it might be better not to give in to begin with."

HYPERSENSITIVITY TO INSULTS

Children must be taught that insulting others is forbidden, but they also should be taught not to take it too seriously if anyone does it to them. Some children take offense very quickly, even when only mildly insulted or ridiculed. You can ask, "How would you feel if someone said to you, 'Ha ha, you have three legs!' Would that hurt you? Of course not — because you wouldn't take it seriously. And if you didn't take it so seriously when someone makes fun of you, you wouldn't get into so many fights about it."

Easily offended children generally suffer from hypersensitivity to negative judgment by others. Help your child get over such hypersensitivity by pointing out that just as it's not his business to judge others negatively, so is it no one else's business to judge him that way. If people do so anyway, it's their mistake, and he doesn't have to feel bad. He must be careful, though, not to judge others poorly for the way they judge him. You might also tell him that our Sages view as real "heroes" those who are able to quietly bear insults. "Who suffer insults without repaying in kind, hear their shame and do not respond."[22]

A good way of handling the problem was presented by this mother:

> When one of my children comes crying that her sister called her "stupid" or "bad," I ask her quietly, "Is what she said true?" As she shakes her head I tell her, "So if it's not true, you don't have to worry about the wrong things she's saying about you." This seems to help a lot.

Another mother showed her children how the rain rolls off her raincoat. Then she said to them, "Be like my raincoat; let all the unpleasant words roll off like rain."

TEASING

Teasing is a common cause of fights. A child who teases should be quietly reminded that he's not allowed to do this since it makes others feel bad. You can influence children to stop teasing by having them put themselves in the other person's position. For instance, a younger child constantly teases her older sister for thumb-sucking. Tell her quietly, "You're teasing her about her thumb-sucking. Now tell me, you (wet your bed, are overweight). How would you feel if she teased you about that? You'd feel bad, wouldn't you? And so does your sister when you tease her about thumb-sucking."

Of course, teasing would never become much of a problem if the one subjected to it would simply ignore it. But with children who react strongly to being teased, telling them to ignore it generally doesn't help. You can teach such a child that, rather than crying and carrying on, he can talk to a sibling who persists in teasing, letting him know how he feels about it and asking him to stop. He might simply say, "I don't like it when you tease me. Please stop it." In the case of an older child whose younger sibling's teasing disturbs him during homework or other activities, you can suggest that he tell the younger child, "You're bothering me. I have a lot of work to get done. Please leave me alone." Children need to be made aware that they may have to repeat these messages several times in order to get them across. They should also be reminded that talking quietly is far more likely to get results.

Some children come crying to the parent because they were hit by a sibling, when the hitting was provoked by their own teasing. Here you might initially empathize with the child; later you can call him aside, saying gently, "You came crying because your sister hit you. But you know, I heard you teasing her before. Maybe that's why she hit you — I guess she didn't like it. So if you don't want to get hit by her again, maybe it would be better not to tease her anymore."

Sometimes it helps if you show a child how his excited reactions to being teased merely provide entertainment. "Do you know why he's teasing you? Because he likes to see you jump up and down and scream — he thinks it's funny — he enjoys it. Are you going to give him that pleasure? How about the next time he teases you, thinking to yourself, 'I'm not going to give him a good time. I'm just not going to react. I'll just ignore him.'"

Here's another way of influencing the child, used by one mother with great success:

> My 9-year-old Sammy would get very angry when teased by Itzik, his younger brother of 6. One day I said to him, "You know, you've made yourself into a puppet and you gave Itzik the strings. Every time you get angry when Itzik teases you, you're giving him the strings."

I told Sammy that this conversation would be a secret between him and me and that his brother wouldn't have to know about it. Then I said to him, "I'm going to help you to get the strings back for yourself, but I know it'll be hard for you to remember. Let's decide on a code word — whenever you get mad because Itzik is teasing you, I'll say 'strings.'" Besides helping him gain control, I think he appreciated the mutuality between us — the idea of a special relationship. I had to use the code word several times during the next few weeks — after that, very little. It really helped!

Another mother finds that humor works best for her. Once one of her children was particularly upset over being teased. She ran over, exclaiming with exaggerated anxiety, "Where's the bleeding?! Show me quick! Let's get the bandages! Shall I call an ambulance?!" The child, greatly amused, quieted down right away. After doing this a few times, he seemed to realize that being teased wasn't so bad after all and that he could survive it.

PROBLEM SOLVING AS A METHOD

In discussions with your children, you can bring up the problem of their fighting, eliciting their ideas on preventing fights. One mother reports a rather amusing but constructive talk with her two small children:

I decided to call my two sons, Chananel, age 4, and Nathan, age 5, for a little discussion about their frequent fighting. We'd had such talks before on this and other subjects. Here's how our conversation went:

ME: *Look here, Chananel and Nathan, your fighting is becoming very unpleasant for all of us. Now do you have any good ideas as to how we could solve this problem?*

CHANANEL: *I think Nathan should move to a different house — he always bothers me and doesn't play nicely.*

ME *Well, that's not a good suggestion because Nathan belongs here — this is his family and Mommy and*

	Daddy love him very much and will not have him living anywhere else.
NATHAN:	*(very seriously) Well, maybe I'll just move into the living room! I'll sleep on the couch and play here.*
ME:	*That's not good because Mommy and Daddy use the living room at night and the lights will be on and there'll be noise. You won't be able to sleep.*
NATHAN:	*So maybe I'll just play here and sleep in my room. We don't fight at night — we sleep!*

Both children thought this over for a moment while I just sat quietly. Then the discussion continued.

CHANANEL:	*I think the best is just to try to be friends and get along because I won't like playing by myself all the time.*
NATHAN:	*That will last exactly one half an hour.*
ME:	*Well, let's see what we could do to make it last for more than half an hour. Let's discuss some of the problems.*
NATHAN:	*Chananel insults me and says things that hurt my feelings.*
ME:	*What could you do?*
NATHAN:	*I could ask him to stop but it won't help.*
ME:	*Well, what do you think would happen if you just walked away?*
NATHAN:	*Good — I'll try that.*

We continued to discuss different tactics which each could use when the trouble started.

Since this talk, I see a certain decrease in the fighting. I remind the kids of our discussion once in a while when things get a little out of hand, and it really helps.

At times you can explore with an individual child ways in which a fight could have been prevented. Tell him that we're not concerned with figuring out whose fault it was, but with finding ways to avoid fights in the future. For example, after he's given you the details about a fight, you can ask, "Let's think — what could you do next time when she...?" or "How could you say it next time so that...?" If the child can't think of anything, you can give suggestions.

Here is a story illustrating this approach:

*Two days after the workshop session on fighting, the week-
ly children's magazine we subscribe to arrived in the mail. My
two daughters, Shira, ages 9, and Tali, aged 11, pounced
upon it and began fighting over it intensely, pulling at the
magazine and yelling.*

"I got it first — Mommy, tell her!"

*"That's not true, I saw it first and I'm going to read it
before you!"*

"Mommy, she's ripping the magazine!"

*At this point the two girls came to my bedroom scream-
ing, the magazine torn in half. In the past I'd have yelled at
them and grabbed the magazine, threatening to cancel the
subscription. Instead, I asked my girls to please leave and settle the matter between themselves.*

*They left. The screaming and shouting continued for
another five minutes. Then suddenly there was quiet. I went
into their room and found Shira and Tali with angry faces, the
magazine torn into shreds. I could see that they were anticipating my reaction, but I said nothing. I merely brought in a
plastic bag and asked that they gather the torn bits. Then I
left. (I found out later that the torn pieces were picked up by
their little sister.)*

*Several hours later I had a chance to talk to Shira, the
younger one. I asked her if she thought the fight over the
magazine (that in the end was ripped to pieces) was worth it.
She began blaming her sister, but I stopped her and asked
that she refrain from discussing what happened and just tell
me how the fight could have been avoided. She thought for a
moment and then said, "Maybe it's better to let Tali read the
magazine first, and then it'll remain in one piece." She suggested donating some money from her savings, and if Tali
would contribute her share, they could buy a new magazine
at the newstand. It would be a shame to miss this week's
installment of an exciting story.*

*That evening I discussed the matter with Tali, who at first
protested: "If that's how she acts, then neither of us will have*

a magazine." But then when I told her about her sister's idea of sharing the cost of a new magazine, to my amazement she sighed a deep sigh of relief. "Okay," she said, "I'll give her the money and she can go buy it. After all, she was the one who started tearing it."

A quarrel now developed between the two of them about who would buy the new magazine, but once again, I managed to stay out of it. To my surprise, the two girls left and came back with the magazine, immediately announcing that it didn't matter who got to read it first. And so it was. The older one got the first turn while her sister was at the computer.

I should add that when the fight broke out, I stopped my oldest daughter of 18 from intervening, taking her away from the scene and explaining that I was trying out a new approach. She gave me a doubting look, saying, "Your approach won't help this magazine, of which soon nothing will be left." When she saw the new magazine that evening, and two quiet girls, she remarked, "I wouldn't have believed it!"

Don't expect that your talks will have a sudden dramatic impact. Be patient, demonstrating toward your child the same tolerance you want him to display toward others. Show understanding with statements such as, "I know how hard it is not to hit back when he punches you like that" or, "I know it's difficult to take when she starts teasing you." If you need to rebuke your child for aggressive behavior, remember to do it gently.

At the close of your discussion, it's a good idea to sum up, "So what are some of the things you're going to be working on?" In this way your child commits himself to work on self-improvement.

THE CHILD WHO KEEPS HITTING

Sometimes a young child develops a habit of going over to other children and hitting them for no apparent reason. Parents are upset to see their child derive pleasure from such behavior, especially if the child acts this way in the presence of other adults. The parents then worry what others are thinking, not only about the child but also about them.

Make every effort to refrain from negative judgments such as, "Why is he so mean to the other children?!" These will only lead to angry criticism of the child. Rather, view the behavior as simply a bad habit. In addition to explaining to him that the Torah forbids hitting, tell the child very quietly that he certainly wouldn't like it if others behaved this way toward him; thus he shouldn't do it to them.

Such a child needs to be handled with patience and understanding. Keep in mind that it may not be easy for him to give up his bad habit; this will help you ward off anger-producing thoughts such as, "I've told him so many times not to hit — why does he keep doing it?" Parents should also worry less about what others are thinking about them because of the child's behavior; such worrying often heightens their anger toward the child.

Occasionally, a teacher will report that a youngster is hitting other children at school. Here's how one mother handled the situation:

> My 3-year-old Channi, a clever and likable child, enjoyed hitting other children at her kindergarten for no apparent reason. She used to hit her brothers and sisters at home; when she started kindergarten, she began doing the same thing there. The teacher would put her into the corner as punishment, but this hadn't helped much. Since a new baby had arrived, the hitting at kindergarten had gotten much worse.
>
> In a discussion of the problem during our weekly workshop meeting, I became aware that Channi had learned to see herself exactly as I saw her. Questions such as, "Why do you like to hit the other children?" had served only to reinforce this notion. It was as if a sign reading "I'm a girl who likes to hit other children" had been pinned to her. I realized too that essentially, I'd come to resign myself to the situation. As a result, so did Channi. I did some thinking about the problem and the next day, had a good opportunity to try out my ideas.
>
> I came to the kindergarten to pick up my daughter, and found her standing in the corner, looking very dejected. On our way home we had the following conversation:
>
> "Why were you in the corner?"
>
> "Because I hit Yaeli."

"Why did you hit her? Did she bother you — take something away from you?"

"No."

"Then why did you hit her?"

"Because I wanted her to cry."

"Do you like it when Yaeli cries?"

"Yes."

"And do you like to cry?"

"No."

"That's right, and I don't think Yaeli likes to cry either."

Now I asked her, *"Why did God create us with hands? To hit others?"* She said no. I asked, *"Why do we have hands?"* She answered, *"To color, cut"*; and I added, *"And to help Mommy to pick up something which falls."* Then I said, *"You know, next time your hand wants to hit, tell it, 'Don't hit — come, let's do something else.' And then quickly give it something else to do."* At that point we arrived home.

The next morning I reminded Channi of our conversation of the day before. When I came to pick her up later from kindergarten, the teacher told me that she had not hit anyone once that day. I told her what I was doing to rid Channi of the habit, and suggested that she use the same method and stop putting Channi in the corner as punishment for hitting.

By the end of the following week, I learned from the teacher that my daughter had almost completely given up her former habit of hitting children!

Another mother used incentives to motivate her child to change his aggressive behavior at school:

Yehuda brought home a note from his rebbi (teacher) that he was hitting every day in school. I discussed it with the rebbi and asked him to send me a note each day to report on Yehuda's behavior. I also asked the rebbi to remind Yehuda that for each good report his mother would give him a star. Ten stars would entitle him to a prize. I explained this arrangement to my son. Over a period of three weeks he improved rapidly to the point where his rebbi said that he never hit anymore!

When I visited the school afterwards, the children greet-
ed me with a chorus of, "Yehuda lo marbitz!" ("Yehuda does-
n't hit!"). Whereas before he had been proud of his image as
a "hitter," now he was equally proud of not hitting.

Sometimes, a child who hits at school can be kept home for a day.

PEACEMAKING

Hillel the Sage taught: "Be among the disciples of Aaron, loving peace and pursuing it."[23] We should teach our children to pursue peace by encouraging them quickly to make peace with each other after quarrels — and without involving their parents.

One mother devised a novel incentive system to encourage her children in this:

> *I've often heard my kids hassling, but sometimes I've heard*
> *them working out a solution too. So we began giving the*
> *Aharon HaKohen Award. If my children made peace with each*
> *other without having to resort to a grownup for help, they*
> *got the award. An Israeli Rosh Hashanah card with Moshe,*
> *Mt. Sinai, and Aharon was pasted onto a square of cardboard;*
> *they got to hang this card in their room for a day when they*
> *earned it. Although they are now bar- and bas-mitzvah age,*
> *they still use the negotiating skills they learned by making*
> *peace together when they were little.*

Children usually do manage to make peace between themselves after a fight, but sometimes our peacemaking efforts are required.

Aaron the Priest had a peacemaking technique which we can use with our children. Whenever Aaron heard that two people had had a quarrel, he would go to each one and tell him that the other was blaming himself for what had happened and was regretful. Then when the two would meet again, they would embrace one another and be friends.[24]

Naturally. we must wait until the children have completely calmed down before trying this.

Chapter Thirteen

CRYING

THE FIRST FEW MONTHS

rying is the baby's distress signal. It can communicate physical distress, such as hunger or indigestion, or emotional distress, such as displeasure over being left alone in the room. Although the average baby cries when he's hungry and, in addition, usually gets into at least one fretful period a day, there's wide variation in how much babies cry. Sometimes this is for purely physiological reasons: For instance, many babies suffer from colic during their first three months and will cry miserably for long spells. A different kind of determinant, however, can be far more crucial:

> Recent studies at the National Institute of Health show that, from birth, children exhibit clear-cut temperamental differences. When subjected to such stimuli as cold disks in their cribs, one child bawls vociferously while another calmly shifts an inch or two.[1]

Mothers are often keenly aware of what seem to be innate personality traits in their babies — sometimes as early as during post-natal care in the hospital. One newborn may seem fussy and irritable, while another is placid and easy going; one is alert and sociable, while another is subdued and withdrawn, and so on.

Keep this in mind when your baby seems to cry excessively or for no reason. When we've checked out everything — the baby isn't sick, he's not hungry, he was burped, he's dry and comfortable, yet he continues to cry — we're apt to fear that "something's wrong." Holding him may comfort him a bit, but he soon starts screaming as before. It's at this point that we have to guard against losing our self-confidence. The baby's crying makes a powerful demand on us to do something, and we're apt to feel inadequate when nothing we try seems to work. We may even feel personally rejected by the baby. Instead, we must assume that the baby is suffering from digestive pains and very possibly also from an innate low frustration tolerance. There's probably nothing we can do to make him stop crying altogether.

Don't become frantic over your baby's crying. Nervously asking, "What's the matter?! Why are you crying?!" is likely to make him cry even more. Instead, try to keep calm by reminding yourself that, highly unpleasant and irritating as it is, the crying is not unbearable.

There are some measures you can take that may at least reduce the baby's crying; a pacifier can often help. A device called SleepTight* was invented by a father who was being driven to the point of despair by his colicky infant who had been crying loudly and incessantly for weeks. A pediatrician recommended that he take his wailing child for a ride in a car, which immediately quieted the baby. SleepTight attaches to the baby's crib, gently vibrating it and simulating the sounds and movements of a car. In a study of the effectiveness of this product, The National Institute of Child Health and Human Development (NICHD) found that out of 60 colicky babies, 85 percent went from an agitated, crying state to a calm state only minutes after SleepTight was turned on.

Some mothers hold their baby whenever he cries, speaking to him in a soothing, comforting voice; others will at times let him "cry

---

* Available from Sleep Tight, Inc., 3613 Mueller Road, St. Charles, MO 63301.

it out" alone. There is no one correct way; you can decide what's best for you.

In the meantime, you don't have to suffer unnecessarily. When you feel the need for some respite, close the door to the baby's room and go listen to some music. (Of course, you should check up on the baby frequently to make sure he's all right.) Don't feel guilty about doing this; you can't function very well if you're worn out from your baby's crying. It's also advisable to have a baby-sitter to relieve you for a few hours once or twice a week, so you can get away from the house.

Spoiling

There's little danger of spoiling a baby during his first two or three months. Feel free to hold your baby when he's miserable without fearing that he'll come to demand this all the time. The fact that he stops crying as soon as you pick him up and walk him around doesn't necessarily mean he's spoiled. More likely, the comfort of being held distracts him momentarily from his pain.

As your baby grows older, be more careful about spoiling him. If you now continue to pick him up and rock him or walk him around every time he cries, he could well become accustomed to such service. It can be difficult to ignore your little one's wails, but it may sometimes be better for yourself and your baby if you harden your heart a bit and let him cry. By now you'll have probably learned to differentiate between types of crying that have to be responded to and those that can be safely ignored. If your baby starts to cry as soon as you put him down, you know that all he wants is to be held. Control your compassion. He needs to learn to accept that you can't hold him all the time. Talk to him soothingly, explaining that you're sorry he's so miserable but you can't hold him right now. He won't understand your words, but your gentle voice will comfort him and help him to accept reality.

BEYOND SIX MONTHS: NIGHTTIME CRYING

By six months, most babies no longer need to be fed at night. Many babies give up their nighttime feeding on their own well before then.

But others continue to cry at night. If you don't mind getting up, you might decide to continue to give the night feeding. But if you find that the nighttime interruptions interfere with your functioning, it will be necessary to train your baby to sleep through the night.

Method One: Let the Child "Cry It Out"

This time-honored method usually takes only a few days. On the first night, the baby is apt to cry for an hour or so, but on succeeding nights the crying quickly tapers off. You can use this method even with older babies who haven't yet been trained to sleep through the night.

One mother had been giving her baby a nighttime bottle for over a year, simply because she felt she didn't have the energy to train him to do without it. When she finally decided that enough was enough, she found that it was much less trouble than she'd imagined. The first night he cried for 50 minutes, the second night for 30; by the fourth night he was down to only 10 minutes. The fifth night he woke up, whimpered a bit, but when he saw that it didn't help, went right back to sleep. By the end of the week the crying had completely stopped.

It's good to keep the door to the baby's room slightly ajar, and position his crib so that you can peek in on him without his noticing. This way you can check to make sure there isn't some serious reason for his crying, such as a hand or foot caught in the crib bars.

Sometimes a baby will cry at night just because he wants your company. This is especially likely to happen if he's been sleeping in his parents' room since birth. In this case, the solution is to move his crib to another room; usually this quickly puts an end to the problem, as this mother found:

> Our 9-month-old baby slept in a crib in our room. At night when he apparently wanted to be with me, he would cry — sometimes several times during the night. As soon as I would pick him up he would quiet down, but if I left him in his crib, he would continue to cry and cry. Time and again I decided to simply ignore the crying, but it was very hard to stick to this and so I usually ended up taking him out anyway.

Finally, when both my husband and I were beginning to feel serious effects from loss of sleep, we decided to seek guidance. The counselor advised us to move his crib to another room and let him cry — it wouldn't take him long to get used to the new set-up and the nighttime crying would stop. I expressed my concern that the move might be traumatic for our baby, but the counselor reassured me that in a baby so young, there is no reason for such fears. She was absolutely right! He cried for one or two nights, and from then on, began to sleep through the entire night. Since then he sleeps well and we too, get our rest.

Method Two: Gradually Accustom the Child to Sleep Through

There are parents who find the method of allowing the child to "cry it out" emotionally very trying. Indeed, some doctors object to this method, seeing it as difficult both for the parents and the child. Instead, they recommend more moderate procedures, such as this one developed by Dr. Richard Farber, head of the Children's Sleep Problems Clinic of Boston Hospital:

1. While he is still awake, put your child to bed in a darkened and quiet room. Don't rock him, or rub his back, or even give him a pacifier. The idea is that when he wakes up at night, he will find himself in the same conditions under which he went to sleep.

2. If the child cries when put to bed, wait five minutes and then go into his room, in order to let him know that you are still there, and have not abandoned him. Talk to him quietly, placing your hands firmly on his back for a moment or two — getting across to him the idea that he must now sleep. If he is standing up in his crib, first get him to lie down. Don't take him out. Don't give him food or drink.

3. If the child continues to cry, wait 10 minutes before going in to him, just for a moment, as before. The next time allow 15 minutes to elapse before going in. From then on wait for 15 minutes each time, until he finally falls asleep.

4. If the child wakes up in the middle of the night, follow the same procedure, starting with waiting five minutes.

5. The next evening, follow the same routine, but instead of going in to your child after five minutes, first wait 10 minutes, then 15, and finally 20 minutes. Every night, add five more minutes to the waiting period.

In Dr. Farber's experience, with this treatment, most children develop a normal sleeping pattern within three or four nights, or, in the worst case, within a week or two. He says that a few nights crying won't harm the child, and it pays because in the end, the entire family will be able to sleep properly. Also, the child and the parents will be calmer during the day.

In the following account, a father describes how the method worked for his little boy:

> At 20 months, we moved Eitan from his crib to a youth bed. Immediately, he began developing serious sleep problems. At first we had to remain by his bedside so that he would fall asleep. After that, he began to wake up and cry in the middle of the night. He quickly learned how to climb over the bed guard and scamper out of bed. We decided to return Eitan to his crib.
>
> But then our real problems began! In order that he fall asleep, we had to stay with him. The moment we'd leave, he would wake up and cry. He would also wake up crying in the middle of the night — and wouldn't stop until we would come to him.
>
> We decided to try Dr. Farber's method. At first, it wasn't so simple at all. Even after several days it still took between three-quarters of an hour to an hour until Eitan would fall asleep. Once it even took an hour and a half! But after this peak, the crying quickly began subsiding. Eitan stopped waking up at night, and also cried less intensely when put to bed in the evening. About two weeks after the beginning of treatment, he returned to a normal sleeping pattern.

There are certain mothers who can't bring themselves at all to train their child to sleep through the night. They feel it's "cruel" and "heartless" to ignore their child's piteous crying. So they run to him the instant he cries, countless times during the night, spending hours with him to the point where they're barely able to function during the day due to lack of sleep. Such mothers need to be helped to see their mistake. Here is one such mother's story:

I nursed my first child "on demand" whenever he cried. When he was 9 months old I was still getting up three or four times a night to nurse him. Although I loved the bonding experience of nursing, the interruption of my own sleep was taking its toll. I was tired and worn. Many of my friends suggested I let him "cry it out" but I wouldn't hear of it. To my mind such an act would be cruel. How could I abandon my own child and ignore his anguish? How could a caring mother do that?

My parenting workshop leader explained to me that a mother's needs also have to be taken into consideration. If a mother lacked sufficient rest, how could she provide quality care? And besides, at 9 or 10 months an infant does not require around-the-clock feeding as does a newborn baby. What we had here was a routine that my child had adopted as habit. His waking and sleeping cycle was just habit, not need, and we needed to help him adjust to new habits.

It made sense, but I was still skeptical. I did not want my child to suffer. And I certainly did not want to be the cause. After much support and encouragement from the group I decided to give it a try. I chose to eliminate the 3 A.M. feeding first. The first night he cried for about 40 minutes. From time to time I did quietly check on him to be sure he was okay, but still it was torture for me! The second night he cried only 25 minutes. The third night he slept through that feeding altogether! I was truly amazed and greatly relieved. I was then convinced that he really did not need the feeding, he was simply in the habit of getting up.

When I felt the time was right, I followed the same procedure to gradually eliminate the other night feedings, one by one. Today, both mother and child get a full night's sleep.

A baby who has been sleeping well through the night may suddenly start waking up again. This often happens after a bad cold, when the baby has become used to having the parents at his bedside. Use the same treatment. It usually takes no more than two or three nights for him to learn that he gains nothing from his crying.

If other children who sleep in the same room complain that the crying wakes them up, explain why the baby is being allowed to cry. If neighbors complain about the noise, drape a heavy blanket over the window to help absorb the sound, and put a thick rug on the floor. Explain to the neighbors that the crying is likely to last for only a few nights.

Occasionally, a high-strung, sensitive baby will keep up the nighttime crying well past the age when other babies give it up. He may scream for hours at a time. His parents become exhausted from sleepless nights; all efforts to break him of his habit fail. Health problems such as allergies and recurrent sickness often predispose a child to such crying. It can sometimes help to go in for a few minutes, talk soothingly to the child expressing empathy for his discomfort, and then put him down gently in his crib. But there may be no one solution to this problem. It's good to keep in mind that these children eventually settle down to a normal sleeping pattern.

AS THE CHILD GROWS OLDER

As long as a child isn't yet able to talk, he'll continue to let you know when he wants something mainly by crying. This is a difficult stage. Try to be patient and to avoid asking the child in irritation, "What do you want?" or offering him various things to make him stop. If it proves impossible — as is sometimes the case — stop trying; just speak to him soothingly. The crying may be unpleasant, but if you stay calm the child is more likely to get over his frustration and eventually quiet down.

By meeting a child's demands while he is still unable to talk, we inevitably reinforce crying behavior. But you can minimize the crying, for example, by taking your child out of his playpen (or high chair) before he becomes too unhappy in it; this way you won't end up having to do it while he's screaming. If your child always gets into crying spells when he's overtired, don't wait until he reaches that state, but put him to bed at the first sign of crankiness.

Dealing With Crying

Empathic responses: As long as our children are small, we must be prepared to tolerate a certain amount of crying. Parents should work on reacting, not with annoyance, but with calm and empathy. It will help them to do so if they remind themselves that showing irritation will only make their child feel worse and cry more. They should keep in mind also that by reacting calmly to the child's crying, they provide him a model of how to cope better with *his* frustrations.

When your child is crying because you refused him something, don't tell him, "It won't help you to cry — you're not getting it"; rather, say quietly, "I'm sorry, but I can't give you what you want." Sometimes a crying child is trying to tell us something, but is so upset that it's impossible to understand what's being said. If you say, "Stop crying — I can't understand a word you're saying!" it comes across as uncaring. An empathic response such as, "I'd like to listen to you, sweetheart, but I can't understand you when you're crying," usually has a calming effect on the child.

Likewise, when a child comes running to us in tears, it's better not to ask, "What are you crying about?" Rather, we should say, with concern, "What happened, honey?" Especially avoid remarks such as, "Come on, it's enough. Stop crying already."

If a child's continuous crying begins to get on your nerves, you can send him to his room. But it should be done with empathy. For example, "You feel so miserable — I know. I'll tell you what — you can go into your room and cry there — when you feel better, you can come out."

Children often scream and carry on about some minor mishap, such as a torn book. Here too, remarks such as, "Come on, that's nothing to cry over," are unlikely to be well received. Show mild sympathy and then allow the child to get over his distress by himself. At times, you might try helping your child to see things in a better perspective. You might say to him, for example, "I can see you're upset about the book, but this kind of crying should be saved for when something *really* bad happens."

Always relate with empathy to a child who is crying because he hurt himself. Because they're impatient to get the child to stop his crying, parents often make light of bangs and bruises or minor cuts, saying, "Come on, nothing happened, it's just a little scratch" or, "Stop crying, you didn't hurt yourself all that much." This usually makes the child cry harder and longer. A sympathetic "Oh, you fell! Where did you hurt yourself?" or, "That must really hurt you!" is far more likely to quiet him. If there are visible marks, examine these seriously as you say, "Come, let's put something on it to make it better." Some ointment, vaseline, or even powder will do.

Anticipating pain, children often cry before a visit to the dentist or doctor. To quiet them, many parents promise, "It won't hurt." This isn't a good idea because if the treatment is painful, the child is apt to feel that his parents weren't honest with him; he learns that he can't rely on his parents' promises. It's better to be as truthful as possible — for instance, "It may hurt" or, "This is going to hurt a little," at the same time providing reassurance such as, "but I'll be with you and I'll hold your hand."

When a child is crying loudly during some painful treatment, he's apt to feel especially resentful if we trivialize his pain with, "Come on now — that doesn't really hurt so much." This adds to the child's misery — in addition to his pain, he now has the frustration of our denying the reality of that pain. When a child is in pain, let him know clearly that you understand it: "I know this hurts." Be careful also not to promise him that the pain will end right away if this isn't true. Instead let him know, "It'll probably hurt for a while." This, together with soothing and comforting words, is the best parents can do to help their child.

Distraction: Small children are easily distracted, and can often be helped over their misery if we quickly divert their attention as soon as they start crying. But be careful not to resort to this method too frequently, because your child might then lack opportunities to learn to recover from upsets on his own.

Problem-solving: Children can often be diverted from crying if we help them adopt a problem-solving orientation. Say to the child, "Let's look for a solution." Once he's busy thinking of solutions, he usually forgets about crying.

Humor: Gentle humor can sometimes distract children from crying. For example, when your child cries because his toy has just broken, you can examine it as you say, very seriously, "Hmm — maybe we'd better call the building company and have them send an engineer to put this together again," and then smile. Or you might say, as you examine some minor scratch or bruise, "Hmm — let me see — how many kisses do you think you need for this? Will five be enough?" Few children will be able to repress a smile.

Other ways of dealing with crying: It can sometimes help to let a crying child know that his noise is disturbing to us. The important thing is that this be done without annoyance or anger. Here's one good way: Hold your hands over your ears as you say, "Oooh! The noise hurts my ears!" Your child may be very surprised by this reaction — while he cries, he's so immersed in his own misery that he never thinks of the fact that the noise of his crying causes you pain! Calling it to his attention may often induce him to reduce his loud crying to a more tolerable whimper.

Common Types of Crying

Nighttime fears. Many small children go through a period of waking up frightened at night. They may have had a nightmare, or simply be afraid of the dark. A few soothing words, with reassurance that we're there to protect them, will usually calm them down. If your child is afraid of some shadowy object in his room which he imagines to be an animal or a "bad man," gently show him that his fears are groundless. One mother describes how she calmed her young daughter:

> My 4-year-old Esti woke up crying one night. I went into her room and found her wide eyed and terrified. I asked her why she was frightened and she said, "There's a bird in my room." I asked, "Where is the bird?" She pointed in the direction of her little kiddie-car and said, "Over there. That's the bird." There was enough light in the room to see clearly, so I picked up the car and asked, "This is the bird? No, this is a kiddie-car, not a bird." She took a few moments and then smiled,

saying, "I thought the kiddie-car was a bird!" Then I told her she must now go to sleep. "Everything is okay," I said. "Daddy's in his bed, the baby is in his bed, you and your sister are in your beds. I'm going to my bed too, and I'm still looking after you. Everything is okay." Satisfied that she was all right, I kissed her and went out of the room.

A child who wakes up frightened at night will often come crying into his parents' room. It may be a great temptation to take him into your bed, but this usually turns out to be a mistake. Once he's used to coming into a parent's bed, it's no easy job getting him out again. It's better right from the start not to allow this, but to take him back to his own bed and calm him there.

Crying when mother leaves: Young children often cry when their mother leaves the house. Although they usually stop two or three minutes after she's gone, some mothers feel terribly guilty about leaving a screaming child. They can't bear to see their child so miserable and think they must be heartless to leave him this way. The child, in turn, often senses his mother's hesitation and guilt and learns to play on it, intensifying his crying so as to keep the mother home.

Once she understands what causes her guilt, the mother will be able to challenge the validity of her thoughts and, as a result, begin to feel more comfortable about leaving the house. The child, too, will find it easier to accept his mother's absence.

My 2-year-old son Gaby was a real Mommy's boy, meaning, he wanted to be near me at all times. This became a big problem whenever I had to leave him with a baby-sitter or at someone else's house. When I did leave him, which was seldom, I would act apologetic and console him; but I would still hear his screams from quite a distance. When I would return, I would hear that he'd screamed a lot, almost the whole time. This made me feel very guilty about leaving him, and I therefore tried not to have to do it, only going out when it was absolutely necessary. If I had to go out, I felt so insecure about it. "How will he manage? How can I do this to him? I shouldn't leave him in such a state! Am I a bad mother if I leave my child screaming?"

Through discussing it in the workshop, I began to identify these thoughts as the ones that were causing my guilt. I realized what my mistake was: the assumption that Gaby was being harmed by my leaving. Of course, this wasn't really true. He was capable of learning to tolerate the fact that I was going away. It was okay for me to go out.

As I got used to thinking this way, I felt more secure about leaving him. The next time I wanted to go out, I just told him in a matter-of-fact way that I had to leave. He cried much less! Now, he cries for no longer than two or three minutes at the most.

Resistant crying: A balky 2-year-old will sometimes resist with vehement screaming your efforts to get him to do something. You can avoid head-on confrontations by firmly taking his hand and leading him through his various routines, ignoring his carrying-on. For instance, if the youngster is screaming because he doesn't want to leave the house with you, pull him along, all the while talking to him in a soothing voice: "I know, you don't want to go — but we're going anyway. Okay — everything's all right." Keep talking to him about other things; this distracts him and helps him forget his distress.

At times, one firm spank will do the trick. It should be given soon after he begins acting up and with conviction, as we say to him, "Okay, that's enough now." Don't postpone the spanking until you're worn out from the child's screaming, because then you're likely to give it in anger.

Temper tantrums: Temper tantrums are common in young children, and are nothing to worry about. Tantrums are an expression of the young child's outrage at having been thwarted in some way. Tantrums generally occur more often in children who have low frustration tolerance, and your reactions can play an important role in helping to minimize this tendency.

You need to experiment to see what approach works best with your child. A bit of comforting, some gentle words and a hug, at the onset of a tantrum can often calm the child down quickly:

My baby of a 1¹/₂, Liat, would work herself into fierce crying fits whenever we didn't give her what she wanted. At first I handled the situation by ignoring her completely. I was very consistent, but it didn't help. Next I tried being firm with her by picking her up, putting her into her crib, and telling her that she had to stay there until she stopped. That helped a bit, but Liat still continued her fits. Then I tried comforting her. I held her and spoke to her soothingly: "I'm sorry — I know you really wanted (such and such) but I can't give it to you. It's not worth making yourself sick over it." We did this consistently and after three days, she stopped it completely!

Or, let the child have a tantrum for a while and then, stroking his cheek, gently ask him, "Are you ready to calm down now?" Often, this is enough to quiet the child.

Little children will sometimes have a tantrum about trivial matters. For example, the child wants to have some toy right next to his plate at mealtime, but you tell him that it has to be further away, whereupon he begins screaming. It's easy to give in to him, to think that it's not worthwhile to make an issue over it when it's so important to him. The trouble is that while this will quiet him for the moment, chances are that in the long run you'll have more tantrums to contend with. Keeping this in mind will help you to remain firm.

With older children, it's usually best to take no notice of their tantrums, except for a sympathetic "I'm sorry, but I can't let you have what you want." Let the child thrash about on the floor while you go about your business as usual. When he sees that the tantrum gets him nowhere, he'll stop.

Sometimes the best way to handle a temper outburst is to lead the child to his room as you calmly say, "I see you're having a tantrum. Come, I'll take you to your room and you can have the tantrum there." Sometimes a child just needs to be by himself for awhile, as this mother discovered:

My son Dudi was in the midst of a tantrum. I told him to please stay in his room until he felt he could restrain himself. I peeked into his room and saw him under his crib. All of a sudden he gave a loud screech. Then there was silence. Two minutes later he emerged from his room and announced, "Mommy, I'm all finished now!"

The right combination of firmness and empathy can sometimes do the trick. This may call for a bit of experimentation:

I picked up my son Meir from kindergarten, and he came up the stairs with some "masterpiece" he had made, which was actually three boxes of different sizes glued together. Suddenly another little boy accidentally knocked into him and the boxes fell to the ground and came apart. His upset was indescribable. Lying on the ground, kicking and screaming, the works!! Well, I recalled all my skills for dealing with this and tried to be very empathic. I sat down with him on a near-by bench and held him close, telling him that I understood how disappointed he must be after working so hard on this project and having it fall apart like that. However, empathy didn't seem to be the right medicine and the crying just got worse and worse until he was quite hysterical, coughing and nearly vomiting.

At this point I thought I'd better try to put an abrupt stop to this severe reaction of his. So I said, "Meir, I know you feel very very upset about your broken art work, but I will not let you make yourself sick about it. You have a choice — either stop this minute with your crying or I'm going to throw the whole thing in the garbage and it'll just be gone." This is not a typical reaction of mine, and throwing away a child's art work does not exactly appeal to me, but on this occasion, I felt that it was most important to stop this extreme tantrum. Well, it worked to a certain extent — his crying became a whimpering, and we made it home.

As we walked in, he burst into tears again and said, "Mommy, you know, Kobi didn't even say he was sorry for knocking into me...." Then I realized that the time had come for empathy. I really tried to put myself in his place and think how I might feel if a beautiful cake I had made just flopped to pieces. This time the empathy did work. I feel that the combination of firmness and empathy was what helped us through this crisis.

More alarming than simple thrashing about in a fit of temper are head-banging and breath-holding spells. If the child is furiously banging his head so that you fear real damage to the brain, of course you must stop him. Hold him firmly, as you talk to him soothingly. Remember to keep calm yourself; this is reassuring to the child and helps him over his temper fit.

> *Whenever something didn't go her way, my 3-year-old would bang her head on the floor or furniture until she was black and blue. Afraid of giving in and spoiling her, I would let her do it; but I felt physically ill watching her. Now that I was advised to hold her and calm her instead, I felt that a weight had been lifted from my chest!*
>
> *I had always been very nervous about denying her things because of her head-banging. When she would come to demand some snack food, I would give in to her more than I felt I should. And so she could end up eating most of the morning. Now I felt more confident. I began responding by stroking her cheek and quietly saying no. If she stamped her foot, I'd quietly hold her foot down.*
>
> *In the past, when I tried to put her to bed for naptime, she would frequently fuss or scream, and I would immediately take her out. Now I softly stroke her cheek, quietly saying, "It's time for a nap now. Put your head down," and she quietly lies down. Within two weeks she's become a different child!*

In breath-holding, the child, who is extremely frustrated and has been crying furiously, suddenly holds his breath. This cuts off the oxygen supply to the brain and the child turns blue (or sometimes white). He may lose consciousness momentarily, or go into convulsions that look like an epileptic fit. Of course, all this is extremely alarming to the parents.

A well-known pediatrician[2] with much experience in the treatment of breath-holding, advises against parents trying to ward off breath-holding by preventing crying fits. Such efforts make for very apprehensive parents and spoiled children. Be very careful not to show alarm at breath-holding; if the child senses parental alarm, he'll use these spells more and more to get his way. Instead, as soon as he begins to hold his breath, go out of the room and leave him alone. Nothing will happen to him. If he faints, his muscles immediately relax so that breathing starts again at once. In fact, when the child sees that he has no audience, his breath often returns to him quickly and he doesn't reach the fainting or convulsion stage. Parents can keep an eye on him through a slightly open door so that, in case he faints, they can go in and lay him down on his side. After the child has calmed down, the parents should make sure to show him warmth and affection.

Parents should always consult with a qualified pediatrician for a proper diagnosis and to rule out epilepsy or other illnesses. It's helpful to know that children usually outgrow this problem as they get older.

Whining and clinging: Young children are likely to be cranky and whiny when they're tired. When you suspect tiredness as the reason for a child's unpleasant behavior, it's best to lead him quietly to his bed as you say, "Come — you're tired. Lie down a bit."

Children who have just recuperated from some illness may also whine a lot, clinging constantly to their mother and demanding the same extra attention they received while they were ill. We have to be prepared to put up with a week or so of crankiness, offering the child comfort while we accustom him to a more normal state of affairs.

Whining and clinging can be very irritating, and parents have to make special efforts to refrain from outbursts such as, "Stop your whining already — it's getting on my nerves!" or, "I can't stand your clinging to me all the time!" When a child is used to saying everything in a whining voice, telling him calmly, "Talk, don't whine," can be an effective way of ridding him of this unpleasant habit. Or, when a child whines, "Mo-o-o-mmy, I'm thirrrsty, I wanna dri-ink," try telling him gently, "You know, when you talk that way it doesn't sound so nice. Suppose you say that again now, in another voice — like this: 'Mommy, I'm thirsty — may I have a drink?'" Now you can tell the child when he whines, "Can you say that again with your *other* voice?" followed by, "See, it sounds so much better when you talk this way."

You can discourage clinging by saying softly, "Honey, I can't work when you cling to me this way" or, "It doesn't feel so nice to have my dress pulled at." Or bring in some toys and let the child play near you on the floor.

Of course, you don't always have to listen to prolonged whining and crying. Tell the child, "I see you're miserable and I'm very sorry about it. But the whining hurts my ears. I'm going to turn the radio on to hear a little music, so the noise won't bother me so much." (A "walkman"-type tape recorder is excellent for this.) Or, the child can be asked pleasantly to go to his room until he's finished with his whining.

Parents sometimes unwittingly reinforce the child's whining behavior. For example, Mother takes Bina out for a walk in her stroller. When she stops to chat with a friend, Bina starts to squirm and whine. Mother tells her friend, "She doesn't like it when I stop to talk to anyone." This is like giving Bina a license to continue acting that way. Instead, Mother should quietly tell her, "We'll be going again right away, Bina. Mommy's just talking to her friend for a minute." Of course, Mother shouldn't try Bina's patience by talking interminably with a friend while the child is strapped in her stroller. If she can walk, let her out, or keep the conversation short.

Chapter Fourteen

THE DIFFICULT CHILD

*I*n past decades, the role of environment in shaping personality has been emphasized to such an extent that the crucial contribution of inborn traits has been almost totally ignored.

In contrast, the Talmudic view of the origins of personality, as summarized some 800 years ago by Rambam, is that "Some traits are present at birth; there are others to which the individual is predisposed...some are absorbed from other people...still others are deliberately acquired."[1]

After years of viewing behavior as pretty much a matter of upbringing, current schools of psychology are now coming around to this Talmudic view. There is increasing evidence that hereditary factors have a far greater share in determining personality than has been realized. While there's no denying the significant effects of early training, new research seems to indicate that children have inborn tendencies which predispose them to certain types of behavior (something mothers have known for centuries!).

This can be reassuring news, indeed, for parents of difficult children. With the old belief in the parent-child interaction as the all-important determining factor in behavior, parents (especially mothers) were blamed for all behavior disorders — and suffered the additional anguish of anxiety and guilt.

A recent long-term study has shown that traits of temperament can be distinguished in early infancy, and that these qualities affect parental behavior (rather than being caused by it). In this study (NYLS — the New York Longitudinal Study, begun in 1956) researchers identified one particular combination of traits — they named it the "difficult child" cluster — which seems to correlate with difficulty in managing the children who manifest it.

In his book *The Difficult Child*,[2] Dr. Stanley Turecki, a practicing child and family psychiatrist, presents the following questionaire for parents:

Do You Have a Difficult Child?

Family Questions

Answer "yes" or "no":
1. Do you find your child hard to raise? _____
2. Do you find the child's behavior hard to understand? _____
3. Are you often battling the child? _____
4. Do you feel inadequate as a parent? _____
5. Is your family life being adversely affected by the child? _____

Child Questions

The headings below identify areas of your child's temperament (his or her basic makeup). Rate your child, in an overall way, on each item, using this scale:

1 = Sometimes
2 = Often
3 = Nearly always or always

High Activity Level
Very active; always into things; makes you tired; "ran before he walked"; gets wild or "revved up," loses control, hates to be confined.　　　　　_____

Distractible
Has trouble concentrating and paying attention, especially if not really interested; doesn't "listen."　　　　　_____

Poorly Adaptable
Has trouble with *transition* and *change* — of activity or routine; goes on and on nagging or whining for something he wants; stubborn; very persistent if he really likes an activity; seems to get "locked in"; tantrums are long and hard to stop; gets used to things and refuses to give them up; preferences for unusual food and clothes.　　_____

Initial Withdrawal
Doesn't like new situations — new places, people, food, or clothes; holds back or protests by crying or clinging; may have a tantrum if forced to go forward.　　　　　_____

High Intensity
A *loud* child — whether miserable, angry, or happy.　　_____

Irregular
Unpredictable. You can't tell when he'll be hungry or tired; conflict over meals and bedtime; moods change suddenly; wakes up at night.　　　　　_____

Low Sensory Threshold
Sensitive to sounds, lights, colors, textures, temperature, pain, tastes, or smells; clothes have to "feel right," making dressing a problem; doesn't like the way many foods taste; overreacts to minor cuts or scrapes; feels warm when everyone else is cold; easily overstimulated; may have a tantrum.　　　　　_____

Negative Mood
Basically serious or cranky. Whines or complains a lot. Not a "happy child."　　　　　_____

What Your Rating Means

FAMILY "YES"	CHILD	CONCLUSION
0-1 points	+ 2-5 points	= Basically easy child with some difficult features
1-2 points	+ 6-12 points	= Difficult child
3 or more points	+ 13 or more points	= Very difficult child

Turecki stresses that temperament manifests itself very early, and is inherent to the child. A child who becomes difficult in his second or third year should not be viewed as a temperamentally difficult child.

Infancy

Parents of difficult children recall that early on even in infancy, they sensed there was "something wrong." Among the symptoms typically reported: extreme restlessness, poor adaptability to changes in routine, irregularity in feeding and sleeping schedules and, most difficult of all, much whining, crying, or screaming, throughout the day and night.

The Early Years

High-activity level becomes more noticeable as the child becomes mobile. The extremely active child is constantly on the go, and the home must be thoroughly childproofed because he gets into everything. Distractibility and poor concentration may show up at this stage. The child with poor adaptability becomes quite stubborn. He gets used to things and won't give them up. This type of rigidity, getting "locked in," manifests itself at every attempt to introduce a change of diet, clothes, playthings, or activities. If he doesn't get what he wants, he'll whine or scream.

When confronted with strangers, new places or new baby-sitters, those children with "initial withdrawal" tendencies will cling to their parents, often becoming upset, even throwing tantrums. High intensity shows up as loudness — whether in excitement, laughter, or weeping. With the irregular child, meals and bedtime are daily and nightly battles.

The School Years

At school, the difficult child may have trouble sitting still or paying attention. The teacher may complain about impulsivity and poor control, and about difficulties in sharing with the other children or joining in group activities.

OTHER POSSIBLE DIFFICULTIES

Low Sensory Threshold and LFT

As was mentioned, children with low sensory threshold are acutely sensitive to sensory stimuli such as noise, bright lights, or pain. They fuss about "clothes that don't feel right," food that "tastes funny," or minor cuts and scrapes. Unlike low frustration tolerance (LFT, discussed in Chapter 1), low sensory threshold is an objective reality — the child is born with it. Low frustration tolerance, on the other hand — the belief that one is unable to endure pain, discomfort, or frustration — may be seen as partly inherent and partly acquired. The predisposition to LFT may manifest itself at birth, but the environment can do much to minimize it or aggravate it.

Clearly, LFT can aggravate a low sensory threshold condition. A child who is sensitive to strange foods or uncomfortable clothing may fuss over them, but when this sensitivity is coupled with LFT, the combination can trigger loud and intense tantrums. The child not only experiences unpleasantness or discomfort — he also thinks he *can't stand it!*

Learning Disabilities

Learning-disabled children generally have normal or even above average intelligence. A learning disability can range from mild to severe. With the severe form, special education is usually required. The deficiency may manifest itself in areas of language comprehension, reading, writing, arithmetic, or in certain nonverbal skills —

such as learning to distinguish right from left and to tell time. Difficulty in sitting still, in concentration, and in paying attention, are also frequently noted.

As we have seen, these latter problems are also characteristic of difficult children. The question arises: Is one dealing with a difficult child, or are these the symptoms of what may later be diagnosed as a learning disability? Concerned parents can have their child tested at an early age so that if any weakness is detected, appropriate learning therapy can be started immediately.

We should keep in mind that learning-disabled children may have to contend with the frustrations of failure, ridicule, younger siblings who are rapidly surpassing them, parental criticism, unsympathetic teachers, etc. This alone is more than enough to give rise to behavior patterns which mimic some of those of the difficult child.

Dyslexia

The term "dyslexia," frequently applied to any learning disability, actually refers to a distinct reading problem. Confusion in diagnosis arises from the fact that there is as yet no universally accepted definition or precise diagnostic criterion for dyslexia. The disorder is associated with deficits in sound discrimination, sound blending, memory for sounds, and sound analysis. Dyslexic children may have problems in other areas such as visual perception, right-left discrimination, and fine motor control — but their chief difficulty is in reading. When this clears up, the child generally does well in school.

In the past, dyslexia was believed to be a fixed, unchanging condition. New research shows that there are gradations of dyslexia — and that the condition *can* change. In one study involving 25 first-graders who were diagnosed with dyslexia, only one in six still had that label by the time they reached the sixth grade.[3] Dyslexia can be overcome.

The Montessori method for teaching reading has proven to be particularly effective for reading problems.

Attention Deficit Disorder

"Attention deficit disorder" (ADD) has largely replaced the formerly popular diagnosis, "hyperactivity." Children with ADD are impulsive and easily distracted. They have trouble paying attention or concentrating on tasks which require sustained attention. In the literature, attention deficit disorder has two forms: with or without hyperactivity.

It should be clear that when we describe a particular child as hyperactive, we're merely saying that he is far more active than "normal."

There are many children who, from babyhood on, evidence a high level of activity. This is no reason for undue concern, but it can make life difficult for the parents. As one mother describes: "Motti's all over the place! I can't take my eyes off him for one minute! In a flash he's at the bookshelves, pulling down books. Then it's into the kitchen where he pulls open the refrigerator and stove doors, tossing around whatever he can get his hands on."

Besides childproofing the house — placing dangerous objects and breakables well out of the toddler's reach — parents should use their ingenuity to protect the child (and their home!) as he exercises his propensity for exploration. Motti's mother, quoted above, attached strips of Velcro to her refrigerator door and inserted a long stick in the stove door handle, to prevent her active toddler from opening them.

But sooner or later, parents must teach the child that there are certain things he must leave alone. The development of basic inner controls is an essential part of his education. (Chapter 2 offers guidance on this.)

The Difficulty of Diagnosis

Difficult children with a high-activity level are often diagnosed as suffering from ADD, as are children who are actually suffering from low frustration tolerance. Don't be overwhelmed or intimidated by an ADD diagnosis (or any other label); adopt an attitude of dealing with the behavior at hand. Don't use a diagnosis as an excuse for lowered expectations. It's all too easy to say, "Well, what do you expect of Susie? After all, she's...." Invariably, Susie senses our expectations and performs accordingly. On the other hand, do be on the alert and don't close your eyes to what are possibly symptoms of a real problem.

Whether we describe a youngster as a "completely normal but highly active child," as a "difficult child with a high-activity level," or as "a child diagnosed as having ADD" (or any of the other possible combinations that overlap) — what matters is that the principles for dealing with his behavior are the same.

Because of the variety of terminologies relating to learning problems, parents of a child having trouble in school often feel confused and anxious. Specialists, though armed with an array of sophisticated tests, don't necessarily come up with clear and reliable prescriptive recommendations. Far too many children with only minor learning problems are diagnosed and labeled as suffering from some disorder. We need a much more conservative attitude. Certainly, there are children with clear difficulties requiring specialized help from competent professionals. But there are many more children with some problems in school who shouldn't be pigeonholed in this way.

EFFECTS OF THE DIFFICULT CHILD ON PARENTS

When a child has only a few difficult characteristics, parents generally manage to stay in control, though they may feel somewhat unsure about how well they are coping. But parents of truly difficult children who are managing poorly are likely to feel guilty, angry, and inadequate. Typically, mothers (fathers, too) will ask themselves, "Where have I gone wrong?" or, "What's the matter with me that I can't handle this child?" As the child becomes more and more difficult to control, hopelessness grows. The constant struggles and ensuing exhaustion may put a strain on the marriage.

Mothers or fathers with low frustration tolerance are in for a particularly rough time, since they tend to be easily frustrated by the many hardships they face in raising their child, and thus regard these hardships as intolerable.

Recognize that your difficult child was born difficult through no fault of yours. With guilt feelings out of the way, you can evaluate your situation objectively. First, make a list:

Which of your child's behavior patterns gives you the most trouble?
In what settings does this behavior occur?
Which traits of temperament are causing the behavior?
How effective are your methods of discipline?

Turecki stresses that this list should include only "relevant" behavior — behavior that objectively speaking, you feel you have to take a stand on and change. As an example, he mentions table manners. Though good table manners may be important to you, is it worth taking a stand on this when there are more serious problems to be dealt with? Perhaps the parents could, for the time being, waive this issue. "One of the main reasons for ineffective discipline with a difficult child is that the parents are so caught up, so irritated by the child, that they respond to virtually *anything* he does."[4]

Parents need to eliminate some of the management techniques they've been using that just won't work with a difficult child (or with almost any child, for that matter). For instance: constant repetition of requests or limits, overexplaining, threatening without following through, excessive or too frequent punishment, or giving in under pressure.

A neutral, objective, attitude is vital. The cognitive approach (presented in Chapter 1, and referred to throughout this book) can make all the difference. It helps parents to zero in on the negative thought patterns which produce those emotional reactions that so interfere with effective discipline.

Dwelling on such thoughts as, "Why is she doing this to me?" for example, can only lead to anger and resentment. Rather, focus on thoughts such as, "How can I understand her behavior?" By learning to *think* differently about your child's behavior, you'll naturally *feel* differently about that behavior. You'll then be in better control of your own behavior, and will find that changing it comes more easily.

MANAGEMENT TECHNIQUES

Methods for managing the difficult child differ little from those already presented for dealing with the ordinary child — except that the difficult child requires more expert handling, and greater patience on the part of the parents. It's crucial to make it clear to the child that while you love him and understand his various difficulties — nevertheless you must limit his behavior and insist that he conform to basic requirements. Love, understanding, firmness, and consistency are the key elements. A reward and punishment system — emphasizing reward more than punishment — can be very effective in the early stages of training, when you're struggling to gain control over your child's behavior and to establish your authority. (See Chapters 4 and 5 for suggestions and guidance.)

There are some special techniques which Dr. Turecki recommends for dealing with particular behavior problems, which are briefly reviewed here:

Wildness

It's normal for children to get out of control occasionally. (The problem is discussed in Chapter 17.) But highly active children progress extremely quickly from excitability to overexcitement, to wildness, to total loss of control.

The trick is to intervene before the child has become wild and has lost control. This can be difficult with some children, who escalate too rapidly to the point of losing control. But in most cases, it's possible to spot the progression and intervene quickly at the crucial moment, to modify behavior.

Turecki suggests methods to extract a child from such a situation. When you catch the escalation early, you may be able to distract his attention with a toy, conversation, or interesting (and quiet) activity. At other times you can let him "cool off" or "blow off steam."

"Cooling off" is a good way of dealing with a child who seems about to become wild. Go up to him, make eye contact, and say, "You're getting too excited. It's time to cool off." If necessary, remove him physically from the environment that has had too stimulating an effect on him. Some "cooling off" activities which Turecki mentions are: sharing a special book with you, sitting on your lap, splashing in the bathtub, or receiving a special snack (without sugar or additives, known to be harmfully stimulating).

"Blowing off steam" is another form of intervention. Take the child to the park — or to the basement, if there is one in the house — and let him run.

Restlessness and Distractibility

With children who have a hard time sitting still or concentrating on an activity for long periods, Turecki recommends the "time out" technique. For example, in the middle of doing her homework Ofra begins to squirm in her seat, stare into space, and fiddle with her pencil and paper. These are clear indications that she's had enough. Tell her, "Ofra, I see you're getting restless." Then give her a short break, perhaps assigning a task that will release some energy, such as emptying the dishwasher, scrubbing vegetables for salad, or helping you to sort the laundry. Or let her play with her toys for a while.

Parents of an easily distracted youngster often complain of difficulty in getting their child to listen. It's important to establish eye contact with such a child, before telling him anything. Say, quietly, "I want you to look at me and listen to what I have to say."

When children have trouble concentrating and sitting still in school, a trial of medication may be warranted, to see if it helps. Once things are going well, dosage may be tapered off, according to the doctor's recommendations. One mother told about her first-grader, who was constantly getting into trouble at school because he couldn't pay attention or sit still. The boy was very unhappy with himself because of his lack of discipline. He was put on Ritalin (for school days only), and it's made a huge difference. He's doing much better at school and is much happier as well. Many parents have reported similar success with medication.

On the other hand, there is a tendency too quickly to prescribe medication as a cure-all for any concentration difficulties or "hyperactivity," without investigating other forms of treatment, such as learning therapy.

Dealing With Change

The key ways of dealing with change are: 1) preparation and, 2) giving the child time to adjust. For example, "This afternoon we're going to visit Aunt Esther. We'll take the bus to the last stop, and then walk from there to her house."

There are, however, situations where no amount of preparation will help. A calm manner — soothing and accepting — is best. Don't cajole; don't change your plans in any way because of the child's difficulties. Simply take him firmly by the hand, in a manner which conveys your expectation of his cooperation. Reassure him — even in the midst of tantrums — that everything's going to be fine. Empathy goes a long way: "I know you're not happy about this. I'm sorry." The following story illustrates this:

> *My 3-year-old Yossi didn't want a kindergarten birthday party. I didn't give in to his refusal but took time to prepare him for the event, explaining that he'd be sharing his party with his friend Avrami and that Avrami's mother was baking a Mickey Mouse-shaped cake. I let him help to prepare the party bags and choose the colors for the birthday candles. Just before the party, I helped him stick the candles into the cake. At the party — despite having been prepared and given time to adjust — Yossi sat in his seat not budging from my side. He wouldn't dance. He wouldn't allow himself to be lifted in his chair (as is customary in Israel). But he did blow out the candles on the birthday cake.*

Yossi's mother acted wisely by allowing him to stay close to her, and by not insisting that he participate in the birthday festivities in his honor. But children often discover — after an initial period of resistance to a new experience — that it's quite enjoyable after all, and end up participating perfectly happily.

THE FUTURE

Dr. Turecki assures parents that, while the influence of temperament does persist into adult life, it becomes less and less important as the child interacts with his environment and as his personality matures. Moreover, he believes that certain difficult children are destined to become exceptional members of society. Because they are often more in touch with their own feelings, these children are freer, more open, intuitive, empathic, creative, and exuberant. He mentions several outstanding individuals — among them Albert Einstein and Eleanor Roosevelt — who, as children, were thought odd. Turecki also cites a book on the childhood years of 400 outstanding individuals. Though not all necessarily temperamentally difficult children, they were, more often than not, considered "different" or troubled. Yet this didn't stand in the way of — indeed, perhaps it contributed to — their very special future.

Chapter Fifteen

THE TEENAGE YEARS

oday's teenagers are in a somewhat unnatural situation. Rapidly developing toward adulthood and with growing capability of doing anything adults can do, they are at the same time hindered by societal norms which require them to undergo lengthy schooling, often beyond the teen years. Deprived of the opportunity to assume the obligations for which they are ready and dependent on their parents for financial support, they are in a sort of "no-man's-land," as neither child nor grownup.

In previous generations the picture was very different. Early in their teens, boys entered the work field, often assisting in their fathers' business, working hard from morning until night in responsible positions. Girls married when barely into their teens. The responsibilities of making a living, managing a household, and raising a family helped mature these young people at an early age.

Today's situation can create problems for the teenager and his parents. On the one hand, the parents expect more mature behavior of him, yet, because he is still in the identical framework he's been in all his life, they tend to continue seeing him as a child and treating him accordingly — which also makes him see himself as a child.

While the adolescent may more or less go along with all this, it can be a source of inner conflict. He may not always be aware of it, but his new maturity can cause him to feel a certain resentment at being "treated like a baby." Needless to say, parents should make every effort to treat their teenage sons and daughters as the young adults that they really are.

Rabbi Samson Raphael Hirsch describes a beautiful ideal for the teen years, when the child enters the age of personal struggle toward manhood or womanhood.

> Sons and daughters will become the friends and comrades, the brothers and sisters of their parents; they will have no closer, more intimate friends in all the world than their parents, from whom they will feel no need to hide even the most secret recesses of their hearts. And by the same token, the parents can have no closer, more intimate friends with whom to discuss their own most personal concerns than their children.[1]

Rabbi Moshe Feinstein has written that, for success in education, mother and father should be in agreement on basic child rearing issues.[2] This is particularly important concerning teenagers, for whom a united front provides a sense of security at this particularly difficult time. The adolescent is more sensitive, more "tuned-in" to parental friction — whether open or hidden. Exposure to such conflict can greatly intensify any tendency toward insecurity. If the parents disagree on some issue concerning their teenage son or daughter, they should settle the matter in private.

It's all too often assumed that the teenage years are inevitably filled with adolescent rebellion, turmoil, confusion — the worst! As one mother reports:

> I used to ask myself, while changing my children's diapers, "Why am I bothering to make all this effort? As soon as they turn 14 they're going to break a chair over my head!" I had

worst-case scenario visions of their running away from home and who knows what else. What actually happened? To my total astonishment and very pleasant surprise — very minimal problems with rebellion or disrespect, and a wholehearted, enthusiastic reception of the world view we're trying to teach them. There were problems, sure. One needed to work on laziness, another dawdled, one was never on time, my girls spent hours in front of the mirror, and their rooms! They could be critical, albeit with humor and even affection, yet it still gave me a slight twinge. Still, on the whole, their relationship to my husband and myself is one of our greatest joys.

PARENTS TALK ABOUT THEIR TEENAGERS

Interviews with parents reveal a wide range of adjustment difficulties encountered by teenagers. Some get through this period easily with no particular problems. Others have only minor difficulties. And then there are those who experience a truly turbulent period.

One mother reports:

My oldest daughter, now 22, is somewhat introverted. She went through her teen years with no difficulties.

But now I see that Chedva, my 14-year-old, is having an entirely different experience. She has become highly sensitive. She has mood swings, sometimes very happy — almost too happy — then she tones down, and sometimes she goes to the other extreme. She is easily hurt by little things.

Though Chedva has always been insecure, now she is much more so — looking for love and approval, at home and with friends. If I haven't spoken nicely to her she'll give me a soulful, hurt look. She is very fine and sensitive. She complains that the other girls are loud, that she feels lost and isn't part of them.

I tell Chedva that she has her own unique personality and should try not to be so dependent on others for approval. I tell her that when she feels lost among her classmates, she should try the technique of changing her thoughts. For instance, not to expect so much from her "chevra" but to open her eyes and watch out for their needs. I say, "Chedva, when you go to a party, have no expectations, and then you'll enjoy it." It really works with her. She goes away happy.

A mother of three teenage daughters had this to say:

I find the teenage years to be wonderful! Gone are the years of constant physical vigilance, when I had to be forever running after them. I love sitting back and just enjoying them. And I feel so rewarded now for not having put them down when they were younger, because now my girls feel good about themselves.

I looked for opportunities to praise them for traits I wanted them to develop. For example, I'm not so neat, but all my daughters are orderly. Whenever they displayed any signs of tidiness, I would praise them highly for it — "Oh, how wonderful the way you cleaned up. I was never like that!"

Yocheved, my 16-year-old, has always been very independent. When she was little she used to drive me crazy. She would make up her mind about something and I couldn't budge her. By the time she was 5, I had given up trying to force her to do certain things which she didn't want to do, such as eating breakfast or putting on the clothes I wanted her to wear (things my mother made me do). She's turned out beautifully — so serenely self-confident and independent. She has a strong sense of self and is not at all into getting approval.

I feel I did right by letting Yocheved's independence flower. I did this with all my children. For instance, cleaning up on Shabbos. On Shabbos I'm a queen. The girls make up between themselves who will do which job — according to their own inclinations. Yocheved sets the table, Chaviva cleans up Friday night, and Edna does the dishes on Shabbos morning. They handle it all themselves.

The most important thing I have learned is to trust their unique natures. Edna is very particular in her mitzvah observance — she'll even tell me what I'm doing wrong! I go along with it. I appreciate it because I feel it comes from a fervor for keeping Halachah.

Chaviva loves to have fun. She used to tease a lot, but now its just a "fun-lovingness." It can be irritating at times, but I try to look at it with a good eye — it comes from an innate joie de vivre.

My girls have fought like crazy over clothes, especially when one borrowed from the other without permission. I'd hear them say that they hate each other, or they would come to me saying, "Mom, I can't stand that kid." But recently, Yocheved left the country for three weeks. At the airport, where we had gathered to see her off, they were all weeping as they said their good-byes.

And from a mother of three teenage sons:

My son Shabtai, just turned 13, is showing some typical teenage characteristics. He is starting to pull away from us and be more independent. He wants to be able to make his own decisions concerning bedtime, when to come home in the evening, household chores. There are homework problems, school-attitude problems. But at this stage it's only mild — I wouldn't call it problematic.

Shabtai has always been very sensitive, but now he is even more so. I can see that he is torn between the need for physical affection and embarrassment over it — he's too big for it. He can come up to me, hug and kiss me, but if anyone comes in he feels very embarrassed.

I see this is a problem with all my boys as they become more mature — they still want the affection, but feel uncomfortable about asking for it. I find I have to give it to them in nonphysical ways that don't intimidate or embarrass them, or they'll pull away. I spend a lot of time "shmoozing" with them, talking to them about their friends. I try to compliment them on the things they are telling me. I also leave them little "love notes," such as, "Dear Shabtai, I like the way you organized your bookshelves" or, "I really enjoyed the conversation we had yesterday. Thank you for sharing with me. I love it."

Shai, 15, is the type of fellow who is very self-confident, very sure of himself. In fact, he's developed into a bit of a smart aleck — he doesn't say it but his attitude, his tone of voice, convey: "What do you know about this? I know best. You're not in my life." You can't really call it chutzpah. I sometimes criticize him for it by saying, for instance, "Shai, when you talk like that, you sound boastful, as if you're lording it over others, putting them down." He doesn't seem to know what I'm talking about. He looks at me and says, "What do you mean, Mom?"

Shai has a lot going for him. He is very bright, very successful, is very highly thought of, gets a lot of compliments. He dresses stylishly. He wants to look like "somebody."

He is a very caring person, very empathic, very thoughtful. He'll go to his grandmother's house before Pesach to clean kitchen cabinets, on his own initiative. I say to myself, "This boy is such an angel! What more can a mother ask? I can't have it all. Maybe I'm expecting too much of him." He'll do anything asked of him, without complaint — he is always willing, more than willing. It's just that I sense that he does it because he wants to impress, to be the "good guy."

Amichai, my oldest, did very well in school until fourth grade. Then we moved and he started in a new school. It was very traumatic for him. Because he was so shy, Amichai had a hard time making friends. He was lost in the large classes of the new school. Because he didn't talk about it, we didn't realize how hard a time he was having and what a beating his self-image was taking. He also had a difficult teacher and was frozen with fear of her. He would close the door to his room, as if locking us out of his life.

As a result of all this, Amichai didn't do well in school. He seemed to be saying to himself, "I'm no good." Once he came home from school and said, "I'm the dumb one in the family." By then, we realized he was in trouble and were really worried. Unfortunately, he sensed our anxiety, which didn't help. Seeing that Shai was so successful at school made things *go from bad to worse. At the end of the sixth grade we saw that Amichai was losing his motivation, and we moved him to a different school again. The new school had a more caring attitude, with more emphasis on character development and less on scholastic achievement. They found opportunities to praise him and give him prizes. Instead of being at the bottom of his class he zoomed up and began believing in himself again.*

Now 17, Amichai is still quiet and very modest, never giving himself credit. "I'm a plain person; I'm nothing special," seems to be his attitude. He actually is something special — fabulous in taking care of his younger siblings, patient, loving and caring, nonjudgmental of them and of us, his parents. He gives you the feeling that he has tremendous appreciation of anything you do for him. He rarely asks for things and is very easily satisfied. For instance, if I give him 100 shekel, he'll give me back 50 saying, "What for? 50 is enough." But grownups have a hard time with him because of his shyness and modesty. They convey the message that there is something wrong with it, and he senses this. They don't see the beauty in it.

Parents of a difficult teenager sometimes wonder whether change is still possible at this late stage. The following is a case history of Chanoch, a young man, whose parents had truly given up on him. Today, Chanoch is a source of genuine joy to them. A change in the parents' basic attitude paved the way for a change in the boy's behavior.

Chanoch's father recalls:

Chanoch was our first son. He'd always been a difficult child. At school he was a weak student, because of poor concentration ability. This was a great disappointment to me — I'd expected this first boy to become a Torah scholar. I yelled at him a lot.

At 15, Chanoch became very rebellious. Once, he ran away from home because I yelled at him for getting up late on Sukkos. When he misbehaved we always got very angry. Sometimes I even hit him.

At 19, Chanoch became a closed person. There were fre-
quent outbursts, especially when we requested something of
him. He would answer back or shout at us. He was lazy and
spent much time in bed. During vacations, he got up late and
went to shul at 10:30. Though with outsiders he controlled
himself — his teachers and friends at yeshiva considered him
a pleasant person — with us he was rebellious and made lit-
tle effort at self-discipline. We felt completely desperate
about him.

Chanoch's mother continues:

Whenever I'd ask for his help, Chanoch would answer, "In
five minutes." When the time had passed, he would say the
same thing. It could take 20 minutes until he finally came.
"I can't rely on you at all!" I would explode. "You're always
running away from jobs!" He would yell back — "I don't
care!"
    On Fridays when Chanoch was home from yeshiva, he
usually went out for the day. We asked him to be home an
hour before Shabbos to help us. He always came in a few
minutes before I lit candles. The same thing happened Erev
Pesach. I got very angry. My thoughts were: "How does he
leave me with all the work?! He's so insensitive, he doesn't
care about me at all!" Still, I heard from a neighbor that he
helped her drag a heavy piece of furniture a long distance.
Also, he helps elderly people. And once when I fell and broke
a rib, he helped me very much — he was really with me. So
he really is a caring person.
    Another good side to Chanoch is that his ambitions is to
improve. For example, he makes resolutions to apply him-
self to his studies at yeshiva. Unfortunately he lacks the self-
discipline to carry them out.

The first stage of counseling focused on helping Chanoch's parents to gain some measure of calm, by teaching them to refrain
from evaluating the situation as intolerable. Instead of seeing their
son in a negative light, they learned to view his poor behavior as a

bad habit, which he needed help to overcome. Chanoch needed to feel that his parents cared about him, and saw him as capable of behaving better.

The parents were also instructed in behavior modification techniques. For example, if Chanoch yelled, "No! I don't want to," or, "I'm not in the mood," they were to point out to him that he harmed only himself with such talk. When he shouted they were to tell him, "We won't listen to you when you yell. Calm down, then we'll listen."

Signs of improvement appeared after the first month. Chanoch's mother reports:

> One night, Chanoch burst out, "I can't talk to you. I don't know how you're going to look for a shidduch for me — you don't understand me at all!" I answered, "You don't let us talk to you about personal matters — all one can discuss with you is politics or gossip."
>
> Later that night I came into his room, sat on his bed and said, "Maybe you and I can start to work together to control our anger?"
>
> "Leave me alone!" he shot back, and added sarcastically, "Maybe you want to put up a star chart on the closet door!?" But then he told me of his willingness to get up for shul at 7:00 the next morning.
>
> The next day at 7:30, I woke him up. It was the usual story: "Soon"..."soon"..."soon." I tried at 8:00 — same thing. My husband tried at 8:30, with no better results. Chanoch was in bed until a 8:45. At last he was ready and left the house for shul. Suddenly he returned, mumbling that he forgot something. Immediately he started fighting with Shlomo, his 12-year-old brother. I tried very hard not to mix in the way I always do. It was quite a fight.
>
> Finally, Shlomo came into my room, telling me that Chanoch had come back to look in the mirror, bumped into him, and that's why they had fought. I told Shlomo, "You know that your brother has had a difficult time lately, but we're trying to work on it, and we hope that things will soon be better."

Chanoch came in right away, having overheard me talking about him. I asked him very quietly what had happened. He answered that Shlomo always left his drawer open, so that when he came back to look in the mirror he bumped into it and hurt himself, promptly smacked his brother, who then threw things at him. Calmly, I said, "It's not right that you fought with him."

Then Chanoch said, "I need money" (he always waits for opportunities when I'm calm). I gave him some. Later on I asked him, "Did you see how I worked on myself not to get angry at you, after all that happened?"

"I loved it," he answered. "You're wonderful!" And then he kissed me. I felt like I was beginning to get my son back.

But there were still plenty of problems. The weeks before Pesach were especially difficult. Last year Chanoch came home from yeshiva two weeks before Pesach and announced that he would clean his father's bookshelves — but he wouldn't help me at all. I couldn't believe it. He knew how much I relied on his help. Chanoch worked on the bookshelves for two days. Then he came to us and said, "You should know that I've taken a job. I'll work all day, and evenings I'll help you a bit." We showed him how disappointed we were at his taking on outside work, when we so needed his help at home.

Chanoch said he would come home early from work, but actually never arrived before 8:00. Yet at least he had changed his mind about not helping me. He even said to me, "Give me a couple of jobs and I'll do them when I get home tonight." I assigned him the refrigerator and stove. That evening he came home at 10:00. He managed to clean only half the refrigerator. All in all, it took him two days to get it finished. When it came to the stove, he decided he had no strength for it. My husband had to help me with it. Chol Hamo'ed, he was with friends every night — he never told us where he was. When he was home, he spent much of his time listening to the radio.

After Pesach a shidduch was proposed — by now Chanoch was 21 — but we never followed through because of the situation. He told us many times that he would take himself in hand during the next study period at yeshiva. We were really hopeful. The tone at home had changed completely. To help things along, we were asking a minimum of him. We didn't get angry when he spoke disrespectfully; we didn't react when he kept late hours or missed meals — during that period he was really more of a stranger than a son.

A dramatic change in Chanoch took place when he went back to yeshiva. Firstly, he had good study partners. In addition, we arranged for someone to study with him, without him knowing that the man was being paid. After two weeks, his teacher reported that our son was learning very well.

Chanoch was definitely opening up. He began coming home more frequently. On Fridays, he was home in time to help, ready to do any jobs. But he requested not to be given fixed tasks — he didn't want me to be a taskmaster, always on top of him telling him what to do, as in the past. He was even available to help out on Motza'ei Shabbos, rather than spending the evening with friends. But he always insisted that he didn't want to be pinned down as to when he'd come, what he would do, etc. By now he had become quite pleasant. One time he came home unexpectedly, and when I asked him why he came, he said, "I missed you," and kissed me.

Another time, Shlomo and Chanoch had gone completely wild, which is very hard on my nerves. With great effort I managed to stay calm. But afterwards I just couldn't bring himself to talk to Chanoch. He couldn't stand that and walked around in circles, until he finally came to tell me he was sorry. Later in the evening he told me, "Mom, I'm so happy with you, because I feel that you're changing." I answered, "Maybe you'll do the same?"

The following year, our son found out about a new yeshiva — one more geared to boys of his type. We were happy with the initiative he had shown and gladly approved of his choice. The new teachers gave him much love and attention and he became one of the most popular members of his group. This gave him much self-confidence.

After that year we reopened the idea of shidduchim, and this in itself made him become more serious about his aims in life. Baruch Hashem, we were able to arrange for a very *suitable match, and the couple is extremely happy together. It's a true joy for us — a real miracle!*

The above stories illustrate widely varying reactions to adolescence. They also illustrate the role which the home plays in easing this transition period. Where the attitude is one of acceptance toward life's inevitable difficulties, coupled with a readiness to deal with whatever problems arise, and where parents relate to each other and to their children calmly and patiently, this period can pass with a minimum of difficulty. As one mother put it:

With my teenagers I used the same principles studied earlier in my parenting group. I had no special problems with them. They seem to have absorbed the basic approach which helped me so much when I first began the class. I once heard my teenage son say to his younger brother, when he was upset over something, "Who says life has to be fair?"

TYPICAL PATTERNS

Teenagers tend to be absorbed in themselves and their particular problems. They want to be like everybody else, to "run with the pack," dress like all the others do, wear the same hair style, etc. This seems to make them feel secure. Try to maintain an empathic and tolerant attitude toward your youngster's "need." If you deem a particular fashion to be immodest or outlandish, convey this in gentle tones, refraining from personal attacks.

In addition to this need to fit in with the group, the following are patterns commonly displayed by teenagers.

Moodiness

Moodiness manifests itself in a variety of ways — sullen silence, withdrawal, crying, banging doors, or other volatile behavior. In the adolescent, moodiness is kicked off by the same things which upset all of us — our negative view of others, of ourselves, or of events in our lives. It's just that during the teen years moods tend to be more intense, and shifts more extreme.

If your teenager seems unusually moody, try to draw him out. Listen, empathize, and be with him. If he really doesn't feel like talking, don't pry. Try to help him see that this state, which is so real to him, is a mood strictly stemming from his view of things and is not objective reality. Chapter 6 discusses this in greater detail.

Low Self-Image

Low self-image was briefly discussed in Chapter 4. Here we discuss the problem as it relates to teenagers specifically.

What causes low self-image? A low self-image means that we see ourselves negatively. It develops from the habit of self-criticism — telling ourselves off for our wrongdoings (real or imagined), for our bad traits, foolish remarks, and from hating things about ourselves such as our (perceived) lack of intelligence, poor looks, bad figure — the list is endless.

This habit of self-criticism is formed early in life. To educate children, parents have to set limits and requirements. But children have minds of their own and don't always go along with their parents' wishes. There's where the trouble begins.

In Chapter 1, we discussed the problem of low frustration tolerance (LFT). Parents with LFT, when confronted with a misbehaving child, tend to jump quickly from thinking, "I can't stand it!" to "They're rotten kids!" Whether the parents merely think this or actually call the child "rotten," or any of a variety of other choice epithets such as "stubborn," "*chutzpadik*," "selfish," or "mean," the message gets across. The child concludes, "Mommy thinks I'm bad because I didn't listen," or, "Daddy thinks I'm awful because I keep coming out of bed," or, "Mommy thinks I'm not nice because I don't share my toys." Parents tend to focus on their child's negative attributes, overlooking his positive traits.

To aggravate matters, children interpret this temporary rejection as a sign that the parents don't love them. From there it's a short step to, "I'm unlovable."

In time, a child — and particularly a sensitive one — internalizes the put-down messages to which he's been exposed. He begins to put *himself* down and see himself as worthless or "no good" when he behaves poorly, does something wrong, acts foolishly, or does anything which he fears might bring on criticism. The habit can generalize to other areas, such as appearance or intelligence. This kind of picking on himself chips away at his sense of worth. Now he has a low self-image. To shore up his self-image, he may turn to others for approval.

While parents probably are a major factor here, other possible environmental influences in this process shouldn't be overlooked.

What can be done about a low self-image: How can a Torah outlook protect us from falling into this negative pattern? Judaism teaches that each individual has inherent value, by virtue of having been created in God's image. Judging our spiritual level is God's domain and not our business. Instead of global self-evaluations such as, "I'm so selfish!" or "I'm bad because I get angry all the time," which accomplish nothing, we should objectively appraise our behavior and then take steps to correct it. For example, we can say, "I sometimes act selfishly. From now on, I'll try to think more about the needs of others." Or, "I have a bad habit of getting angry. I'm going to work hard to control myself."

Since a poor self-image develops from putting oneself down, to correct it, a person has to stop putting himself down. But as with all bad habits, this one isn't easily broken. Persistent effort is required. (Chapter 1 offers guidance on this.)

If your teenager has a low self-image (frequent mood swings are a tip-off), you can help him by conveying your unconditional love and acceptance of him as a worthy individual. If in the past you haven't restrained yourself from verbal attacks, you need to begin now. This, as pointed out above, starts in the cognitive approach, with being aware of how anger is triggered by specific thoughts. Practice convincing yourself that you *can* tolerate the difficulties that this budding adult is causing. (Refer to Chapter 1 for more details.) In addition, you can help him by introducing him to the basic principles discussed above. (You might have him read this section.)

Don't fall into the common trap of trying to prove your teenager wrong, when he sees himself negatively. For instance, if your daughter tells you she's not nice, don't jump in right away with: "That's not true. You *are* a nice person," going on to point out all the nice things about her. First, hear her out. Then, try to find out *why* she sees herself as not nice.

Whatever faults she mentions, your reaction should be basically: "I'm not sure if everything that you say is true, but let's assume that it is. So you haven't always *acted* so nicely. That doesn't mean that you, yourself, are not nice. Besides, when we have shortcomings — and who doesn't? — our job is to correct them. There's no point in trying to judge ourselves. That's Hashem's business. We stick to judging our *behavior* only. Instead of thinking, 'I'm not a nice person,' it's much more helpful to think, 'What I just did really wasn't very nice.' Try to do what you can to correct it, and plan ways to be nicer from now on. Don't even judge yourself 'nice.' Rather, tell yourself, 'My *behavior* was nice. It's really improving.'"

The main objective is to help her develop an attitude of self-acceptance, along with the acknowledgment that she could do better.

Fear of Failure

Adolescents, especially those of high-school age, can be very troubled by fear of possible failure, whether academic, social, or in any area important to them. Anxiety begins with the thought, "What if (I fail at school, I do poorly in gym, my friend rejects me, etc.)...." From there the person goes on to "awfulize" about these possibilities. Again, avoid the trap of arguing the youngster out of his fears. To begin with, these fears might actually be realized — and he knows it. More importantly, this is missing the point. Anxiety over failure has its roots in the mistaken perception that our value as human beings is linked to our accomplishments, and/or in the perceived inability to tolerate the practical difficulties which failure would bring.

After hearing him out, suggest a "worst-case scenario" approach. Tell him to imagine that his worst fears would be realized. How would he view that? You can ask him, "Do you see failing as something awful?" He'll probably say that he does. You then ask him why it would be awful. What would it mean? If he's unable to put his finger on the exact meaning that failure holds for him, you can help him out with some possibilities: he might see himself as deficient or inferior, others might view him this way, people might be angry with him or they might ridicule him. He might see having to repeat a failed course, etc. as unbearable. The trick is to get him to face these fears and come to grips with them — to see that as unpleasant as failure might be, it wouldn't be the end of the world; he could tolerate it. Finally, emphasize that failure in a certain area doesn't say anything about his value as a person. (For a discussion of anxiety associated with schoolwork, see Chapter 16.)

Let's face it, success — being outstanding in some area — feels pleasant. But one negative side of this is that inevitably there will be some other area in which we don't succeed. Then what happens? If we equate self-worth with success, we'll be "down in the dumps." Teenagers are particularly susceptible to this. They'll say, "I'm no good at math." The parents' tendency is to jump in with reassurances: "That's not true. You *are* good in math," or, "Maybe you're not so good at math, but you're terrific in history." Many teens will say, "I'm no good at anything."

We should certainly seek ways to help our teenager to develop any potential abilities or talents and to improve any weaknesses. But this alone doesn't treat the root of the problem. We need to help him understand that whether his perception of lacking ability, looks, etc. is correct or not, this really isn't the issue. The underlying fallacy here is that the youngster is, consciously or unconsciously, basing his worth (partial or entire) on the level of his achievements or talents. It is as if lack of success in some area diminishes his worth. Or he believes that he must shine at *something* in order to be "somebody."

Western society strongly encourages the development of these beliefs, and reinforces them constantly. They have, most unfortunately, even seeped into our Torah society and its educational system. It is vital for us to counter this influence, by stressing that an individual's worth is intrinsic. We should utilize every opportunity to develop this more constructive and objective Torah viewpoint.

Looks

The problem of teenage daughters (sometimes sons, too) who are miserable over their — real or imagined — unattractive appearance must be handled delicately. A woman recalled how as a girl of 13 she hated her looks, and would cry whenever she viewed herself in the mirror. More than anything else, she wanted to be beautiful like her popular, older sister. Actually she wasn't bad looking at all — in fact, she had delicate beauty, but a poor self-image. On top of that, she wasn't good in social relationships. Her well-meaning parents comforted her: "Never mind that you're not pretty — you're smart." This only made her more miserable.

Often, with teenagers who think they are bad looking, what they're really looking for is the popularity and admiration which they think would surely be theirs if only they were beautiful. Parents can point out that there is not only physical, external beauty, but inner beauty as well. There's more to beauty than perfect facial features. A smile does so much to light up a face. And we all know individuals who aren't at all good looking, yet are well liked and have many friends. Although at this age, especially, external beauty can indeed make for superficial popularity, what ultimately counts is having true, good friends who see others for what they really are.

Still, a plain-looking girl can do much to make herself prettier. A flattering hairdo can help, facial blemishes can be covered up, and glasses can be exchanged for contact lenses.

When excess weight is a problem, be careful to avoid making derogatory remarks about it. Adolescents who are overweight are usually very self-critical because of it, hating themselves for their poor self-control. This is the vicious cycle of acting counterproductively, hitting oneself for it but not doing anything about it, and so on. Counseling can sometimes help, or the teenager might join a Weight Watchers group. Don't nag or make remarks like, "You don't really want another serving of spaghetti!" Your acceptance of your teenager as he is will help him to accept himself as he is. Then, hopefully, he'll eventually be motivated to change his eating habits. Ultimately it's a matter of self-discipline, which is especially difficult when it comes to food.

Parents who share this problem and who work to keep their own weight down can be an inspiring example to their teenager in this respect. Preparing low-calorie meals and banishing "junk food" from your home can also help — all providing that the boy or girl is motivated to diet. (For a fuller discussion on overweight, see Chapter 17.)

Teenagers sometimes complain about having few friends, when it's lack of social skills that's the real problem. You can explain that in order to have friends, one needs to show interest in others and be a good listener. You might suggest doing some role playing, to provide practice and help them feel more comfortable in social relationships.

It is important to stress to your teen that being beautiful, popular, or admired, has nothing to do with our value as individuals. These traits may make us feel good but they aren't what count in life, and at best, give us temporary pleasure only. Genuine and lasting joy comes from living a Torah life — doing God's will, seeing ourselves attain higher levels in character refinement, feeling deep down that we're fulfilling our purpose in life, and occupying ourselves with mitzvos and deeds that increase others' happiness and well-being.

Overblown Ego

Teenagers who have a lot going for them, such as 15-year-old Shai described earlier, are apt to develop an overblown ego. Almost invariably, a show of superiority masks an underlying uncertainty about one's worth. A person who is truly secure about himself has no need to convince himself that he's better than others.

Help your child by teaching him to be thankful for the abilities and talents with which he's been blessed. Point out, "You've been fortunate to have received so many wonderful qualities and abilities. But being blessed in this way doesn't make you better than others. Just the opposite — it obligates you to feel grateful to Hashem for these precious gifts, and to use them to benefit other people."

COMMON BEHAVIOR PROBLEMS

Many problems which parents face in dealing with adolescents are no different from those encountered with younger children. Parents can refer for guidance to specific topics in this book.

In dealing with any problem behavior, be realistic. If your teenager's behavior in a particular area has thus far been unsatisfactory, this won't change for the better overnight.

Imagine yourself in your adolescent's position and try to understand how he sees things. (This shouldn't be that hard, since all of us were adolescents at one time.) Blaming your youngster for all the trouble you're having on his account will only make you angry at him, and will get you nowhere.

As cognitive psychology teaches us, the crucial ingredient for keeping the relationship on an even keel is tolerance. This doesn't mean that you should ignore objectionable behavior. It does mean refraining from *personal intolerance,* as expressed in thoughts such as, "I can't take these moods!" or "She's driving me crazy!" Even if we don't *say* these things, the irritation triggered by such thoughts is bound to come across to the adolescent and have a negative effect on him. Parents need to work on convincing themselves that, while things may be difficult, they very well *can* take it.

Also to be avoided is nonconstructive self-blame, taken on in an effort to account for the child's difficult behavior. By eliminating both anger and guilt, parents will gain a measure of calm with which to deal with difficult situations effectively.

Disrespect

The problem of disrespect was dealt with in Chapter 2. Here we focus on special aspects of disrespectful behavior in teenagers.

Your adolescent has more definite opinions now and, in discussions with you, he may forget about being respectful to you when he expresses them. Thus he treats you as his equal, contradicting, criticizing, ridiculing, and the like. This disrespect can express itself in any area. For example, when asked to perform some chore he may yell, "Why me?" or, "Why not (so and so)?" or, "I did my share — I'm not doing any more!"

In dealing with disrespect, a basic rule is: *Avoid anger.* Try to identify the thoughts which are bringing it on, such as, "How *dare* she talk like that to me!" or, "What *chutzpah!*" or, "I won't stand for this!" If such thoughts aren't dealt with, you'll surely "blow your top," causing your youngster to yell back or retreat in sullen resentment. What have you accomplished? Remind yourself that this isn't such unusual behavior and that you *can* deal with it.

Here's how one mother dealt with her daughter's impertinence:

> *Over a period of about half a year, I was becoming increasingly exasperated as my 13-year-old daughter, Tamar, became progressively more chutzpadik (especially in her challenging of family rules). When she spoke disrespectfully, I inevitably got angry and yelled at her (about her chutzpah), causing her either to yell back or to retreat and sulk resentfully.*
>
> *Freshly armed with new insights from our group workshop, I resolved to handle the next situation more effectively. My chance came the following evening when Tamar began to carry on disrespectfully at my suggestion that it was time for bed. I bit my tongue to refrain from lashing out verbally, as Tamar yelled, then stomped off to her room.*
>
> *About five minutes later, figuring that Tamar had had enough time to cool off, I went into her room. Sitting down on the bed next to her, I took her hand in mine. "Tamar," I said very gently, "you know, it isn't right for you to speak to me this way. I've had to point it out to you over and over lately. It isn't right."*
>
> *"I'm sorry," Tamar whispered, as her eyes filled with tears.*
>
> *Later, I could not stop marveling at the clear-cut difference caused by my controlled behavior. For the first time in half a year, I had gotten the regretful response which I had all along been unable to draw forth using anger!*

Generally, it's better not to correct disrespect on the spot. But if necessary, it needn't be a problem to do so if you remember to keep your voice very low. A father told how this worked with his 18-year-old son:

> *I was looking for the thermometer, which I knew Yechiel had used the day before. I called out to him, "Where's the thermometer?"*

"How should I know?" came back his answer.

I walked over to him and said, very quietly, "First of all, you didn't answer me nicely." Yechiel grinned sheepishly in recognition. Then we resumed the discussion about the thermometer, with Yechiel talking especially quietly and respectfully.

Thirteen-year-old Sa'adia's mother reported:

I was putting Sa'adia's laundered shirts away, when I came upon one drawer of underwear with everything topsy turvy. "Sa'adia," I called out, "come in here, please. Your drawer is in total chaos!"

"Are you calling me about the room again?" he said in a complaining voice as he walked in.

I said nothing for a moment, and then replied in a very friendly way, "That was a complaint, Sa'adia."

"I didn't like the way you called me," Sa'adia said, somewhat apologetically.

"Then you could have told me respectfully," I answered gently.

Sa'adia smiled, and then went on to explain why the drawer was such a mess. (He had worn several undershirts, one over the other, for extra warmth while on a hike, and since he would need them the next day he saw no reason to fold them up again.)

Contradicting and Criticizing Parents

Contradicting parents is a transgression of the mitzvah of reverence.[3] Teenagers tend to forget this. For instance, Tami has been monopolizing the phone. Father says to her, "Please Tami, you've been on the phone for over an hour. No one can reach us." She answers, "That's not true. I made only two calls and they didn't take longer than half an hour." Father may be tempted to prove her wrong, in which case a fruitless debate ensues. In the process, Tami's disrespectful contradiction of her father is totally overlooked. The father shouldn't argue with his daughter. Rather, he should wait a moment and then, in a friendly tone, tell her quietly, "You know, you just contradicted me."

When confronted with a shouting child or adolescent, never shout back. Sixteen-year-old Chava, is screaming at her mother who has asked her to help with the Shabbos cooking, when she wanted to go out with her friends. Mother should tell her daughter that she must stay to help, and furthermore, that she won't listen to her until she calms down. This is *not* the time to reflect back with, "I see you're very angry at me," which will almost surely result in the rejoinder, "You bet I am!" While the girl's anger is accepted as a reality and she is not condemned for it, her mother must avoid encouraging her expressing it.

When Chava quiets down, her mother should point out in a friendly way, "I know you were upset before, Chava, but you're not allowed to shout at your parents. You can tell me quietly and respectfully that something is bothering you, and I'll try to understand you." At an appropriate time, Mother should explain to Chava that she is not being kept home just for her mother's convenience, but for her own benefit as well. Helping parents is an opportunity to perform the mitzvah of *chesed*. Also, life requires a certain amount of self-discipline, a readiness to do things even when they are not to our liking.

Faced with parental unwillingness to grant some wish, teenagers often try to weaken the parents' position by wailing, "But all my friends' parents let them!" This form of disrespect, too, is frequently overlooked. It shouldn't be.

Seventeen-year-old Eliezer asked his parents to let him take driving lessons. The parents had no objections, but told their son he'd have to finance the lessons himself. "But all the other boys' parents pay for their lessons!" Eliezer argued. Nevertheless, the parents stuck to their decision. But Eliezer didn't let up. On visits home from yeshiva he raised the issue again and again. After several weeks of this, it occurred to his parents that they were entirely overlooking the implied disrespect in Eliezer's arguments. He was, in effect, criticizing his parents for not measuring up to the other boys' parents. They calmly pointed this out to their son, and it put an end to the arguing. Then, to show their good will, they offered to subsidize the lessons in part.

Disorder

An area of major conflict is parents' unhappiness with the disorderly appearance of their teenager's room. Generally, this has been the state of affairs for years, and it shouldn't be expected that such a longstanding habit will change easily. The youngster needs your encouragement to help overcome a negative attitude toward cleaning up.

You might say pleasantly, "Sharon, I *know* how much you hate to clean up and how hard it is for you to bring yourself to do it. You know, there are times when I don't feel much like cleaning up either — I just force myself to do it anyway. Afterwards, I feel good. I've found that the trick is not to think about what an awful job cleaning is, but just to do it. Afterwards when I've finished, I realize it wasn't so bad after all. Then I have the reward of a nice, neat room, and I have the additional pleasure of a sense of victory over my lazy inclinations. Remember, Sharon, how much trouble you had last Friday looking for your necklace? Think how nice it would be to have a room with everything at your fingertips, instead of a mess which makes you feel disgusted with yourself every time you look at it."

Offer your help, getting things started with a general reorganization of the room, showing how to keep small items in boxes and so on.

Remind your teenager — but not more than once a day — to straighten up his room. If you do this in a friendly way, without complaints or criticism, he'll generally make some effort. If the room is still in bad shape, first commend him for what he achieved — then tactfully specify what remains to be done. For example, "My, Asher, how nice that bookshelf looks! Now I'd like to see you tackle the pile of clothes on your bed, and the papers on your desk."

Another way to handle the problem is to make a list of the remaining tasks and post it on the door or a bulletin board. For example, "Asher, your desk looks terrific! Please get started now on..." Don't allow yourself to start thinking, "I shouldn't have to tell him all this — he knows it." The fact is that if you don't tell him, he won't do it. You might as well accept this fact and not disturb yourself with mulling over how things *should* be.

Try to avoid upsetting yourself with thinking, "They don't even notice what a state their room is in!" or "They don't seem to care at all about the mess!" Unfortunately, this may well be the reality of the situation. In that case, it is better to accept it and then go on from there; it's useless to try to *force* teenagers to notice or care more about the appearance of their room. Nonetheless, don't let up on your efforts to impress them with the importance and advantages of neatness; hopefully, with time these lessons will sink in.

There's no harm done, however, if you tell your teenager at times that it upsets *you* to see disorder in his room. With this, you let him know that even if a messy room doesn't bother *him*, he should keep it neat out of consideration for you. Naturally, this shouldn't be said in an excited or angry tone of voice, as this would convey intolerance.

Keep in mind though, that much as your children may want to please you, they may be loath to make the necessary effort. Typically, they'll answer, "Yes, Mom," yet still make little effort to improve. In that case, you might ask for some assurance — for example, "I'd feel better if I could have some kind of commitment from you — like telling me right now about a specific time which you plan to set aside regularly for cleanup."

It's a good idea to reach a compromise whereby the rooms have to be neat and tidy at least once a week. To provide additional motivation, the youngster, after being forewarned of the consequences, can be denied his weekly allowance if the room doesn't pass inspection.

Late Hours

The problem of teenagers coming home at all hours can be worrisome indeed. Ground rules are essential. Decide on an appropriate curfew, depending on the age of the youngster. (It goes without saying that parents must keep an ever-watchful eye on their children's activities and the company they keep.) If for any reason they can't be home by the hour agreed they *must* call, to spare you anxiety.

The Phone

The telephone is a major bone of contention in homes with teenage children. What's to be done? The problem can be alleviated by installing an additional phone line. But this isn't dealing with the root cause — and in any case, if there are several phone-users in your family, the phone may very well still be tied up, just when you need it!

Call a family meeting and establish ground rules for phone usage. For example: If the phone is in use when you need it, you'll *politely* request that the conversation be ended in, say, five minutes (or whatever period of time is agreed upon), with no recriminations. If needed urgently, the phone should be relinquished quickly (again, the exact amount of time needs to be agreed upon). If your teenager reproaches *you* for tying up the phone, remind him that this is disrespectful.

As for incorrigible "schmoozers" who have difficulty with these rules, be empathic (after all, how about your own lengthy chatting?) but at the same time, be very firm that they observe whatever rules have been established.

Loud Music

You don't have to tolerate loud music blaring constantly from your teenagers' rooms — especially if it's loud music that's not to your taste. When the tape player is on full blast, you can ask pleasantly that it be turned down, or turned off. (You'll have to go into their room to ask so that they will hear you!) Don't give them a long tirade about how you can't stand the noise. On the other hand, don't suffer silently, out of guilt about depriving your teenagers of their youthful pleasure. This is essential training for them to learn consideration for others, and for their parents in particular. (Earphones can be a big help here.)

Chapter Sixteen

THE SCHOOL: ASSISTING IN THE EDUCATIONAL ENDEAVOR

*U*ntil the Talmudic period, Jewish children were educated exclusively by their parents. They were taught Torah and some trade or craft by which to earn a living. Because of a danger that Torah might be forgotten, Yehoshua ben Gamla established, at the beginning of the Talmudic period, an innovation of major importance — the world's first system of public education.[1] Whereas parents previously bore the sole responsibility for teaching their children, now they could delegate some of this responsibility to others. It must be kept in mind, however, that in the area of moral training, all the school can do is help parents in their work. Here, the parents' job remains primary. The home is the ideal environment for molding children's character.

ASSUMING A SUPPORTIVE ROLE

In choosing a school, it is important to make extensive inquiries in order to find the best possible learning environment for your child. Once your decision is made, you must entrust your child to the school's care and assume a supportive role. Naturally, a school is only as good as its teachers, and teachers, sadly, are not always the perfect examples we would like for our children. Often they are far from the prescribed ideal: "If the teacher is like an angel of God, they shall seek Torah from his mouth; if not, they shall not seek Torah from his mouth."[2] Still, try to be tolerant, difficult though this can be sometimes. However dissatisfied you may be, never talk about it in front of your children! This is likely to foster disrespect for their school and teachers.

In addition to giving the school your full support, you should maintain contact with your child's teacher on a regular basis to discuss his progress and find out about any problems he might be having.

PLAYING SICK

Some children simply hate school and try to get out of going by complaining of various aches and pains. Try applying some logical consequences. Two mothers relate their experiences:

> My 9-year-old Yisrael, who isn't too keen on school, to put it mildly, complained one morning that he couldn't stand on his legs. I was pretty sure he was faking to get out of going to school. So I said to him, "All right, I'll bring you over in the stroller." I'm sure that at that point he would have been willing to walk, but by now he was caught! To his great mortification, Yisrael went to school that morning in his baby brother's stroller — but I think he learned something from the experience.

> Our Yechiel, nearly 13, often woke up complaining of a stomach ache. Our doctor could find nothing wrong. Yechiel had been very excited about our upcoming trip to Israel for his bar mitzvah, so I said, "How can we possibly go to Israel with a sick child? No way! We'd have to worry about you every day!" That put a quick stop to the stomach aches.

With a child who insists he's too sick to go to school when it's clear that he's looking for an excuse to stay home, you can try calling his bluff by saying, "Okay, you can stay home. But I have to put you in pajamas and you must stay in bed." One mother who tried this reported that within five minutes her youngster said, "I feel better already," got dressed, and went to school. (Obviously, this won't work with children who love the idea of staying in bed.)

WHEN TO START NURSERY SCHOOL

Many children just love nursery school and can't wait to go every day. They thrive on the social setting which nursery school offers, the songs, games, arts and crafts, and other fun activities. If a child, though very young, seems eager to start, there's no reason to delay enrolling him.

But many other children suffer separation trauma, sometimes prolonged, leaving parents in a quandary — should they force the issue? It depends. If the mother has taken on an outside job, or if other, younger children are making it hard for her to function with everyone at home all day, it would seem that there is little choice but to weather the daily weeping, hysteria, tantrums, etc. Keep in mind that no real harm is being done to the child. He's miserable, true. Accept this, but don't let it plunge you into guilt feelings. It's essential also to refrain from impatience or annoyance about these morning ordeals. Try to display a matter-of-fact, cheerful attitude, at the same time expressing empathy with soothing words: "I know, you don't want to go. Okay, sweetheart, Mommy will be here when you come home." Drag the child along if you have to, and remind yourself that eventually, this will pass.

But if there's no real need for nursery school as yet, consider postponing it. If the child still wants to be close to you, you'll save him and yourself needless upset.

Here's a mother who decided to begin with an informal play group setting as a way to get her daughter used to the idea of playing with other children on her own:

> Shortly after the birth of our third child, I started a play group for Tammi, our oldest (nearly 3 at the time), in our

largely Hebrew-speaking neighborhood in Jerusalem. The group, with three other English-speaking children, met in various homes, including mine. She went happily the first few times; in fact, it was even hard to get her to come home again. But the following week she threw up at my friend's house (I think it was because she was coming down with a cold). I ran over to bring her home.

After that experience Tammi wouldn't go at all to anyone's home, not even to her grandparents', unless my husband or I stayed with her. Also, whenever I left her with a baby-sitter (even with her father), she cried and got hysterical to the point of throwing up. If I so much as mentioned the play group, she would say, tearfully, "No, no, Ima stay with me!" We decided not to insist that she go, although she did participate in the play group when it met in our house once a week.

Five months later, the summer before she was to go to "gan" (in Israel, this term is used interchangeably for nursery and kindergarten — virtually all children begin gan at age 3¹/₂), we decided to start Tammi again with the same play group, except that now one of her regular baby-sitters was running it as a little four-week day camp (known as "kaytana" in Israel) — right in our building upstairs on the third flour.

Even when she went to the kaytana, Tammi didn't go happily. She would cling to me weeping, "No, I don't want to go!" but I would only answer, matter-of-factly, "It's time to go, Tammi. All the other children are there."

"Then don't go, Ima. Stay with me."

"Ima has to go downstairs to be with the other children. I'll pick you up soon."

As we'd climb the stairs, Tammi's tears would subside somewhat. She would say, "Ima, hold my hand," but once inside she'd resume her crying. Each time, I left quickly with a friendly but final good-bye.

It was hard for me to leave her like that. Sometimes I would stand outside the closed door, hoping the crying would soon stop — which it often did. The girl who ran the kaytana told me that after I would leave, Tammi usually would settle down within five minutes.

Gradually Tammi was accepting the reality of being separated from me, but she still wouldn't stay at anyone's home unless Ima or Abba were with her.

After summer she started gan. It was a large, Hebrew-speaking gan, with only one other child whom she knew — fortunately, English-speaking too. I anticipated difficulties but my husband and I felt it was the right thing to do.

Tammi didn't want to go to gan. Sometimes she'd cry along the way, but I would hold her hand firmly, with an attitude of "This has to be done — it's important for her." When we'd get there, she wouldn't want to stay, but she knew she had to. "Ima, come and get me soon," she'd beseech me, weeping pitifully. But at least she no longer said, "Stay with me." I think my firm attitude made it easier for her to accept reality.

It took a good two months until Tammi stopped crying altogether (even then, when there was a substitute teacher, she went back to her crying). Now, half a year later, Tammi goes off happily to gan each morning. She feels good about herself for having overcome her anxiety, though she still prefers that I, rather than her Abba, take her to gan. She's made friends, is comfortable with the Hebrew, and is managing nicely.

MISBEHAVIOR AT SCHOOL

Parents naturally measure their own success by their children's behavior. This is why, when they hear that their child misbehaves at school, they see it as a sign of *their* failure. Knowing that others, too, see them as having failed, increases the pain.

Parents' reactions vary. Some get angry at the child and punish him for bringing such disgrace upon them. Others get angry at the teacher, blaming him for the problem. Neither approach is constructive.

To deal effectively with the situation, we have to begin by identifying the true sources of our anger — our sense of failure and our feelings of shame — and deal with these. When we evaluate ourselves negatively because of our child's poor conduct, it's because we're assuming that it must be our fault. But the child's misbehavior at school could be due to other reasons. Remember that even if parents were to do everything right (if that were indeed possible!), it still wouldn't guarantee them perfectly behaved children. In any case, it's best not to be involved with global evaluation of ourselves, nor with the concomitant worry about what others think of us.

Once we're feeling calm, we should talk to the child and let him tell his side of the story. We might say gently, "You know, I heard some unpleasant things about you from the teacher. Could you tell me what's happening?" Whatever problems the child raises, we should relate to them seriously. Perhaps some of these can be solved by tactful intervention on our part. But no matter what difficulties he's having, he must know that he has to respect his teachers, especially his Torah teacher.[3]

Often the misbehaving child is only trying to have fun. In that case you need to have a serious talk with him about this. An incentive system can sometimes motivate him to improve his behavior. One mother shares her story:

> My son was bringing home bad conduct reports from the teacher nearly every day. It came to a point where I was willing to try almost anything. I knew that my son loved money, so I promised him a quarter for every day that he didn't bring home a bad report. His behavior improved immediately and I was able to gradually discontinue the payments. I know that most people wouldn't think it a good idea to pay a child for good behavior, but I was just desperate. In retrospect, I think it was the right decision in this situation.

In serious cases, you can try punishment, but it's usually better to leave disciplinary action to the school.

Don't immediately blame the teacher for the child's faulty conduct, but do keep in mind that poor teaching skills or poor control of the class are often at the bottom of the problem. However, the child should never see himself as the one in the right. Certainly, as already mentioned, he must never hear you berate the school or belittle the teacher.

HANDLING COMPLAINTS ABOUT THE TEACHER

If children come to you with complaints about their teacher, don't get involved in a discussion over who was right or wrong. Hear your child out first, keeping in mind that it's halachically forbidden to accept what he tells you as the absolute truth. After you've listened to his story, ask him, "Are you telling me this because you think I can help you in some way? Then I want to know about it. But if you're telling me because you're angry at the teacher and you want me to know how mean he is, then it's *lashon hara* and you're not allowed to tell me."

Help your child to realize that anger always comes from judging others negatively, and teach him to judge his teacher's actions favorably. At the same time, you can help him to be more accepting of the situation if you show empathy. You might say, for example, "I'm so sorry you're having a hard time, but you're not allowed to tell me *lashon hara* about the teacher." Even if you have sound reasons for believing that the teacher was at fault, you can still say, "Maybe the teacher made a mistake, but...."

Encourage your child to talk over any problems with the teacher himself. He can ask to talk to him during recess. If the child hesitates because he's afraid the teacher will regard this as *chutzpah*, you can rehearse with him what he'll say, making sure it will be said respectfully.

LEARNING DIFFICULTIES

Many educators today still believe that children don't enjoy learning, that when left to their own devices they'd prefer to play, and that they must therefore be stimulated to study by grades and other forms of competition. To realize how untrue this notion is, one has only to visit a Montessori kindergarten and observe children of 3 and 4 at work without any external incentive. (One mother took her children out of such a kindergarten because, as she put it, "All they wanted to do when they came home was wash the walls and windows!") Maria Montessori, the Italian founder of this system of education, maintained that children feel a great need to do constructive work: "It is certain that the child's aptitude for work represents a vital instinct."[4] Apparently, when God blessed the newly created first couple with the commandment to "fill the earth and conquer it," He implanted in them a drive to control and shape their environment, a drive which can be seen even in young children.

The saying "The jealousy of *sofrim* increases knowledge" is frequently quoted to justify the use of competition among students. But the word *sofrim* refers here to teachers and not students. The correct interpretation of this saying — which is merely an observation about human nature and in no way a recommendation — is that jealousy among teachers causes them to become better educators.[5]

The grading system, thought by so many to be necessary to stimulate students to better achievement, actually causes much harm. It creates in children's minds a false association between accomplishment and esteem. Objectively viewed, a grade on a test or report card is nothing more than a rating of a child's knowledge in a particular subject. But teachers generally convey to their pupils quite a different meaning: A high grade is something to be proud of; it shows that the child has paid attention and studied well; thus he is a "good" student and worthy of esteem. A low grade, on the other hand, is something to be ashamed of; it indicates that the child has not applied himself sufficiently; he is therefore a poor or "bad" student and consequently held in low esteem. What is entirely overlooked here is that success in learning depends as much on intellectual ability as on diligence.

Unfortunately, this attitude is frequently carried over into the home. Parents express pride and satisfaction in the child who is a good student, but show disappointment and displeasure toward the child who does badly in school. This is contrary to the Jewish approach, which values the individual according to his righteousness and not according to his intellectual achievement. God has seen fit to endow us with different levels of intellectual ability. Only in respect to righteousness do we have equal opportunities. God doesn't measure our righteousness by any absolute standard but only relative to our potential. A person who was born with a pleasant disposition to parents who provide him with a good upbringing is expected to have a better character than one who is less fortunate. A child who was raised among thieves and who, by a tremendous effort, overcomes his background to become an ordinary law-abiding citizen, may be more righteous than the son of a great rabbi who merely follows in his father's footsteps without any effort. It's surely in this sense that Rambam wrote: "Every person has the ability to be as righteous as our teacher, Moshe,"[6] although certainly not as wise.

Of course, there are youngsters who do poorly in school not because they lack ability but because they lack self-discipline; other children can't achieve because of a learning disability (see below). But all too often, the poor student is a child of mediocre intellectual ability who, though he tries hard, can't really do any better. Unfortunately, in most cases there is no recognition of this. Both parents and teachers urge the child to make greater effort. The child, who does try harder but still fails to do much better, inevitably concludes that it is his fault and that he must be somehow inferior. In such a situation, he naturally loses much of his motivation for learning and is unlikely to continue exerting himself for long — thus making it easy to point to the child's lack of effort as the reason for his poor performance!

But even a good student may be harmed by a system that stresses competition. Some successful students develop such a strong need to be held in high esteem that they strive excessively to excel. They become terribly upset at any mark less than 100, and are dissatisfied unless they're always on top. Such perfectionism often makes children tense and anxious about their studies (see the discussion below).

The ideal solution to these achievement problems would be a highly individualized learning system that permitted each student to advance at his own pace, a system in which grades — if given at all — would reflect achievement *relative* to the child's ability.*

> The teacher can help each child set his own standards of performance for what he would learn, and reward *every* child for making progress toward his particular goals. A test is merely

---

* High school marks which serve as a basis for admission to institutions of higher learning must, of course, be based on absolute standards.

a way to find out what the child has learned so he can be rewarded for it and a way to diagnose what difficulties the child may have so he knows what he has yet to learn.[7]

Interestingly, in the old-time *cheder* the practice was for the *rebbi* (teacher) to test each child separately. Written tests and report cards were unheard of. The Jewish approach to education has always stressed the need for individualization in education: "Teach the lad according to his nature."[8] The Talmud tells the story of Rav Preida, who had a student with whom he had to review each lesson 400 times.[9] Maharsha views this not as an example of unusual patience and devotion, but as the fulfillment of an *obligation* for all teachers to teach the lesson over and over until the student knows it thoroughly.[10] Moreover, we find in the *Shulchan Aruch:* "A teacher must not become angry with his pupils if they don't understand him, but must repeat his explanation as many times as necessary until they understand."[11]

Schools that live up to these ideals are rare. It is up to us, the parents, to foster in our children a serious attitude toward their studies, but without setting up standards of accomplishment that are too high. For instance, don't tell a child who got an 85 on a test, "You could have done better." Praise children for diligence rather than for high marks. Encourage them to study in order to acquire knowledge, not in order to get praise, recognition, or high grades.

When a child with mediocre learning ability shows unhappiness over his low grades, tell him, "To us it doesn't matter what marks you get. The main thing is that you're doing your best." Emphasize that the merit achieved through Torah study is not measured in terms of success, but in terms of the extent to which we exert ourselves.[12] The more effort we make, the greater the reward.[13]

The Underachiever

The underachiever is a child with good intellectual ability who lacks the self-discipline to apply himself to his studies. He hates the school regimen and, though forced to sit in the classroom, usually absorbs little instruction there. Teachers find it frustrating to have such a child in their class, a capable youngster just frittering his time away.

Parents may worry over what will become of their under-achieving child, but there's actually less reason for concern than one might think. After wasting most of their elementary school years, these children usually start buckling down to their studies later in high school. As long as they've acquired basic skills such as reading and arithmetic, they can easily make up for the lost years since most of the missed material will be reviewed.

In the meantime, the best thing you can do is to commiserate with your child about his dislike of school, while at the same time encouraging him to apply himself more seriously. The message should be, "I know how much you hate school, but since you have to be there anyway, why not try to learn something." Don't make critical remarks about his low grades. Instead, note any improve-ments, no matter how small, and comment on these. For example: "I notice you're doing better in *Chumash* — you went up from a D to a C."

The Learning-Disabled Child

Learning disabilities can range from mild to severe. Here we will focus only on the milder form; with the severe form, special educa-tion will usually be required.

To most parents, it comes as a shock to hear that their child has a learning disability. Typically, nothing is noticed until he starts first grade, and doesn't learn to read as the other children do. Often he has difficulty in writing and arithmetic as well. Fortunately, most schools today have special "mainstreaming" programs for these chil-dren, in which they leave their regular class for only an hour or so a day of specialized educational therapy.

Learning disability must not be confused with mental retarda-tion, where the child functions poorly because of an inherently lim-ited intellectual capacity. The typical learning disabled child has nor-mal or even above-average intelligence; his problems stem from a perceptual handicap.

Learning disability must also not be confused with so-called developmental lag. The learning-disabled child cannot be kept another year in kindergarten with the expectation that he'll "out-grow" his problem; he must receive specialized educational help with a trained teacher. With early detection and treatment, there is every hope that he'll eventually overcome his disability completely.

The learning-disabled child needs strong support from his parents. Talk about his problem openly and frankly; inform his siblings of it as well. If they ridicule him for asking inappropriate or naive questions, or show lack of understanding of his problems in other ways, remind them of his disability and help them to develop a more sympathetic attitude.

The Striving and Tense Child

This child can do well, but he pushes himself to the point where he becomes tense and nervous. This is because he believes that a person must achieve outstandingly in order to have worth. Before an exam he worries incessantly; afterwards he upbraids himself over every wrong answer, wondering, "How could I make such a stupid mistake?" Parents often unwittingly contribute to the child's problem by telling him, even when he's done reasonably well, that he should have done better. If he sees that he can't maintain the standards of perfection he's set for himself, he may even give up and become an intellectual "dropout," physically present in the classroom, but mentally elsewhere.

To these children, too, stress that a person is rated according to his righteousness, not his intellectual achievement, and that striving for excellence is commendable as long as the goal isn't acclaim or recognition. Show pleasure over the fact that your child enjoys learning, rather than praising him for his high marks.

HOMEWORK

Homework should be seen as the child's responsibility. Parents should remain in the background, giving support and perhaps some minor assistance now and then. Never let homework become a daily affair of reminders, unpleasant nagging, scolding, or threatening.

For homework to have meaning, it must be geared to the child's capacity so that he can work independently with little assistance. If your child's assignments are too difficult for him, ask the teacher to adjust the work accordingly.

If your child is negligent about doing his homework, have a quiet talk with him in which you convey your concern, and explain the importance of school assignments. But tell him that you won't remind him about homework since it's his responsibility. You might ask your child to decide on a convenient time for doing his homework, but then stay out of the picture. If the teacher complains about the child's negligence, you can say that you're very sorry about it but, while you encourage your children to do their assignments, you prefer not to let it become an issue at home. This leaves it up to the teacher to deal with the problem.

Certainly it's desirable that children do their homework. But is it worth your while to be engaged in daily battle over it, making everyone miserable and spoiling the home environment?

There are teachers who rely on the parents' active involvement in the child's homework to supplement their classwork. For instance, the teacher will introduce a particular multiplication table, but then depend on the parents to drill the child at home. Parents who feel overwhelmed by the teacher's expectations of them, because of unfamiliarity with the material, difficulty in "deciphering" the children's scrawled homework assignments, or pressing household demands, can consider approaching the teacher (possibly along with other parents as a group), to convey concern about their child missing out on fundamentals. But if this doesn't help, there seems no choice but to come to terms with the situation and be prepared to struggle through patiently, sitting with each child who needs you. Of course, the help of older siblings, or even of a neighbor's older child, can be enlisted.

In the case of a child with a mild learning problem, the parent's help may be necessary to provide encouragement and practical help. Experienced tutors can ease the tension that is often present in homework sessions with such a child. Parents need to be in constant contact with the teacher, deciding together on adjusting the homework to suit the child's capacity.

Chapter Seventeen

COMMON PROBLEMS

EATING

I n his book on baby and child care, Dr. Benjamin Spock writes:

Why do so many children eat poorly? Most commonly because so many mothers are conscientious about trying to make them eat well. You don't see many feeding problems in puppies, or among young humans in places where mothers don't know enough about diet to worry. You might say jokingly that it takes knowledge and many months of hard work to make a feeding problem.

One child seems to be born with a wolf's appetite that stays big even when he's unhappy or sick. Another's appetite is more moderate and is easily affected by his health and spirits. The first child seems to be cut out to be plump; the second is apparently intended to stay on the slender side. But *every* baby is born with enough appetite to keep him healthy, keep him gaining at the proper rate for him.[1]

Parents can spare themselves much unnecessary misery over feeding problems by following one basic rule: Don't urge and certainly never force a child to eat. Children have a natural, inborn desire for food. When they are hungry enough they'll eat.

A mother might hesitate to put this advice into practice for fear that if she allows her child to eat only what he pleases, he may develop some nutritional deficiency. Dr. Spock notes that there is rarely any such danger:

> It's important to remember that children have a remarkable inborn mechanism that lets them know how much food and which types of food they need for normal growth and development. It is extremely rare to see serious malnutrition or vitamin deficiency or infectious disease result from a feeding problem.[2]

Dr. Spock describes Dr. Clara Davis's well-known experiments in appetite. Babies of eight to ten months were allowed to choose their own diet from a variety of wholesome, unrefined foods. The babies developed very well over a period of time, choosing what any scientist would agree was a well-balanced diet.

Nevertheless, parents of a child who is eating poorly are advised to have a doctor check him from time to time, to evaluate his diet for what it provides and what it lacks, and to recommend substitute foods or supplements if necessary.

Avoiding Feeding Problems

From the very beginning we should show confidence in our children's inborn capacity to judge what's good for them. Don't try to make a baby finish more of his bottle than he wants. Introduce solids gradually; when a baby refuses food, take it away. You can try offering it again after a few weeks. If the baby's appetite wanes for a while (sometimes due to teething), make no effort to get him to eat more. Children should come to think of food as something *they* want, not as a favor they do *you*. Mothers often make the mistake of continuing to feed a baby when it's obvious that he's lost interest in his food. When an infant begins to fool around or turns his head away from the spoon, assume he's had enough; take him out of his highchair and end the meal.

Or there may be one particular food — usually some vegetable — which the baby dislikes. The mother insists on his taking it anyway, trying by hook or by crook to get it down him — even mixing it with some other food which she knows the child likes. Usually, children are not so easily fooled. Even if he eats it, he may notice something strange about its taste and start to become suspicious of food in general. Is it worth it? After all, many adults, too, have a few foods that they just don't like. The child's aversion is probably very real, and we cause him real suffering (and ourselves much trouble) every time we put him through this ordeal.

As they grow older, children's tastes and appetites will continue to vary, resulting at times in balkiness about eating. This can easily develop into a feeding problem. The worried mother urges the child to eat more — but the child eats even less. The mother's anxiety may turn into anger, as she begins to feel increasingly frustrated by the child's refusal to eat; this only serves to further reduce his appetite. Mealtimes become scenes of conflict and wrangling. The child not only comes to view eating as something he does to please his mother, but he often starts to see himself as bad for not eating as his parents want him to.

To avoid these problems, make a determined effort to stop worrying so much about your child's food intake, and rely on his natural appetite to establish a pattern that's right for him. Keep in mind that there are no "good" or "bad" eaters, only children with big or small appetites. Don't measure your success by how much your child eats. Once your anxiety is gone, you'll be less likely to become upset over your child's poor eating habits.

My 9-year-old was always choosy with food. I always tried to persuade him to eat the food for the "vitamins," "calcium," "protein" or whatever, but he ate what he wanted anyway and I wound up frustrated and sometimes exhausted from the effort. Slowly he began becoming more choosy, eating only uncooked food. Many times he'd come to the table, take a look and say, "There's nothing for me to eat." I tried using all kinds of methods to make him eat, but he just kept narrowing down his food choices and losing a lot of weight.

When it got down to yogurt and fruit, I became really worried and made an appointment with a counselor.

She advised me not to say anything at all, no comments whatsoever concerning his food choices no matter how weird they seemed to me — just not to get involved. With great effort, I tried. (I kept saying to myself that he wasn't sick, just not eating what I wanted him to.) Very slowly he added more foods to his "repertoire." Today he is 12, with normal weight and still eating choosily, but he does also eat the food which I cook for the family. I realize that it was largely my emotional involvement which had caused this problem.

It is unnecessary to battle with children who have trouble finishing what's on their plate. Avoid the entire problem by simply allowing your child to help himself, or by first asking him how much he wants and giving him *only* what he specifies. (In fact, in general it's best to give very small servings so that he has to ask for more.) With the child in control of what's on his plate, you shouldn't have to insist that he finish. If he still doesn't want to eat the food, tell him, "Okay, I guess you're not hungry now; you can eat it later." (Cold food should be reheated for palatability.) Children should be taught that it's wrong to throw away food.[3]

The Fussy Eater

Some children's problems with eating go beyond a vegetable or two; the fussy eater refuses to touch a wide range of foods. Try your best to be tolerant and to refrain from comments about his fussiness. Don't coax him or try to make him eat "just a little bit"; don't offer him something special if he eats; don't threaten to deprive him of his dessert. If there's nothing he likes at a particular meal, he can always have bread with some prepared spread. (Five slices of bread contain nine grams of protein!)

Some parents believe that children should learn to eat everything. Certainly this is desirable; the question is how to accomplish it. Fussy children are serious about their dislikes; if we try to force them to eat something we're going to have a fight on our hands.

From time to time you can suggest that a child try something he's rejected until now. You might explain that tastes frequently change and, if we give ourselves a chance, we often discover that we like something we thought we'd never eat.

You don't have to go out of your way to cater to such children. Be considerate and try to include foods in the menu which your child likes, but don't prepare special foods just for him. A firm policy here will also help him to eat more foods eventually.

If your child hasn't eaten at mealtime, be sure not to let him fill up afterwards on "junk" food or even on fruit. Tell him beforehand that no food (beyond a regular snack) is served between meals; that way he knows what to expect if he chooses not to eat. This must not be said in a threatening manner, such as, "If you don't eat now, you're not getting anything else until supper!" Let him have crackers or fruit with everyone else at snacktime.

A mother may feel terribly guilty at the idea of letting a child go hungry. After all, it's her responsibility to provide him with food; isn't she a bad mother if she sees her child go hungry and does nothing about it? But she should realize that it was the child's choice not to eat. The small amount of hunger which he may feel (much exaggerated, to get us to pity him!) will do him no harm; it will teach him to eat when everyone else does — at mealtimes. Sympathize with him when he complains of being hungry, but, for his own good, stick to your decision.

Fussy children often express dislike for a particular food by saying, "Yuch!" or "I hate this!" Although a child may say that he does not care for something, he should never show disgust for food as this demonstrates lack of gratitude for what God provides. If he doesn't want to eat something that's being served, he can say, "No, thank you" or, "I'd rather not have any."

Illness

Children generally have poor appetites while they are ill. Even after recovery, it may take a while until they begin to eat normally again. Feeding problems often begin here, when an anxious parent starts to push food on the child prematurely. Offer him only the drinks and solids he wants, and wait patiently until his appetite returns to normal. There's no need to worry about weight loss;

when the child's appetite comes back he's usually ravenous and quickly gains back whatever he may have lost.

The Thin Child; the Overweight Child

Thinness is usually a matter of constitution, but consult your child's doctor to rule out any medical problems. Dr. Spock's opinion is that as long as your child doesn't seem to show any special problem, has been slender since infancy but gains a reasonable amount of weight every year, you can relax and leave him alone. No doubt he was meant to be that way.

As for overweight, an important factor behind it is heredity. Your child's chances of being overweight are highest if both parents tend to plumpness, less if only one of his parents has this tendency. If the propensity exists, the only way you can fight it is to regulate his food intake. If while he's young you accustom him to eating low-calorie foods, this can greatly decrease his risk of being overweight. This means not serving fatty or sugary foods and drinks, or rich desserts. Instead of cookies, pretzels, cola, and the like, serve snacks of fresh fruit or even raw carrot and cucumber sticks.

Well fed often means overfed. There's no reason to worry about a little "baby fat"; but if an older baby looks as if he's getting heavy, it would be wise to cut down somewhat on starchy foods and concentrate more on fruits and vegetables.

If your child is fat, encourage him to be sensible about what he eats. But don't tell him things like, "You're too fat — you shouldn't eat so much bread." Also, don't keep him from eating the rich foods served for special occasions, such as Shabbos; he'll certainly feel enormously deprived and it may even increase his craving for those foods.

Some children don't seem the least bit troubled about being fat, but others are very unhappy about it, very critical of themselves for eating too much, blaming themselves for their poor self-control. The typical pattern of the overweight person is to tell himself as he reaches for some calorie-rich food, "I really shouldn't eat this, but...."; afterwards, he reprimands himself. To help your child, get him to understand this cycle and teach him first to stop telling himself off for indulging. He should realize how difficult dieting is and that it takes tremendous will power to lose weight. Sympathize with his difficulties in losing weight; certainly don't add to his misery by calling attention to how he looks.

It usually doesn't help to push a child (or grownup) to lose weight. But older children, adolescents in particular, can often be persuaded to consult with a doctor or nutritionist who can prescribe a suitable diet.

LYING

We must distinguish between the young child's tendency to confuse fantasy and reality, and deliberate lying. The former is common among children with lively imaginations. Rather than expressing disbelief, it's better to respond with mild amazement. For instance, if your 4-year-old tells you, "I saw a lion on the street!" you might simply answer, "Really!"

Deliberate distortions of truth are another matter. Most children will resort to lying on occasion to avoid scoldings or punishments, or to evade responsibilities. Some children will also conjure up stories about themselves to gain acclaim.

If you suspect that your child is lying, be careful not to accuse him of it right away. Confront him gently; if he insists he's telling the truth, give him the benefit of the doubt.

But if you're sure he's lying, have a quiet talk with him about it. Tell him that you know he isn't telling the truth and explain that lying is forbidden by the Torah.[4] In addition, impress upon him how important it is that you be able to rely on what he tells you.

The child has to be taught that he is forbidden to lie, but don't frighten him about it. Keep in mind that though a child knows lying is wrong, he may at times resort to it anyway. If too big an issue has been made over it, he might then feel terribly guilty.

When a child denies having done something because he fears you'll reprimand or punish him, assure him that you'll do neither. It's more important that he be encouraged to tell the truth. Afterwards you can say, "I'm glad you told me the truth. Please, never be afraid to admit it when you did something wrong." In general be careful that your reprimands for misdeeds be mild, so that your child won't be frightened into lying.

Much defensive lying can be prevented by steering clear of the kinds of questions that so often provoke it. For example, if you notice that your child has run off right after finishing his meal, don't ask him "Did you say *Birkas HaMazon* (Grace After Meals)?" but say instead, "You'd better come back to the table — you forgot to say *Birkas HaMazon*."

When their child lies a great deal, parents naturally worry that he'll become a confirmed liar. There's usually no reason for such anxiety. Though children do sometimes go through a phase of persistent lying, with proper handling they gradually give it up. The important thing is to react calmly and continue to impress upon the child how important it is for him to always tell the truth.

STEALING

Young children often lack a clear sense of what belongs to them and what doesn't. When they want to take home an attractive toy from the store or from a playmate's house, don't call it stealing. Just explain to the child that the toy doesn't belong to him, gently persuading him to give it up. Likewise, when he helps himself to candy in the supermarket just tell him that it belongs to the store and make him put it back on the shelf. By age 6, children are capable of understanding what stealing is and that it's wrong.

When parents learn that their child has carried out a more serious theft, they usually react with alarm. Stealing, after all, is a crime and it's frightening to associate their child with it. After their initial shock the parents may look for motives. They may even blame themselves: "Where have *we* gone wrong that he needs to steal?"

Seeking psychological explanations for the child's behavior is usually not helpful. The most simple and logical reason for stealing is that the child badly wants something which doesn't belong to him and, though he knows it's wrong, takes it anyway — or steals money in order to buy it. Neither is it constructive for parents to try to figure out where they've failed. Instead, they should focus on the problem itself and what to do about it.

To begin with, make sure that the child understands that stealing is a serious transgression.[5] One mother discovered that her 5-year-old was taking money from her purse. She reacted by reprimanding him sharply; yet the child continued taking money. She then had a serious talk with him, calmly explaining that stealing isn't allowed. This made a strong impression on the child and he stopped taking money.

It is also important, if you're sure your child has stolen something, to confront him directly. For instance, you notice that a $20 bill is missing from your purse. That same day your son comes home and shows you a brand new watch which he claims to have found on the street. Don't ask, "Are you sure you found it?" Tell him, very quietly, "Twenty dollars is missing from my wallet. You took that money and bought the watch with it, didn't you?" If the child denies having taken the money, don't get drawn into an argument, but quietly persist. When he does finally admit the theft, make him return the watch and give you back the money. (If stolen money was spent on candy or other treats, discuss with the child ways to reimburse the person from whom the money was stolen.)

Never shame a child who has stolen something or call him a thief, and don't frighten him with visions of ending up in jail one day. Also, don't ask him, "Why did you do it?" — this is likely only to set off self-denigrating thought patterns.

Even if you avoid these mistakes, children who steal will often still feel enormously guilty about it afterwards. In helping the child to cope with these feelings, first try to get him to talk about them. You might start by asking, "You feel very bad about what you did, don't you?" The child may hang his head and say nothing; usually, this is a sign that he feels too ashamed to answer. Nevertheless, continue by gently reminding him that even though he did something very bad, it doesn't make *him* a bad person. Rather than thinking how terrible he is, he should just be sorry and make up his mind not to do something like this again. Then he can be sure that Hashem will forgive him. Advise the child to come and talk to you from now on, whenever there's something he wants badly.

In the following story we see how one mother, using the approach just outlined, was able to handle the situation successfuly when she discovered that her daughter was stealing.

My suspicions that my 7-year-old Mimmy was stealing were first aroused when she came home from school one day with a marzipan bar in her hand. "Mommy, take a bite," she said, offering some first to me and then to the others — "Tirtza, take a bite — Ezra, try some — isn't it delicious? Isn't it good?" When I asked her where she got the candy she answered, "Dina gave it to me." "She gave you a whole marzipan bar, just like that?" I asked — "It's hard to believe." "Yes," Mimmy insisted, "she bought it, she didn't like it, and so she gave it to me." I was rather skeptical but decided that I would believe her and didn't pursue the matter further.

Four days later I came into the bathroom and saw a half-eaten wafer bar in the bathtub with crumbs all over the tub (this, with only a week-and-a-half until Pesach!). My suspicions were now further aroused — especially since in our house eating is allowed only in the kitchen and so I couldn't imagine who could have eaten in the bathroom.

Five minutes later Nachum, my 11-year-old, came to tell me the following: He and Mimmy had been playing a game while I was out of the house. Suddenly she said to him, "I'm hungry — let's buy some candy." "What do you mean?" he said — "You can't — you have to ask permission." Then he saw Mimmy go over to my purse, open it and look inside. "You can't do that!" he told her, "It's Mommy's!" She closed it and didn't take anything.

Then Nachum told me, "I think she was down at the grocery store before, buying things." I rushed down with him to the grocer's, asked to look at our charge account, and saw Mimmy's name signed next to about 20 or so small charges. I asked the store owner, "What's going on here?" We both laughed as he told me, "Today she drove me absolutely crazy! Now I'm not letting her buy anything anymore." I found out that she had been bringing little neighborhood children into the store, letting them choose whatever candy they wanted, and charging it to our account! I asked the grocer to please continue not allowing Mimmy to charge anything for the time being, and left the store.

Once home, I began planning how I would handle the situation, keeping calm by reminding myself that this wasn't a serious offense.

Right after supper I told Mimmy, "Please get ready for bed — I want to speak to you soon." A few minutes later I went into her room, closing the door behind me. Holding up the wafer bar, I said to her, in a quiet voice, "You ate this in the bathroom today, didn't you?" She yelled, "I did not!" but I ignored her, pressing on softly. "You know, Mimmy, maybe you don't realize it but taking money from a mother's purse or charging things at the store without permission are wrong things to do." She immediately began protesting, "But I didn't do that!" and then, in an effort to explain, stammered, "but...but...but...I...I...I...." I knew that it was important to continue confronting her and so, cutting her off so as to avoid any arguing, I said, "Look, I'm not going into any details about exactly how I found out, but I know that you did some wrong things and I'm sure you feel bad about them." Now I continued, reassuring her over and over in a gentle tone, "You did a bad thing, Mimmy, but it doesn't mean that you are bad. But if you feel bad about it and decide never to do it again..." — At this point I smiled at her, saying very lovingly, "I'm sure you won't do it again. I'm sure the reason you did it was because you really wanted the candy very much, and from now on if you ever want something very much, just come and tell me."

Afterwards Mimmy felt so relieved — she was so happy — she kissed me and I kissed her back. The next day, too, she seemed especially content and I could tell that she was grateful as well. Since then there has been no recurrence of stealing.

BAD LANGUAGE

Children use bad language chiefly because of the reaction it gets from grownups. Frequently they have no idea what the words mean; all they know is that by saying them, they have the power to shock everyone around them.

It's important to avoid these reactions. The first time your child uses inappropriate language, let him know quietly that those are not nice words and that you don't want him to use them. Your reaction should be very low keyed. If he does it again, tell him calmly, "I asked you not to use that word." The child might also be told, "These are garbage words — they don't belong in your mouth." For older children a mild rebuke such as, "I don't expect you to talk that way," can be helpful. They should be taught also that obscene language (*nivul peh*) debases both speaker and listener and is condemned by the Torah in the strongest terms.[6]

This doesn't mean that you must react each time the child uses bad language. If you have the impression that your remarks are encouraging him to keep it up, it may be best to ignore him for awhile. Whichever way you choose to handle it, the main thing is to stay calm.

One mother told of her way of dealing with this problem. When her children use unfit language, she tells them, "We have a medicine for children who use bad words." Then she puts a tiny amount of black pepper (two grains) on their tongues. That usually ends it.

WILD BEHAVIOR

All children tend to get out of control occasionally. They start running around the house, over and under the furniture, tumbling over each other, screaming at the top of their lungs. For the kids, it's great fun; but not for the grownups, who are usually left feeling exhausted and at their wit's end.

Call the children to one room, saying that you have something important to tell them. Once they're together, say, "Kids, I know you're having a lot of fun, but I can't let you run around here like this. It's okay for outside but not in the house. Now, if you can play quietly — fine. If not, I'll have to put you into separate rooms. You decide, okay?" If this doesn't help, tell them, "All right kids, into separate rooms — you can come out when you're ready to play quietly," and lead each one to a different room.

Some mothers hesitate to stop their children from making noise, telling themselves, "Kids have to run around and let out energy, and I shouldn't let it bother me so much. I should be able to tolerate it." They'd do better to be less demanding of themselves; why let their nerves take a needless beating? In the end it's bound to come out in yelling at the children. Other mothers feel guilty about breaking up their children's fun. Interestingly, one sometimes gets the impression when watching kids running wild that they've had enough, but have gotten into a state where they can't stop themselves. In other words, we might actually be doing them a kindness by stopping them.

SHYNESS

Shyness, when not exaggerated, is actually a positive character trait. It is one of the three outstanding good qualities which characterize the Jewish people.[7]

Some children seem to be born with a tendency toward shyness. In contrast to the outgoing youngster who has a ready grin for any stranger, the shy child is apt to draw away from a visitor's friendly overtures. Don't chide him, out of embarrassment about his behavior, with remarks like, "Why are you so shy?" or, "Someone talked to you — why don't you answer?" Also don't excuse him with, for instance, "He's always like that with visitors." This will most likely only reinforce his shyness. Moreover, by calling attention to the child's shyness in this way, we make him come to see it as something bad.

Try not to be concerned about the impression your child makes. Encourage him to be friendly, but don't make an issue of it if he fails to respond to someone's "Hello" or "How are you?" If a visitor thoughtlessly remarks, "My, isn't she shy!" answer, "No, she's not shy. She'll talk in a little while, when she's gotten used to you." Even the normally outgoing youngster may feel overwhelmed at times by a grownup's overly enthusiastic show of friendliness, especially when he's being bombarded with questions which he doesn't feel like answering at the moment.

The less you say about a child's shyness, the better. As they grow older, these children generally lose much of their shyness and become more sociable.

Chapter Eighteen

IN CONCLUSION

ost parents want more than anything else for their children to behave properly and in accordance with Torah values. They are often not quite as successful at this as they'd like to be. This may be, in part, because they don't realize how obstructive their own negative emotions are. Armed with the cognitive methods presented in this book, they can now use Torah principles to achieve their goal.

But a word of caution: Reading this book, or any other guide, is only a beginning. Understanding parenting principles is relatively easy. *Changing* our behavior is slow and difficult. Don't feel guilty when, despite all your new knowledge, you continue to get upset and behave counterproductively. Don't tell yourself, "I'm not supposed to act like this anymore; I should be able to keep my emotions in check and stay calm by controlling my thinking!" While you may have a good understanding of cognitive principles, it doesn't mean that you'll always make use of them. It's unreasonable to demand that because you've learned these concepts, you'll be able to apply them at all times. Emotional habits are difficult to eliminate. Yet we can go far in freeing ourselves of them, sometimes even after an amazingly short period of time. Here are some sample letters from grateful mothers:

> I feel that the most obvious change for me is that I am much more *aware* of a potential blow-up. I can now stop at those crucial seconds which can make the difference between yelling or talking quietly and firmly. I have really seen the change in my children, and I am much more in tune with them.

> ...Incredibly, I have begun to realize that a great deal of the anger which I had been grappling with just isn't *there* anymore. To a very great extent, I have succeeded in challenging the underlying causes of the anger. I truly feel *freed* of an enormous burden!

In the past I had been yelling at my children quite a bit. Now that I had been been going to the workshop for several weeks, I was making a great effort to control myself and speak calmly. It seems that my two sons noticed the change. They went out and bought a package of hot and spicy taco chips (they had asked me earlier if I like them) and left it together with the following note under my pillow:

For keeping cool and
not blowing up with anger keep the same
P.S. We hope you enjoy it without
blowing up from taco.
Yours sincerely,
Hillel
Shaika

...The tone of my household has changed, so much so that my very independent 12-year-old son, who never wants to be kissed, is now willing sometimes, and has even kissed me back! I feel that my newly found self-control has freed my affection for my children, and it is being reciprocated.

Just as I was about to leave for my workshop meeting, my 11-year-old son stopped me with, "Hey, Mom, are you going to that lady again? Tell her thank you, it's been awfully quiet around here lately!"

When I heard at the first workshop session that we'd be given tools to have a happier, quieter household, I was hopeful but somewhat skeptical. I had heard such things before. I had gone to many lectures on child education (I go to everyone I hear about), full of enthusiasm, only to come home without a concrete set of rules or suggestions to implement. Within a short time I was always back to square one.

This workshop has given me the tools. Within three weeks, I have reduced my rating on the anger scale from 9 to 1. Situations have occurred that would normally have me tearing out hair (theirs, not mine), yet I have managed to keep my cool and talk to them rationally instead.

I no longer feel the tremendous guilt I used to feel about my shortcomings as a parent. Baruch Hashem, I'm beginning to feel like a good mother who is going to be even better!

Notes

Introduction

1. *Midrash Mishlei* 31:10.
2. The parents' obligation to educate their children has several aspects. Their obligation to accustom them to fulfilling the mitzvos is a Rabbinic commandment (*Sukkah* 42a, *Chaggigah* 4a) and the father's obligation to teach his son Torah is a Divine command (Deuteronomy 11:19). In addition, the father is obliged to teach his son good character traits and a trade (cf. Rambam, Commentary on the Mishnah, *Makkos* 2:3). See also Rabbi Samson Raphael Hirsch, *Horeb*, vol. 2, trans. by Dayan Dr. I. Grunfeld (London: Soncino Press, 1975), sec. 548.
3. *Even Sheleimah* 6:5.
4. Rabbi Samson Raphael Hirsch, *The Collected Writings*, vol. 7 (New York: Phillip Feldheim Inc., 1995), p. 132.
5. *Sefer HaChinuch* 16.

Chapter I

1. Walen, DiGuiseppe, and Wessler, *A Practitioner's Guide to Rational Emotive Therapy* (New York: Oxford University Press, 1980).
2. *Sotah* 3b, and Rashi there.
3. *Nedarim* 22a.
4. *Pesachim* 113b.
5. *Shabbos* 105b. The reference here is to the *yetzer hara* as the cause of anger and not necessarily to the anger itself. However, the

metaphor is so striking and appropriate that we incorporated it into the text in that sense.

6. Loc. cit.; see Rambam, *Mishneh Torah, Hil. Dei'os* 2:3.

7. Personal communication.

8. Carol Tavris, *Anger: The Misunderstood Emotion* (New York: Simon & Schuster, 1983).

9. See Chapter 2, notes 33, 34.

10. *Leviticus* 25:17; *Bava Metzia* 58b; *Shulchan Aruch, Choshen Mishpat* 228.

11. *Sefer HaChinuch* 338.

12. *Shabbos* 105b; Rambam, op. cit., 2:3.

13. *Avos* 2:4.

14. Rambam, op. cit., *Hil. Teshuvah* 3:2.

15. *Avos* 1:6.

16. Rabbi Samson Raphael Hirsch, *Horeb*, vol. 1, trans. by Dayan Dr. I. Grunfeld (London: Soncino Press, 1975), sec. 138.

17. Cited in Rabbi Zelig Pliskin, *Love Your Neighbor* (Jerusalem: Aish HaTorah Publications, 1977), pp. 287-288.

18. *Ecclesiastes* 7:20.

19. *Avos* 2:16.

20. Rambam, op. cit., 7:3.

21. See Rambam, op. cit., 6.

22. *Jeremiah* 31:18.

23. *Der Israelit* (8 IX 36).

24. Dov Katz, *Tenuas HaMusar*, vol. 1, p. 284.

25. *Avos* 2:13.

26. Rambam, Commentary on the Mishnah, *Avos* 2:13.

27. Rabbeinu Yonah, commentary, *Avos* 2:13.

28. *Avos* 3:14.

29. Mishnah *Sanhedrin* 4:5.

30. All but the most severe transgressions (those entailing *kares,* "cutting off," or worse are forgiven upon *teshuvah* and the passing of Yom Kippur (*Yoma* 86a).

31. *Yoma* 86b and *Iyun Yaakov* in *Ein Yaakov,* there.

32. This seems to be implied by the verse cited there ("... like a fool reciting his foolishness," Proverbs 26:11).

33. The two sides of this issue appear to be the subject of a Talmudic debate (*Yoma* 86b). However, Rif and Rosh accept both

sides as relevant, implying that they are reconcilable. The above paragraph is an attempt at such reconciliation.

34. Mishnah *Yoma* 8:9; Rambam, *Mishneh Torah, Hil. Teshuvah* 2:9.

35. Rudolf Dreikurs, *The Challenge of Parenthood* (New York: Duell, Sloan & Pearce, 1948), p. 96.

36. Rabbi Samson Raphael Hirsch, op. cit., vol. 2, Sec. 519.

Chapter 2

1. *Menoras HaMaor* 163, referring to *Kiddushin* 30b.

2. *Kiddushin* 30b.

3. *Sefer HaChinuch*, 33.

4. Rabbi Yaakov Kamenetzky, personal communication.

5. *Shulchan Aruch, Yoreh De'ah* 240:19.

6. Cited in Rabbi Meir E. H. Munk, *S'char V'ha'anasha B'chinuch* (Bnei Brak: Hamesorah, 1982), p. 38.

7. *Exodus* 20:12.

8. *Leviticus* 19:3.

9. *Kiddushin* 31b; *Shulchan Aruch, Yoreh De'ah* 240:1-4.

10. Mishnah *Kiddushin* 1:7.

11. *Shulchan Aruch, Yoreh De'ah* 240:14.

12. Mishnah *Kerisos* 6:9. Though in principle the honor due the mother is equal that due the father, in practice, if both parents have asked for the child's help, the father is to be given precedence because he has a right to the mother's services. When this obligation falls away due to a divorce, the child may assign precedence according to his own judgment.

13. Rambam, Commentary on the Mishnah, *Kiddushin* 1:7.

14. Rabbi Eliezer of Metz, *Sefer Yerei'im*, sec. 56 (in R.Y.I. Goldblum's edition, sec. 221-2); R' Menahem Ha-Meiri, *Beis Ha-Bechirah, Kiddushin* 31a (in R.A. Sofer's edition, p. 181).

15. *Aruch HaShulchan, Yoreh De'ah* 240:8.

16. *Sefer Chareidim*, Pos. Commandments of the Torah 1:26.

17. *Shulchan Aruch, Yoreh De'ah* 240:2.

18. Chazon Ish, *Yoreh De'ah*, 149.

19. Rabbi Yoel Schwartz, *Ben Yechabed Av* (Jerusalem: Jerusalem Academy of Jewish Studies, 1980), p. 91.

20. *Shulchan Aruch, Yoreh De'ah* 240:2.

21. Loc. cit.

22. *Pischei Teshuvah*, Ibid., 240:2.

23. *Igros Moshe, Yoreh De'ah*, vol. 1, sec. 133 (p. 272).

24. *Chayei Adam* 67:11.

25. *Deuteronomy* 27:16.

26. Rambam, *Mishneh Torah, Hil. Mamrim* 5:15.

27. *Sheiltos* 60; *Ha'amek She'elah* there, no. 6.

28. *Chayei Adam* 67:3.

29. Rambam, op. cit., 6:3.

30. Rabbi Yerucham F. Perla, commentary to *Sefer HaMitzvos* of Rabbi Sa'adiah Gaon, Com. 9, s.v. *ume'atah nomar.*

31. *Bereishis Rabbah* 65:16.

32. *Sefer HaMiknah* on *Kiddushin* 31b.

33. *Teshuvos Rabbi Akiva Eiger, Pesachim* 68.

34. Loc. cit. Indeed, it appears that this question is subject to a dispute among early authorities. For an extensive discussion, see above, Note 30, s.v. *ela sheraisi.* Rabbi Perla concludes there (s.v. *ve-amnam afilu*) that obedience is included in the mitzvah of reverence.

35. Personal communication.

36. *Avos* 4:12.

37. Rabbi Samson Raphael Hirsch, *The Collected Writings*, vol. 7 (New York, Philipp Feldheim, Inc.), p. 426.

38. Rabbi Samson Raphael Hirsch, *Yesodos Ha-Chinuch*, vol. 2, trans. by A. Wolf (Bnei Brak: Netzach Publishers, 1968), pp. 54, 57.

Chapter 3

1. Cf. Rambam, Commentary on the Mishnah, *Makkos* 2:3.

2. J. and H. Krumboltz, *Changing Children's Behavior* (New Jersey: Prentice-Hall, 1972), p. 243.

3. *Midrash Rabbah, Koheles* 1:13, s.v. *v'nasati es libi.*

4. *Ecclesiastes* 5:9.

5. James Dobson, *Dare to Discipline* (New York: Bantam Books, 1970), p. 31.

6. Rabbi Samson Raphael Hirsch, *Yesodos HaChinuch*, vol. 2, trans. by A. Wolf (Bnei Brak: Netzach Publishers, 1968), p. 54.

7. See Introduction, Note 2.

8. Rabbi S. R. Hirsch, *Judaism Eternal*, Vol. 1, trans. by Dayan Dr. I. Grunfeld (London: Soncino Press, 1956), p. 230.

Chapter 4

1. Cited in Rabbi Zelig Pliskin, *Love Your Neighbor* (Jerusalem: Aish HaTorah Publications, 1977), p. 374.
2. *Shemos Rabbah* 20:10.
3. *Mechilta Shemos* 19:5.
4. *Avos* 2:8.
5. *Avos* 2:16.
6. *Sotah* 22b.
7. *Avos* 1:3.
8. *Ta'anis* 24a.
9. Rambam, Commentary to the Mishnah, *Sanhedrin*, chap. 10, introd.
10. Rabbi Yoel Schwartz, *The Eternal Jewish Home* (Jerusalem: Jerusalem Academy of Jewish Studies, 1982), pp. 78-79.

Chapter 5

1. *Proverbs* 3:12.
2. *Proverbs* 13:24.
3. Rabbi Shlomo Wolbe, *Alei Shur* (Be'er Yaakov: 1972), p. 261.
4. *Proverbs* 29:17.
5. *Job* 11:12.
6. *Sotah* 47a.
7. Rabbi Samson Raphael Hirsch, *Yesodos HaChinuch*, vol. 1, trans. by A. Wolf and S. Pushinsky (Bnei Brak: Netzach Publishers, 1968), pp. 65, 66.
8. *Midrash Rabbah, Exodus*, beginning.
9. James Dobson, *Dare to Discipline* (New York: Bantam Books, 1970), pp. 2-3.
10. *Leviticus* 19:17; Rambam, *Mishneh Torah, Hil. Teshuvah* 4:1; *Shulchan Aruch HaRav, Talmud Torah* 1:6.
11. *Proverbs* 3:12.
12. Rambam, op. cit., *Hil. Dei'os* 6:7.
13. *Yevamos* 65b.
14. *Lev Eliyahu*, vol. 2, pp. 26-27.

15. Rambam, op. cit., 6:7 and 8.

16. *Semag* prohibition 6 and *Bris Moshe* there.

17. *Shabbos* 105b; Rambam, op. cit., 2:3.

18. *Avos de'Rabbi Nasan* 12:3.

19. *Derashos HaRan,* No. 9, beginning.

20. Cited in Rabbi Yoel Schwartz, *The Eternal Jewish Home* (Jerusalem: Jerusalem Academy of Jewish Studies, 1982), p. 63.

21. Haim G. Ginott, *Teacher and Child* (New York: Avon Books, 1975), p. 83.

22. Rabbi Samson Raphael Hirsch, op. cit., p. 69.

23. *Even Sheleimah* 6:5.

24. "Even though he learns, it is a mitzvah [to hit him]" (*Makkos* 8a), presumably only when it is necessary for his character development. This is implied by the verse cited there (Note 4 above). For confirmation of this interpretation, compare Rambam, Commentary on the Mishnah, *Makkos* 2:3.

25. Rabbi Shlomo Wolbe, op. cit., p. 260.

26. Ibid., p. 261.

27. "[God] never punishes without previous warning" (*Sanhedrin* 56b) and we are to emulate God's ways (Deuteronomy 13:5; *Sotah* 14a).

28. *Semachos* 2:6.

29. *Reishis Chochmah, P. Gidul Habanim,* s.v. *v'tzarich ha'adam.*

30. *Sanhedrin* 85a from *Deuteronomy* 25:3; *Shulchan Aruch, Choshen Mishpat* 420:1.

31. *Shulchan Aruch HaRav, Choshen Mishpat, Hilchos Nizkei Guf Va'nefesh* 4.

32. Rabbi Samson Raphael Hirsch, op. cit., vol. 2, trans. by A. Wolf, p. 65.

33. *Bava Basra* 21a.

34. *Even Sheleimah* 6:4.

35. *Shulchan Aruch, Yoreh De'ah* 240:20.

36. *Leviticus* 19:14.

37. Rabbi Akiva Eiger on *Yoreh De'ah* 240:20.

38. *Yoma* 48b, *Mishnah Berurah* no. 38.

Chapter 6

1. *Leviticus* 19:18.

2. Rambam, *Mishneh Torah, Hil. Eivel* 14:1.

3. Rabbi Shlomo Wolbe, *Alei Shur* (Be'er Yaakov: 1972), p. 93.

4. *Yerushalmi Nedarim* 9:4. See also *Psalms* 89:3.

Chapter 7

1. *Kiddushin* 29a; *Shulchan Aruch, Yoreh De'ah*, 245:1. cf. Rambam, Mishnah commentary, *Makkos* 2:3 and *Mishneh Torah, Rotzei'ach* 5:5.

2. *Kiddushin* 29a; cf. *Shulchan Aruch, Orach Chayim* 306:6.

3. *Be'er Heitev, Orach Chayim*, 47:4; *Mishnah Berurah*, ibid., 10.

4. *Sedei Chemed, Kelalim, Ches* no. 59.

5. *Shemos Rabbah*, 28:2.

6. *Minchas Ani, Ha'azinu*, s.v. *V'niftach*.

7. *Deuteronomy* 6:7.

8. *Shulchan Aruch, Yoreh De'ah* 245:4.

9. *Sotah* 21a.

10. Rambam, *Mishneh Torah, Talmud Torah* 1:13.

11. *Likutei Halachah l'Ba'al Chafetz Chayim, Sotah*, chap. 3, text and footnote.

12. *Hilchos Talmud Torah* 1,6.

13. *Deuteronomy* 30:20.

14. Rabbi Yehoshua Neuwirth, *Shemiras Shabbos K'hilchasah*, first ed. (Jerusalem: Feldheim publishers, 1965), chap. 32.

15. *Igros Moshe, Yoreh De'ah*, vol. 3, sec. 76.

16. *Deuteronomy* 31:12.

17. *Yerushalmi Yevamos* 1:6.

18. Rabbi Yehushua Neuwirth, op. cit., chap. 32, sec. 54.

19. *Avos* 2:16.

20. Rabbi Samson Raphael Hirsch, *Horeb*, vol. 2, trans. by Dayan Dr. I. Grunfeld (London: Soncino Press, 1975), sec. 554.

21. Rabbi Samson Raphael Hirsch, *The Collected Writings*, vol. 7 (New York, Phillip Feldheim, Inc.), pp. 133-134.

22. Ibid., p. 136.

23. Rabbi Yoel Schwartz, *The Eternal Jewish Home* (Jerusalem, Jerusalem Academy of Jewish Studies, 1982), p. 119.

24. Rambam, *Hilchos Dei'os* 6,1.

25. Rabbi Samson Raphael Hirsch, *Yesodos HaChinuch*, vol. 2, trans. by A. Wolf (Bnei Brak: Netzach publishers, 1968), p. 71.

Chapter 8

1. *Leviticus* 25:17.
2. *Avos* 1:2.
3. *Tosefta Pe'ah* 4, 18-19.
4. *Michah* 6:8.
5. Rabbi Yisrael Meir Kagan (Chafetz Chayim), *Ahavas Chesed*, part 2, Chs. 1 and 2.
6. *Bava Metzia* 58b.
7. "That which is hateful to you, do not do to your fellow. This is the entire Torah; the rest is commentary" (*Shabbos* 31a).
8. *Psalms* 89:3; see also *Avos* 1:2.
9. Rabbi Eliyahu E. Dessler, *Michtav MeEliyahu* Vol. 1, ed. by Rabbi Aryeh Carmel, Rabbi Alter Halpern, pp. 34-35.
10. *Sefer HaChinuch* 16.
11. Rudolf Dreikurs, *The Challenge of Parenthood* (New York: Duell, Sloan & Pearce, 1948), p. 156.
12. Cited in "How to Raise a Happy Child," *Reader's Digest*, Jan. 1986, p. 95.
13. *Avos d'Rabbi Nasan* 11. See also Yehudah Levi, *Sha'arei Talmud Torah* (Jerusalem: Feldheim, 1981), pp. 195-199; 3rd ed., (Jerusalem: *Olam HaSefer HaTorani*, 1987), pp. 218-223.
14. Netziv, *Ha'amek Davar*, Genesis 2:4.
15. *Avos* 1:10.
16. Rabbi Yoel Schwartz, *The Eternal Jewish Home* (Jerusalem: Jerusalem Academy of Jewish Studies, 1982), p. 78.
17. *Isaiah* 58:7; *Tanna D'vei Eliyahu Rabbah* 27, begin.; see also *Shulchan Aruch, Yoreh De'ah* 251:3.
18. *Shabbos* 31a.
19. *Yoma* 86a.
20. *Berachos* 6b. Under certain circumstances, one should even interrupt the reading of the *Shema* to greet a person (*Mishnah Berachos* 2:1).
21. *Avos* 5:7.
22. *Chagigah* 5a.

Chapter 9

1. *Sefer HaChinuch* 16. See also *Mesilas Yesharim* 7.

2. *Gittin* 67a; Rashi, s.v. *otzar balum*.

3. *Sanhedrin* 86a.

4. Cited in Rabbi Yoel Schwartz, *The Eternal Jewish Home* (Jerusalem: Jerusalem Academy of Jewish Studies, 1982), p. 80.

5. *Avodah Zarah* 20b and Maharsha there.

6. *Shabbos* 50b; *Vayikra Rabbah* 34:3.

7. *Berachos* 53b, based on *Leviticus* 11:44.

Chapter II

1. *Shabbos* 10b.

Chapter 12

1. *Psalms* 133:1.

2. *Sanhedrin* 58b; *Shulchan Aruch, Choshen Mishpat* 420:1.

3. *Shulchan Aruch, Choshen Mishpat* 421:13; *Shulchan Aruch Ha-Rav, Choshen Mishpat, Hilchos Nizkei Guf Va'nefesh* 2. See also note 11, below.

4. Ibid., 4.

5. *Leviticus* 25:17; *Shulchan Aruch, Choshen Mishpat* 228:1.

6. Loc. cit.; *Bava Metzia* 58b; Rambam, *Mishneh Torah, Hil. Dei'os* 6:8 & *Hil. Teshuvah* 3:14.

7. Maharshal to *Semag* (Neg. 6).

8. *Shabbos* 31a.

9. Rabbi Yisrael Meir Kagan, *Chafetz Chayim* I 4:10-11.

10. Ibid., 8:11.

11. *Pesachim* 118a, based on Exodus 23:1.

12. Rabbi Yisrael Meir Kagan, *Chafetz Chayim* I 6:4, *Be'er Mayim Chayim* 7.

13. *Leviticus* 19:18. From a passage in *Yoma* 23a it appears that one may bear a grudge over a physical attack or an insult, until an apology is received. However, revenge is never permitted. See also Rambam, op. cit., *Hil. Dei'os* 7:7: "...in all matters of the world." Other authorities permit even revenge for physical or verbal attacks. We have based the text on the conclusion of Rabbi Y. M. Kagan (*Chafetz Chayim*, Introduction, note 8-9), who discusses the issue at length.

14. *Avos* 1:6 and *Shavuos* 30a.

15. Rambam, op. cit., 6:6-7.

16. *Avos* 2:4.
17. *Leviticus* 19:17; Rambam, op. cit. 6:6-7.
18. *Yevamos* 65b, brought by Rosh, there.
19. *Mishnah Yoma* 8:9; Rambam, op. cit., *Hil. Teshuvah* 2:9.
20. *Avos* 4:1.
21. Carol Tavris, *Anger: The Misunderstood Emotion* (New York: Simon & Schuster, 1983).
22. *Shabbos* 88b.
23. *Avos* 23.
24. *Avos d'Rabbi Nasan* 12:3.

Chapter 13

1. Cited in Albert Ellis, *How to Raise An Emotionally Healthy Child* (California: Wilshire Book Co., 1978), p. 5.
2. Dr. Uri Levi, Poria, Israel.

Chapter 14

1. *Hilchos Dei'os* 1:1.
2. Stanley Turecki, *The Difficult Child* (New York: Bantam Books, Inc., 1985).
3. Cited in *Science News*, 141:37 (January 18, 1992).
4. Stanley Turecki, op. cit.

Chapter 15

1. Rabbi Samson Raphael Hirsch, *The Collected Writings*, vol.7 (New York, Phillip Feldheim Inc., 1995), p. 314.
2. *Igros Moshe, Yoreh De'ah*, part 3, note 76.
3. *Kiddushin* 31b; *Shulchan Aruch, Yoreh De'ah* 240:1-4.

Chapter 16

1. *Bava Basra* 21a.
2. *Mo'ed Katan* 17a.
3. *Shulchan Aruch, Yoreh De'ah* 242:1.
4. Maria Montessori, *The Secret of Childhood* (New York: Frederick A. Stokes, 1939), p. 208.
5. *Bava Basra* 21a.

6. Rambam, *Mishneh Torah, Hil. Teshuvah* 5:2.

7. J. and H. Krumboltz, *Changing Children's Behavior* (New Jersey: Prentice Hall, 1972), p. 195.

8. *Proverbs* 22:6.

9. *Eiruvin* 54b.

10. *Chiddushei Aggadah, Sanhedrin* 91b, s.v. *kol ha'monei'a.*

11. *Shulchan Aruch, Yoreh De'ah* 246:10.

12. "The one who accomplishes more is equal to the one who accomplishes less, as long as his intention is to do the will of Heaven" (*Berachos* 5b).

13. *Avos* 5:22.

Chapter 17

1. Benjamin Spock, *The Common Sense Book of Baby and Child Care* (New York: Duell, Sloan & Pearce, 1962), pp. 423-424.

2. Ibid., p. 426.

3. *Shabbos* 129a; Rambam, *Mishneh Torah, Hil. Melachim* 6:10.

4. *Exodus* 23:7; *Sotah* 42a.

5. *Leviticus* 19:11.

6. *Isaiah* 9:16; *Shabbos* 33a.

7. *Yevamos* 79a.